Programming with

Python

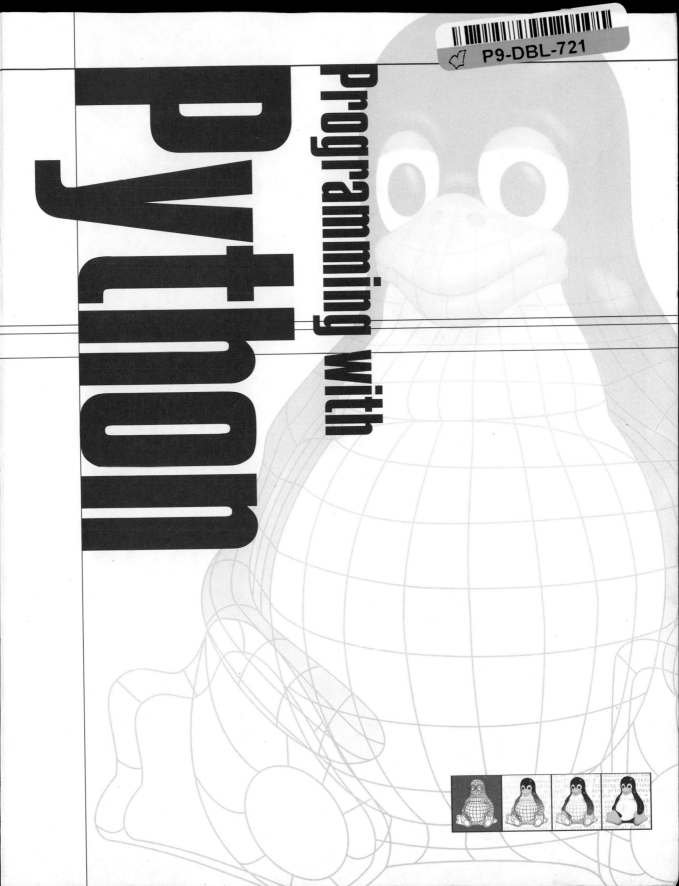

Send Us Your Comments:

To comment on this book or any other PRIMA TECH title, visit PRIMA TECH's reader response page on the Web at **www.prima-tech.com/comments**.

How to Order:

For information on quantity discounts, contact the publisher: Prima Publishing, P.O. Box 1260BK, Rocklin, CA 95677-1260; (916) 632-4400. On your letterhead, include information concerning the intended use of the books and the number of books you wish to purchase. For individual orders, visit PRIMA TECH's Web site at **www.prima-tech.com**.

Programming with Python

Python

Tim Altom

With Mitch Chapman

A Division of Prima Publishing

A Division of Prima Publishing

Prima Publishing and colophon are registered trademarks of Prima Communications, Inc. PRIMA TECH is a trademark of Prima Communications, Inc., Rocklin, California 95765.

The Open Source Initiative board has voted to certify the Python license as Open Source. Python was created by Guido van Rossum.

Linux is a registered trademark of Linus Torvalds. The Linux penguin is used with permission from Larry Ewing (**lewing@isc.tamu.edu**). Ewing created this image using The GIMP (www.gimp.org).

Windows, Internet Explorer, and Microsoft are registered trademarks of Microsoft Corporation. Netscape and Netscape Navigator are registered trademarks of Netscape Communications Corporation.

Prima Publishing and the authors have attempted throughout this book to distinguish proprietary trademarks from descriptive terms by following the capitalization style used by the manufacturers.

Important: If you experience problems running Python, check Python's Web site at **www.python.org** for support and technical information. Prima Publishing cannot provide software support.

Information contained in this book has been obtained by Prima Publishing from sources believed to be reliable. However, because of the possibility of human or mechanical error by our sources, Prima Publishing, or others, the Publisher does not guarantee the accuracy, adequacy, or completeness of any information and is not responsible for any errors or omissions or the results obtained from the use of such information. Readers should be particularly aware of the fact that the Internet is an ever-changing entity. Some facts may have changed since this book went to press.

ISBN: 0-7615-2334-0

Library of Congress Catalog Card Number: 99-65006

Printed in the United States of America

99 00 01 02 03 BB 10 9 8 7 6 5 4 3 2 1

Publisher
Stacy L. Hiquet

Associate Publisher
Nancy Stevenson

Marketing Manager
Judi Taylor

Associate Marketing Manager
Jody Kennen

Managing Editor
Sandy Doell

Senior Acquisitions Editor
Kim Spilker

Senior Editor
Kevin Harreld

Copy Editor
June Waldman

Technical Reviewer
Mitch Chapman

Interior Layout
Danielle Foster

Cover Design
Prima Design Team

Indexer
Sharon Hilgenberg

To Richard Stallman, Linus Torvalds, Guido van Rossum, and the hundreds of other innovators, volunteers, and contributors who have made Free/Open Source one of the most exciting environments in the history of computing.

Dedication

Contents

Chapter 3:
Modules 61

Chapter 4:
Tkinter 81

Part II:
"I'll Just Have a Look 'Round the Back of the Shop, Then . . ."

Chapter 5:
Running Python

Chapter 11:
System Operations and Programming 235

Chapter 12:
Games and Artificial Intelligence 261

Kudos to Kim Spilker of Prima, who has a wonderful vision of Linux/GNU books, and Kevin Harreld, an editor who put up with a heck of a lot.

Contributors include:

Mitch Chapman

Andrew Markebo

Sam Rushing

Joe Strout

Michel Vanaken

And some who preferred to remain anonymous. Thanks to each and every one of you.

Special thanks to Mitch Chapman, who worked extensively with me honing and testing scripts. May his tribe multiply.

Acknowledgments

Tim Altom spent the first 15 years of his adult life as an electronics technician and industrial programmer. It was imperative for him to achieve balance, so he sought and won a degree in English/journalism from Indiana University. For the last several years he's been a technical communicator, project manager, author, and vice president and chief technodude of Simply Written Inc. in Indianapolis. He is a jack of all languages, master of none. He's worked in Visual Basic for Applications, assembly, C, JavaScript, Java, Boolean, Basic, Lisp, and now Python.

Tim is a senior member of the Society for Technical Communication and past president of the Hoosier chapter. He has spoken at numerous conferences about Simply Written's documentation methodology and is the author of several professional articles on subjects ranging from the history of using "big" words to designing documentation for dyslexics. He is the coauthor of Prima Publishing's *Hands On HTML*, as well as other books.

He is married, with two daughters and a stepson, and lives on the northeast side of Indianapolis in the pleasant independent community of Lawrence, Indiana. Lawrence is the proud new possessor of Fort Benjamin Harrison, a victim of the Base Closure Act. Simply Written is pleased to have authored the Reuse Plan that was partly responsible for convincing the federal government to sell Fort Harrison to the community, where it's currently being made into a center of Lawrence community life.

Mitch Chapman has been programming since his parents gave him a TI-55 calculator in 1980. He earned a degree in computer science from Wright State University in Dayton, Ohio, then went to work, maintaining aerodynamic modeling software at Wright-Patterson AFB and later helping automate flight testing of the Swedish JAS-39 Gripen.

Mitch spent the past six years at Ohio Electronic Engravers, where he barely hampered efforts to produce the world's most advanced publications gravure systems.

Mitch has developed software in C, C++, Pascal, Assembler and Fortran, and has played with many other languages. In 1996 he discovered Python. It is his favorite by far.

Mitch's current employer is Bioreason, a chemo-informatics startup located in Santa Fe, NM. Bioreason is automating the analysis of high-throughput drug screening data, and they use Python for everything from AI to GUI applications.

Mitch is a member of the IEEE Computer Society and is proud, through dumb luck, to be member number six of the Python Software Activity.

It isn't every day that I get to write a book about something really, really fun. Oh sure, technology itself is usually interesting, often addictive, and occasionally even remunerative. But fun isn't often part of the equation.

Python is fun. Really fun. It's powerful, flexible, and simple. But most of all, it's a kick to use.

I'm a communicator. I'm pretty good at it, good enough to earn a living doing it. I'm also a confirmed geek. So it's only natural that I'd write, speak, and train within technology. But much technology is at best engaging, and at worst agonizingly boring. Most software isn't exactly scintillating when it pops to the surface within its interface. And so much of what I'm called upon to document is a closed system, locked away from me by a compiler. How much fun is it to document the windshield wiper controls when you want to pop the hood and tinker?

Python is different. It's open. The source is available, and indeed is supplied on the CD. It's simple. The people who write in it are helpful and have a good collective sense of humor.

I first stumbled onto Python about the time I loaded my first Linux distribution years ago. At Simply Written Inc., we work mostly in Microsoft Windows, which is a confession I'll make here and then leave the subject alone. Our clients are largely running Windows variants, so that's what we use. As soon as Adobe ports FrameMaker to Linux, we'll talk seriously about a wholesale conversion.

Python is still a minority player in its little scripting language universe, and that too I'll readily concede. Perl was there first and is still the scripting language of choice for most UNIX/Linux users. Python, compared to Perl, is rather analogous to Linux/GNU up against the WinTel leviathan. Python is nimbler than Perl, more object-oriented, and easier to learn. But vast numbers of users have learned Perl, and haven't learned Python. Many haven't seen Python or played with it. Yet Python can be a godsend to administrators and Webmasters who are being increasingly harried by deadlines and by burgeoning demands on their time. Python could ease the pressure if only those who need it could learn and apply the rudiments of Python quickly while they were gradually becoming more steeped in its subtleties.

This book is intended to help those poor souls. It differs from prior Python books in that it doesn't teach you the language in any kind of gradual tutorial manner. Other excellent books can do that job for you, if you want.

Instead, this book presents the bare bones of Python: its statements, modules, data types, and so forth. If you're already familiar with C, database terminology, and other administrator-type technology, you'll recognize most of Python.

Then the book gives you scripts. Some are short, and others are long and involved. In my experience, what newcomers to a language cry out for is examples. Most of us learn a language more quickly with a good supply of sample code that we can puzzle through and try. You can even pluck the code right from the page or CD and adapt it to your own needs.

How This Book is Arranged

Chapters 1 through 4 are introductory. You'll read about the Python statements and see a listing of Python's modules, along with some explanation of how Python is put together. Don't expect a dissertation here, though; I'm saving room for the code.

The Python version I'm usually working with and testing in is 1.5.2. Another version may be out by the time you read this, so check **www.python.org** for updates. Many of the contributed scripts are written for older versions, which makes it necessary to offer updates in some cases.

The remaining chapters are code examples. These range from the simple, such as string handling, to the obscure that only advanced users may be able to understand.

Each script is accompanied by an analysis/explanation of the code. I break down the script's operations so you can see what's going on. This peek into the inner workings can get you jump-started into Python.

There's also an appendix with a Python FAQ. You can access the Python Web site at **www.python.org** for the latest FAQ. The Python.org FAQ is a masterpiece and deserves its place here. All FAQs should be so well organized, so comprehensive, and so informative. You can almost learn Python from the FAQ. It's on the companion CD in HTML format, too.

For More Stuff

The central switching point for Python is python.org. Downloads, documentation, SIGs — it's all there.

A major source of day-to-day help is comp.lang.python. Before posting anything, check the FAQ. It's on the companion CD, in Appendix A, and on python.org. List participants tend to get irritated if they need to write notes saying "check the FAQ." As two of the Monty Python characters say in one famous skit:

"I've told you once."

"No you haven't!"

"I most certainly did?"

Where the Scripts Came From

You'll notice that most of the scripts aren't mine. Most of the scripts in this book were donated. Some are in use by their authors, while others are fun programs that were written and posted for others to enjoy.

I solicited scripts from Pythoneers because, no matter how much I write, my code will always be in my style. Others are much better at writing Python code, so I figured that it would help you more to have a wide variety of code from experienced programmers. These scripts are in the public domain. Use them as you will. However, most of the authors would like to know if you're using their code in anything commercial. Where I was permitted to, I note the programmer's name and organization. You might want to get in touch, just to say thanks.

Python is a part of the Free/Open Source world. That means you can obtain, load, run, and tinker with Python all you want. This approach is in stark contrast to the proprietary software universe in which you're given a package, pay for it, and then struggle with it as best you can. Lots of Python programmers like Python precisely because it isn't proprietary. With Python, the tool is every bit as malleable as the product. Python programmers are often as open and available as Python itself. They're usually generous with advice and help, and the programmers who contributed here are no exception. They deserve recognition.

Although the authors of the scripts are helpful, they aren't foolish. They take no responsibility for what you do with the code. It's your job to try code and bug-zap it on your own machines.

I've edited some of the scripts to suit my purposes. In these cases, I show the original version first, then my retool. I've generally tried to start each script section with a simple example that I analyze more heavily than the rest, to give you a better entry point.

Python and Platforms

Python is available for just about every moderately popular platform, including the Amiga. However, all platforms aren't Pythoned equally. For this book I used a WinTel Python distribution and one for Linux. There are differences. Some scripts didn't run the same way on both. Shaney.py, for instance, wouldn't stop running when I ran it on WinTel. It just kept pumping out text. It ran properly on the Linux machine.

For this reason, beware of just copying a script and expecting it to fly. You may find a problem here or there with your own implementation. A basic Python script should run anywhere, but when you leave utmost simplicity behind and try for more, scripts can vary in reliability.

All in all, I prefer to write scripts on the Linux machine. My distribution is Caldera's, and I wrote mostly on Xemacs 20.4. It has a Python mode that makes it easy to keep track of indentations. You can test a script right in Xemacs. Beware, however, of testing a script in Xemacs that uses Tkinter because, in my experience, Xemacs may slow to a stop if you try to execute out of Xemacs. Ah, well?

The scripts in this book were written specifically on and for Linux/GNU. The scripts may or may not run well elsewhere.

A Taste of Python

Okay, if you've come this far with me, you're probably itching to see some code. Here's a simple example that I edited from a submitted script by Joe Strout.

```python
#! usr/bin/python
# dog.py
### get the original age
def doggie():
    try:
        age = input("Enter your age (in human years): ")
        print # print a blank line
### do some range checking, then print result
        if age < 0:
            print "Negative age?!? I don't think so."
        elif age < 3 or age > 110:
            print "Frankly, I don't believe you."
        else:
            print "That's", age*7, "in dog years."
### pause for Return key (so window doesn't disappear)
        raw_input('press Return')
    except SyntaxError:
        print "Why didn't you type anything? Try again."

if __name__=="__main__":
    doggie()
```

Anything in the script preceded by a pound sign is a comment. In this script, the other two pound signs are for effect; only the first one does anything.

Notice the use of indentation. Python doesn't use parentheses or curly brackets to enclose code. It's done solely with indentations. def indicates the start of a function.

If, while, for, and def statements are finished with colons, which tell the interpreter to look below for code to execute in these blocks. The if statement has an else and an else if that's contracted to elif.

There are other aspects to this script, but you get the idea. You can probably dope out its operations without knowing any more about Python. With a few minutes of study, you could write your own script based on this example alone. I did mention that Python was simple, didn't I?

Running this script in the interpreter isn't much harder. Start the interpreter by typing **python** at the command line or in a terminal window. If Python is installed correctly, you should get a Python prompt that looks like three angle brackets:

```
>>>
```

Make sure that the script is accessible to Python. The easy way to do this is to copy dog.py into the Python library directory. On my Linux machine, this directory is at usr/bin/lib/python1.5/.

To run this script, at the shell prompt type

```
python dog.py
```

The script fires up and runs. To play again, type the same thing again at the prompt.

You can also import the script into a Python session. That's done with

```
>>>import dog
```

You'll get back to the Python prompt. dog.py is now in the Python namespace. To make it do its doggie trick, type this:

```
>>>dog.doggie()
```

This makes the interpreter run the function doggie() in dog.py. You should get this on your monitor:

```
Enter your age (in human years):
```

Go ahead. Type in your age. Just don't try to confuse the script with any age less than 3 or more than 110. It knows better, you see. If you type 12 and press the Enter key, you'll get back:

```
That's 84 in dog years.
press Return.
```

Press the Enter key and you're back at the prompt.

If you want to run this little program again, just type **dog.doggie()** again and press the Enter key.

This example doesn't begin to graze a molecule on the surface of Python, but it does illustrate the most basic principles.

Ready for more? Tally ho!

This part is an introduction to the scripting language Python. It doesn't have Python scripts; those are in Part II. In Part I, you'll see how Python is put together, its statements, data structures, modules, and widgets. And in Chapter 1 you'll read an utterly irrelevant introduction to Python the troupe, languages in general, and Python in particular.

PART I

"Well, What've You Got?"

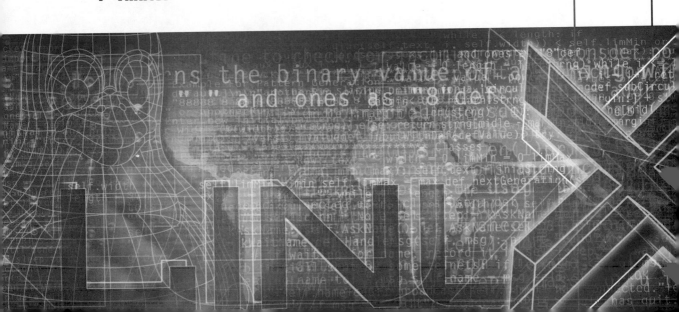

"It's..."

Chapter 1: A Day at the Circus: An Introduction to Python

The question that opens Part I occurs in the first few seconds of one of the most famous television sketches of all time: the Spam sketch from episode 25 of *Monty Python's Flying Circus*. This short television bit makes no rational sense at all; its elements include a woman café owner played by a man, a Spam-loving customer, his Spam-hating wife, and singing Vikings. Other sketches by Monty Python have featured a man arriving home to find a dead bishop on the landing, a concessionaire hawking an albatross, and singing philosophy dons at the University of Walamaloo, all of whom are named Bruce.

Monty Python was the work of six loony actors in England who had their own television show on the BBC from 1969 to 1974. The success of the show spawned albums and movies even after the show faded from the airwaves. Legions of fans have memorized the entire script of *Monty Python and the Holy Grail,* a massively irreverent movie about King Arthur and his knights' quest for the Holy Grail in medieval England. Many of these rabid fans are programmers. And yes, I know that Arthur didn't live in medieval England. Monty Python didn't exactly revere reality.

The actors, even in real life, were somewhat unconventional. Graham Chapman, one of the six, was a doctor before he succumbed to the acting bug. He died of cancer at the age of 48. John Cleese's father reportedly carried the last name Cheese until he enlisted in the army, whereupon he apparently decided to avoid barracks embarrassment by changing his name to Cleese.

Monty Python was the naming inspiration for the programming language Python, although the connection isn't readily apparent. Other than its name, the language Python shares almost nothing with the famous group of television nutcases. However, it does give Python developers no end of delightful asides and sly allusions. Those unaccountably curious about Monty Python can become jaded at **www.stone-dead.asn.au**.

Python the language was the creation of Guido van Rossum. He's still the guru and godfather of the language, and its ultimate decision maker. Van Rossum (the *van* is capitalized per Guido's request when it occurs at the front of a sentence) has been writing languages for some years. Python's origins date back to 1989, although van Rossum didn't release Python until 1991. Since then it's been retooled a bit, but it's still basically the same language that he created back then. Van Rossum's home page is at **www.python.org/~guido/**. Read his entire home page before sending him e-mail, because you may find the answer to your question before you ask it.

There is a fair amount of information about Python at the aptly named **www.python.org**. This is the official Web site for Python and the home of the Python Software Activity. Membership is only $50 US, but you can use the site if you're not a member. Here you'll find documentation, sample scripts, and lots of other Pythonalia.

Python is currently on version 1.5.2, with rumors of version 2.0 materializing soon. 1.5.2 is free for downloading from **www.python.org**. It's available for Linux, Windows 95/98, Windows NT, Amiga, BeOS, QNX, VMS, Windows CE, Sun Solaris, SGI IRIX, DEC UNIX, IBM AIX, HP-UX, SCO, NeXT, BSD, FreeBSD, and NetBSD. It comes standard in most Linux packages. Python is true open-source software, too, with its source code readily available.

If you haven't written code in an object environment or if you haven't written scripts before, Python may take some explanation. I can't tell you everything about Python here, but you can download enormous amounts of information from **www.python.org** to supplement what's in this book. With the Python download, you'll also get a tutorial, a language reference, and other materials.

Scripting: Now for Something Completely Different

If you've written scripts before, just skip this section. Go ahead. I won't be offended. Scripts are programs written in a scripting language. I know that's a circular definition, but the line between scripts and interpreted languages is vague at best.

In general, scripting languages like Perl, Tcl, or Python are written for specific purposes and have limited uses, unlike full-blown languages like C or Java that are more universally useful but are harder to learn and use. Scripts are usually written for special purposes and don't hang around all the time. You might, for example, write a script to search a file once a day for a special URL. That's all it does, and then it goes away. A scripting language that's part of an application is sometimes called a "macro" language, and its little programs are called "macros" rather than "scripts." Same thing, really.

The Linux world, of course, is loaded with scripting languages. Shells have their own scripting capabilities, and you usually get awk, Perl, Python, Tcl, and even StarBasic with Linux. In addition, you can use JavaScript and VBScript in browsers.

Scripts are interpreted, rather than compiled. An interpreter has to be running to figure out what the script commands are and then interpret those commands for the system. A compiled program, by contrast, is ready to go straight to the system without any intervention. C and C++, for example, are compiled. Perl, Python,

Tcl, and other scripting languages aren't. Interpreted languages take longer to run than compiled languages do, as a rule, but they're easier to use and maintain.

Scripts are often used for donkey work like filtering data and restructuring files. Most of the smarts that lie behind Web sites are contained in scripts. Scripts can interrogate databases, perform calculations, validate data, check permissions, write HTML on-the-fly, simplify connections between networks, and draw pictures, among many other things. Scripts can be run from the command line by typing their names. They can also be called to life by events such as logins. And scripts can even be used with a GUI (*Graphical User Interface*) like Tk or Tkinter to produce a true application.

Oh My, How to Choose?

With the clutter of possible scripting languages, how do you choose? And why pick Python?

In general, Linux scripting languages come in these types:

- Shell
- Application specific
- General use

The Linux BASH shell has a particularly useful scripting language that does most of the basic things you want any language to do: manipulate variables, evaluate conditionals, input and output data. However, the scripting language is used most often as a way of shortcutting laborious shell operations. By the way, if you want to know more about the BASH shell, type **man bash** at the Linux command line. Make sure you have a few hours set aside.

Application-specific scripting languages are used for operations within the application itself, with no thought to making the script work outside of the application. StarOffice has StarBasic, for example, as its macro language.

Python doesn't compete directly with these first two categories. It's more of a general-use scripting language. Unlike shell scripts, Python scripts are often portable to other operating systems. Python scripts are generally more flexible and high level, less concerned with system commands. And Python scripts are not normally used within applications, although Python could certainly be used that way if you were willing to do the work to embed it.

Python shares the general-use category with, among others, Tcl and Perl. Perl came along long before Python and is probably the most commonly used scripting language on servers around the world. However, although Perl is powerful and flexible, it's also much harder to master than Python and isn't inherently object oriented, as Python is. Further, Perl's syntax is almost impenetrable until you learn the language thoroughly. Python's syntax is remarkably intuitive, which makes it easier to figure out and maintain. This simplicity is also a big plus when you're learning your first scripting language.

Tcl (pronounced "tickle") is also popular, although less powerful than either Python or Perl. Unlike Python, Tcl wasn't designed to be a general-purpose programming language. Despite that, Tcl wizards have wrought remarkable things with it.

Python is particularly good at interfacing with other environments and languages. Modules are often written in C, but they don't have to be. The Python interpreter appears to other programs as an API (Applications Programmer Interface), making it relatively easy to embed. Lots of programmers use Python scripts as wrappers, or for CGI (*Common Gateway Interface*) scripts. But Python isn't just a good playmate for other applications; you can write entire applications in Python, too. Grail, a fully functional browser, is written totally in Python. You'll find it on the companion CD, or you can download it for free from **grail.cnri.reston.va.us/grail/**, the Grail home page. Grail is totally open, so you can extend or modify it as you like. It is rather slow compared to its compiled cousins. On the plus side, Grail can use Python scripts as applets.

When you look at the Grail code for the first time, you may be surprised to see how short the main program is. Python programs are often short because they can use the services of lots of other programs, as you'll see next.

Object-Oriented Programming in Python: Putting Things on Top of Other Things

In Pythonese, everything is an object. *Objects,* in programming parlance, are self-contained units of code that expose only parts of themselves on their surfaces. They're reusable and portable. Object-oriented languages make it easy for programs to reach out and use other programs' internal machinery without actually knowing anything about how that machinery works.

For example, consider a program that has several abilities inside of it. These abilities may have nothing to do with one another. They're like tools lying around in a toolbox. You can call these abilities "classes," "functions," or "methods."

It may, for instance, have mathematical functions that calculate planetary orbits, create fractals, calculate pi, and figure the beer required for any size of fraternity party.

The math operations are all very nice, but it's the beer function you're interested in today. You're preparing an orientation for graduate students, and the beer calculator would do nicely for planning the beer purchase. You don't need to write a beer calculator of your own. Instead, you write a short piece of code in Python that invokes the beer-calculator part of the calculator program. You don't know or care that the calculator program does other things too. You can just get to the beer calculator and ignore everything else. In fact, in Python, it's possible to invoke the beer calculator with two lines of code. It's as simple as that.

In this example, both your orientation program and the calculator program (which I'll call a "module" from here on) are objects. Your orientation program doesn't need to know how the calculations are done.

You can just use the beer calculator in the calculator module the same way you'd use the radio in your car without a thought to how the cigarette lighter works, even though they're both on the same electrical system.

There are lots of other aspects to OOP (*Object-Oriented Programming*), and you'll see some of them as you look through the scripts in this book. Python makes it so simple to work with objects that you may never need to know all the deep, dark secrets of how OOP works. Nonetheless, it's helpful to know a bit about how object calling is done in Python code.

Much of Python's power comes from the large collection of modules that come with the Python package. You can sometimes literally build your own programs by invoking first one module, then another, and then another until you're done.

Here's a typical Python program, using an imaginary module:

```
#! /usr/local/bin/python
import mathmodule  #This brings in the math module
beer_needed = mathmodule.beerbust(100) #This starts the beer function
#and returns the result to the variable "beer_needed"
print beer_needed #Print the result to the screen
```

And that's all there is to it. Other modules are used in much the same way. A list of the modules and what they do is in Chapter 3.

Guido van Rossum, the oracle on all things Pythonish, has said that one of Python's great strengths is that it's a blast to use. As usual, he's right. I'd add, though, that another of Python's great strengths is its evocative name. You can only do so much with *Perl* or *tickle*, but the world of the Python is endlessly rich with allusion and pun.

How to Use the Scripts in this Book

The scripts in this book are intended for two purposes: education and adaptation. The best way of learning a language is to use live code to do things and then to see what happens when you change things here or there. As you grow more adept, the scripts also give you a scaffolding on which to build your own special scripts in your own environment.

Each script is accompanied by analysis and comments. And each script has its creator's name and other information as available or warranted.

The scripts are largely aimed at Linux/GNU. Some can be run on any platform. All have been tested, but remember that successful script execution is often heavily dependent on a number of other factors. For example, a script written to interface with a GDBM database probably won't work if all you have available is DBM. However, the principles of database work are the same in both even if the statements are a little different. You'll see more about databases in Chapter 7.

One of the marvelous things about the Free/Open Source world is that people in it share and usually play nicely together. If you decide to write some interesting Python scripts, especially if you use some of the scripts herein to get started, I urge you to post them somewhere and make them available to others.

Most of the scripts in this book are short. There's a reason for that. You see, slices of dead trees with ink on them are expensive to produce and distribute. Some of the longer scripts submitted for the book would print out at a dozen pages or more. Put several of them into a single chapter, and you have a book thick enough to stop a mortar round. I had to make a choice. I could publish a few really, really long scripts, or several more short ones with different styles and approaches. I chose the latter option. Besides, size by itself is a formidable obstacle to understanding. When you have a script that runs to hundreds of lines, after a certain point you lose the thread of the logic. It's better to learn on short scripts that are more easily analyzed.

This emphasis on shorter and more varied scripts does have a drawback. Python scripts written for single, simple purposes are quite different in thought pattern from scripts written to answer big, ambitious needs. Few shortie scripts use class definitions, for example, which is a Python strength. Modules use class definitions routinely. When you need a class, you can often find one in the library, so you'll see few scripts in this book that define classes. However, a few scripts here do define classes, just so you can see how it's done. You'll see numerous examples of modules being imported and used, though. Making clever use of the Python library can shortcut hours of work.

Enjoy your trip through Python. If you have scripts you'd like to contribute to a future version of this book, or maybe tips or gotchas, feel free to e-mail them to me at **taltom@simplywritten.com**.

> "What do they mean to you?
> What do they mean to me?
> And what do they mean to
> the man in the street?"

Python is a kind of colony animal because much of its power comes from its ability to seamlessly use modules, rather than having to incorporate hundreds of commands into its own corpus. Modules can add an infinite variety of additional commands that are called just as easily as Python's intrinsics. Dozens of such modules come with Python, others are available on the Web, and you can readily write your own. However, Python has a large number of intrinsics that don't require external modules. This chapter covers these intrinsic operations.

Most of the intrinsic statements and functions work right from the keyboard in interactive mode. In this mode, you can often get returned values immediately. For example, inputting the statement chr(100) works immediately in interactive mode, printing the value to the screen. The little examples with the entries in this chapter are mostly given as if you're typing them in interactive mode.

On the other hand, in real scripts most of the statements are used by assigning outcomes to variables. Instead of having a statement print right to the screen in interactive mode, a self-starting script might use the syntax:

```
character=chr(100)
```

Statements

abs (number)

Returns the absolute value of an integer or a floating-point number.

Example

```
abs(-6)
returns
6
```

apply (function, tuple), apply (function, tuple, dictionary)

Allows an argument sequence to be assigned at run time, rather than having to be pre-defined. If the "tuple" argument isn't already a tuple, it's converted before it's used.

Example

The three-argument form is:

```
apply(do_something, (people), mydictionary)
```

In this example, do_something is a defined function, (people) is a tuple, and mydictionary is a defined dictionary. The dictionary must have strings as keys.

Where to Find It

Chapter 6: regexer.py

assert

Checks for the truth (or, more helpfully, the falsehood) of a specific debugging expression that you've inserted expressly for debugging purposes. This statement works only if the __debug__ variable is true.

Example

In interactive mode:

```
assert 1>2
```

produces

```
Traceback (innermost last):
File "<stdin>", line1, in ?
AssertionError
```

break

Halts execution of a while loop and makes execution "fall through" the loop. If the current loop was within another loop, break sends execution to the nearest enclosing loop. See also *while, continue*.

Example

```
while x != 0:
    y = doit(n) # Function that does something
    if y > 45:
        break   # Get out if y gets too large
    x = x - 1
```

callable(object)

Checks to see if an object is callable. The function returns true if the object is callable and false if it's not. Callable functions include functions, classes, methods, and built-in functions.

Example

```
callable(string)#Test to call a variable
```

returns

```
0
```

```
callable(callable)#Test to call a function
```

returns

```
1
```

chr(x)

Returns a single-character string that's the equivalent of the ASCII number x. See also *ord(x)*.

Example

```
chr(100)#Return the equivalent of ASCII 100
```

returns

```
'd'
```

cmp(x,y)

Compares the two objects *x* and *y* and returns an integer that reflects the equivalence. cmp() can be used to compare numbers or strings. The value returned is negative if x is less than y, zero if x is equal to y, and positive if x is greater than y. If the two compared objects are strings, Python compares them in standard alphabetical order.

Example

```
cmp(2,3)
```

returns

```
-1
```

```
cmp("Graham","Cleese")
4
```

coerce(x,y)

Returns a tuple consisting of the two numeric arguments converted to type that's common to both. Python doesn't permit numerical operations on unlike numerical types. They're converted to common types with coerce(x,y). Python prefers longs to simple integers, and floats to both longs and simples. Remember that you have to convert one or both back if you need the original data type elsewhere.

Example

```
coerce(12, 12L)
```

returns

```
(12L, 12L)
```

compile(string, filename, kind)

Compiles the string into a code object, read (if used) from the file filename. Python code is compiled into bytecode before submission to the interpreter. The compile statement precompiles an object, thereby saving the time of compiling at run time. The kind of object produced is determined by the kind of code being compiled: evals, execs, or singles. Execs are objects containing a sequence of statements, which do not return a value. Evals are objects that evaluate a single expression. They can return a value, but cannot assign values to variables. A single is a single interactive statement, which may or not be an expression statement. See *eval()*, *exec()*.

Example

```
mycharacter=compile("chr(100)", "", "eval")
#Compile the string into an eval()
```

Calling mycharacter

```
eval(mycharacter)
```

yields

```
'd'
```

continue

Stops execution of subsequent operations within an iteration of a while loop and sends execution back to the next iteration.

Example

```
while x != 0 :
    a = a+1 #Accumulate counts by one
    if a<10: #If you're not to 10 yet?
        continue #Go back for another iteration
```

del

Deletes a variable or item from a list. See also *lists, variables.* Also statically deletes an attribute from a class, instance, or module in the namespace.

Example

To delete an item from a list:

```
del mylist[0] #Deletes the first item from a list.
```

To delete a variable:

```
del mylist #Deletes both variable contents and name
```

To delete an attribute from an object:

```
del mymodule.yourattribute
```

Where to Find It

Chapter 6: dictEdit.py

delattr (object, name)

Dynamically deletes an attribute of a class, instance, or module in the namespace. See also *del, setattr(), getattr(), setattr().*

Example

```
delattr(mymodule, "haircolor")#Dynamically deletes
#the attribute "haircolor" from mymodule
```

dir()

Returns a list of names in the local symbol table. dir() returns a list of modules, classes, and instances. dir(name) returns a list of (name)'s attributes. This function isn't complete by any means; for example, it doesn't return methods from class instances.

Example

```
import mymodule
dir()
```

produces

```
['__builtins__', '__doc__', '__name__', 'mymodule']
dir(mymodule)
```

yields

```
['yourattribute']
```

elif

Shorthand statement for "else if." Used when an if statement has multiple possible outcomes. Note that colons must follow elif statements, just as with if statements. elif can be optionally followed by an else statement. See also *if, else.*

Example

```
if myvariable<10:
    doit()
elif myvariable>10:
    dosomethingelse()
```

else

Gives an alternative action for an if statement.

Example

```
if thisvariable != purchaseprice:
walkout()
else:
punch()
```

eval(expression[, globals[, locals]])

Invokes the Python interpreter at run time for single-statement objects or other expressions. See also *exec(), compile.* The expression argument is either a string containing a Python expression or a compiled code object produced with the compile() statement, using "eval" as its third argument. The other two arguments are optional dictionaries.

If the globals argument is supplied, then it will be used as the global namespace when evaluating the expression. If the locals argument is also supplied, then it will be used as the local namespace; otherwise the globals argument will be used as both the global and the local namespace. If neither dictionary is supplied, the expression will be evaluated using the namespaces in which the eval() is being performed.

Example

To evaluate a precompiled expression:

```
mycharacter=compile("chr(100)", "", "eval")#Creates mycharacter
eval(mycharacter)
```

results in

```
'd'
```

To evaluate an expression on-the-fly:

```
myvariable=1
eval('myvariable+1')
```

gives you

```
2
```

execfile (file[, globals[, locals]])

Reads and executes a file but without importing it into the namespace. The globals and locals arguments are optional dictionaries. If the globals argument is supplied, it is used as the global namespace when executing the file's contents. If the locals argument is also supplied, it is used as the local namespace when executing the file's contents; otherwise the globals argument is used for both global and local namespaces. If neither dictionary is supplied, then the file's contents are executed in the namespace in which execfile() was invoked.

Example

```
execfile('module1.py', mydict)#Executes the file
# using the dictionary mydict as both global and local namespace.
#"module1.py"
```

filter (function, sequence)

Eliminates the need for convoluted if statements to produce a filtered set of data, based on a definition. Requires both a filter specification and a sequence to test. If a function is given as an argument, filter() returns a list of the true elements. If the function None is used, the sequence is tested for "true" and all false or empty elements are not returned.

Example

To set up and test a list:

```
mylist=[1,2,3,4,5,6,7,8,9]
filter(mydefinition, mylist)#Apply the filtering definition
#mydefinition to the variable list mylist
```

for

Constructs a for loop. In Python, the for loop is optimized for iterating over sequences. For constructing loops that use counts, the while loop is a better bet. See also *while, if*.

Example

```
forexample = ("Come in", "Look around", "Call the cops")
for x in forexample: #Iterate over the sequence
    print x #Print the sequence variable
```

This results in the printing of

```
Come in
Look around
Call the cops
```

Where to Find It

Chapter 6: Andy's Widgets

float(x)

Converts a string or a number to a floating-point type. The argument may be a plain or long integer or a floating-point number. See also *int(), long()*.

Example

```
float("-12")#Float of a string
```

returns

```
 12.0
float(12)#Float of an integer
```

returns

```
12.0
```

getattr(object, name)

Dynamically returns an attribute of a class, instance, or module in the namespace. See also *setattr(), delattr(), setattr()*.

Example

```
getattr(mymodule, "haircolor")#Dynamically gets
#the attribute "haircolor" from mymodule
```

globals()

Returns a dictionary of the current global symbol table.

Example

```
globals()#Get a dictionary of the global namespace
```

hasattr(object, name)

Checks to see if a given object has a stated attribute. Returns a 1 if true, a 0 if false.

Example

```
import math #Import the math module
hasattr(math, 'sin')#Ask if the math module has "sin" attribute
1
```

hash(object)

Returns the hash value of the object if the object is hashable. Hash values are integers and are used to compare dictionary keys during a dictionary lookup.

Example

```
hash("cheese shop")
```

returns

```
666332922
```

hex(x)

Converts an integer to a hexadecimal string.

Example

```
hex(12)
```

yields

```
'0xc'
```

id(object)

Returns the "identity" of an object, which is actually the address. The ID is an integer that's unique for the lifetime of the object.

Example

```
id(math)#Ask for the id for the math module
```

gives, for this session

```
7870496
```

if

Constructs an if expression. An if expression examines a condition and acts on what it finds. See also *while, for, else, elif.*

Example

```
if thisvariable < thatvariable: #Compare two variables
    jumpup() #Do the function jumpup.
else:
    jumpdown() #Do the function jumpdown
```

Where to Find It

Almost any script.

import <module>
from <module> import <module methods>
from <module> import *

import <module> imports the module's name into the namespace and initializes it. When this form is used, access to the module's functions is in tree form: module.method(). from <module> import <module methods> doesn't import the module name itself, but imports only those module functions by name that you list. These functions are then called directly. from <module> import * imports all the functions in a module, but not the module name itself.

Example

```
import math #Imports the module math by name
from math import sin #Imports only the sin function from math
from math import * #Imports all of math's functions
```

Where to Find It

Any script that uses a module.

input(prompt)

Equivalent to eval(raw_input(*prompt*)). Displays a prompt and allows an expression to be evaluated.

Example

```
input("Want me to add those for ya?")
```

gives

```
Want me to add those for ya?
```

and you can then type something like

```
Want me to add those for ya? 4+5
```

and Python comes back with

```
9
```

Where to Find It

Chapter 10: dog.py

int(x)

Converts a string or number to a plain integer. See also *long(), float()*.

Example

```
y=int("34")#Make a variable y and load it with the integer result
y #Get the value of the variable
34
```

intern(string)

Places a string into a special table of "interned" strings and then returns the string. An *interned string* is a little faster to use in lookups. Interned strings are never garbage collected.

Example

```
intern("Doctor, where's my intern?")
Doctor, where's my intern?
```

isinstance(object, class)

Returns true if the object is an instance of the argument class. Returns false if it isn't.

Example

```
isinstance(myobject, myclass)
1
```

issubclass(class1, class2)

Tests both classes to see whether class1 is a subclass of class2. Classes are subclasses of themselves.

Example

```
issubclass(myclass1, myclass2)
1
```

len()

Returns the length of a string, list, tuple, or dictionary. These can be variables or literals.

Example

```
simplestring = "12345" #Assign five elements to variable
print len(simplestring) #Count the variable's elements
```

This prints

```
5
```

list(sequence)

Provides a convenient way to create a list from a sequence. The created list is in the same order as the sequence. If the sequence is already a list, Python returns a copy of the list.

Example

```
list("12345")
```

gives back

```
['1', '2', '3', '4', '5']
```

locals()

Returns a dictionary of the local symbol table.

Example

```
locals()#Get a dictionary of the local symbol table
```

long(x)

Converts a string or number to a long integer. See also *int()*, *float()*.

Example

```
long(2e3)
```

prints

```
2000L
```

map(function, sequence)

Applies function to every item in sequence, producing a new list to hold the results.

The function should be a single argument. If the function takes several arguments, then several sequences may be supplied to map(); the function will first be called with the first argument from each list, then with the second, and so on.

Example

```
1 = [1, 2, 3]
map(float, 1)
```

yields

```
[1.0, 2.0, 3.0]
```

For functions with more than one argument

```
def expound(stepNumber, step):
    return stepNumber + ": " + step


stepNumbers = ["One", "Two", "Three"]
steps = ["Grasp the holy hand grenade.",
         "Holding it firmly, pull out the pin.",
         "Count to three."]
map(expound, stepNumbers, steps)
```

yields

```
['One: Grasp the holy hand grenade.',
 'Two: Holding it firmly, pull out the pin.',
 'Three: Count to three.']
```

Where to Find It

Chapter 11: python2c.py

max(sequence)

Returns the largest item in the sequence. See also *min()*.

Example

```
max(7,8,78)
```

produces

```
78
```

min(sequence)

Returns the smallest item in the sequence. See also *max()*.

Example

```
min(7,8,78)
```

gives back

```
7
```

oct(x)

Returns an octal string from an integer argument. See also *hex()*.

Example

```
oct(9)
```

returns

```
'011'
```

open(name)
open(name, mode)
open(name, mode, bufsize)

Creates a new file object from an existing file. open(name) opens a named file. open(name, mode) opens a file in one of three modes: read, write, or append ("r", "w", or "a", with "r+" being read/write). open(name, mode, bufsize) allows you to specify the size of the buffer for the file.

Example

```
open("bruce.txt")#Makes bruce.txt into an object
open("bruce.txt","w")#Opens bruce.txt with write privileges
```

Where to Find It

Chapter 7: dbase3.py

ord(x)

Returns the ASCII value of a character. ord() inverts chr(). See also *chr()*.

Example

```
ord('d')
```

gives you back

```
100
```

pow(m,n)
pow(m,n,z)

pow(m,n) returns m to the power of n. pow(m,n,z) returns m to the power of n, modulo z. You could alternatively do modulo with pow(m,n) % z, but pow(m,n,z) is more efficient.

Example

```
pow(34,5)
```

comes back with

```
45435424
```

pass

A null statement, doing nothing. Pass fills in when a statement is required for proper syntax, but nothing should be done.

Example

```
while variable1 > variable2:
    pass #Pause for variable update
```

print

Puts the programmed text on the screen.

Example

To print one item:

```
print myvariable
```

To print several items on the same line:

```
print name, address, phone
```

To print several items on successive lines:

```
print name, address, phone,
```

range(upper limit)
range(lower limit, upper limit)
range(lower limit, upper limit, step)

Returns all the integers within a given range as a list. range(upper limit) generates a simple sequence from zero, with upper limit being the stopping point. range(lower limit, upper limit) generates a sequence of integers with the lower limit being the starting point. range(lower limit, upper limit, step) produces a sequence of integers starting at lower limit and counting to upper limit by the number of integers in step. See also *xrange()*.

Example

```
range(10)
```

Prints as

```
[0, 1, 2, 3, 4, 5, 6, 7, 8, 9]
range(5,10)
```

Prints as

```
[5, 6, 7, 8, 9]
range(5,10,2)
```

Prints as

```
[5, 7, 9]
```

raw_input()
raw_input(prompt)

Gets input from the standard input device, most often the keyboard. If raw_input(prompt) is used, the prompt is printed ahead of the expected user input area. The typed input is returned as a string.

Example

```
name=raw_input("Please type somebody's name: ")#Save the input as variable "name"
```

This statement produces

```
Please type somebody's name:
```

When the user types a name, it's saved into variable "name".

Where to Find It

Chapter 7: nickname.py

reduce(function, sequence)
reduce(function, sequence, initialization)

reduce(function, sequence) applies the function argument progressively to the items in the sequence argument, which reduces the sequence to a single value. This process is done cumulatively to each item in the sequence. reduce(function, sequence, initializer) adds an optional initial object that starts the sequence and is the default if the sequence is empty.

Example

To add a sequence of numbers together:

```
x=reduce(lambda a, b: a+b, [1,2,3,5,7,11])#x becomes the final result
#of the lambda function
```

x is now 29.

This example creates an algebraic operation ((((1+2)+3)+5)+7)+11).

To multiply a sequence of numbers together:

```
x=reduce(lambda a, b: a*b, [1,2,3,5,7,11])
```

x becomes 2310.

```
x=reduce(lambda a,b:a+b, [1,2,3], 60)
```

results in

```
66
x=reduce(lambda a,b:a*b, [1,2,3], 'bruce')
```

oddly results in placing this in x:

```
'brucebrucebrucebrucebrucebruce'
```

Gotcha

The multiplication operator (*) works differently on strings and numbers, but it works on both. For numbers, it multiplies the numbers. For strings, it duplicates the string the number of times called for. The one thing the multiplication operator won't do is multiply two strings. Sorry.

reload(module)

Reloads and reinitializes a previously loaded module. Often used to reload a module after it's been modified. The module must have been loaded already at least once, or at least a module with that name has to have been loaded.

reload() comes with a slew of warnings and special considerations. Check with the official Python documentation you get with Python.

Example

```
reload(mymodule)
```

repr(object)

Returns a string that's a conversion of the object argument. An alternative is to use reverse quotes ('object').

Example

```
repr(123)
```

creates

```
'123'
```

return

Used in function definitions to return a value from the function. If there's no expression after return, the special value None is returned by default.

Example

```
def example(a,b):
    total=a+b
    return total #Return the variable total
```

round(number, places)

Returns a floating-point value, rounded to the argument-defined number of places. The default places argument is zero.

Example

```
round(1.4567, 2)
```

returns

```
1.46
```

setattr(object, name, value)

Dynamically sets an attribute in the named object. 'setattr(sweetshop, "product", "spring surprise") is equivalent to sweetshop.product="spring surprise"'.

Example

```
setattr(test_module, "coolattribute", "albatross") #Sets the attribute
#"coolattribute" to read "albatross".
```

str(x)

Returns a converted string from x. It's used pretty much the same way as repr().

Example

```
str(6*3)#Make a string out of the result of 6*3
```

comes back with

```
'18'
```

tuple(sequence)

Converts a list sequence to a tuple. This action makes the list, which is mutable, into an immutable tuple. Often used for making dictionary keys.

Example

```
tipple_tuple = ["rum", "merlot", "gin"]#Create a list
tuple(tipple_tuple)#Convert to a tuple
tipple_tuple #Print the contents of the variable
```

brings back

```
('rum', 'merlot', 'gin')
```

type(object)

Returns the type of the argument object.

Example

```
import math #Import a module into the namespace
type(math) #Check the module type
```

which returns

```
<type 'module'>
```

vars(object)

Returns a dictionary of the object's values. The object must have __dict__ attributes.

Example

```
class demothang #Make a demonstration class
    cat="hairball factory"
    dog="loyal companion"
vars(demothang)#Get demothang's attribute values
```

comes back with the dictionary

```
{'cat':'hairball factory', 'dog':'loyal companion', '__doc__':'none',
'__module__':'__main__'}
```

while

Creates a while loop that continues to perform an operation so long as a test condition exists.

Example

```
def loop(x,y): #Function with a while loop
while x>y: #Tests for x greater than y
        print y #Print the variable y
        y=y+1
    return y
```

This example loop is called with

```
loop(6,3)
```

which evaluates the function loop(6,3) and produces

```
3
4
5
6
```

xrange(upper limit)
xrange(lower limit, upper limit)
xrange(lower limit, upper limit, step)

Returns an xrange object of the integers within a given range as a tuple. xrange(upper limit) generates a simple sequence from zero with upper limit being the argument value. xrange(lower limit, upper limit) generates a sequence of integers with lower limit being the starting point. range(lower limit, upper limit, step) produces a sequence of integers starting at lower limit and counting to upper limit by the number of integers in step. See also *range()*.

Example

```
xrange(10)
```

Prints as

```
(0, 1, 2, 3, 4, 5, 6, 7, 8, 9)
range(5,10)
```

Prints as

```
(5, 6, 7, 8, 9)
range(5,10,2)
```

Prints as

```
(5, 7, 9)
```

Arithmetic Operations

Like other languages, Python has simple arithmetic operations.

a+b

Adds two quantities. Works for both strings and numericals.

Example

```
2+3
```

results in

```
5
"stark"+"naked"
```

comes back

```
'starknaked'
```

a*b

Multiplies two arithmetic quantities. It works for strings, integers, and long integers. If the end result is likely to be a long integer, you must make the operands long integers.

Example

```
89898L*999L
```

yields

```
89808102L
```

a-b

Subtracts b from a.

Example

```
17-6
```

gives you

```
11
```

a/b

Divides a by b. If a and b are integers, the remainder is discarded. For a remainder, see *modulus, next.* As you might expect, if b is zero, a DivideByZero exception is raised.

Example

```
12/5
```

makes Python return

```
2
```

a%b

Modulus of a divided by b.

Example

```
13%5
```

gets a modulus back of

```
3
```

-a

Makes a negative (unary minus).

Example

```
x=-6 #Make x equal -6
x #Print the value of x
```

gets back

```
-6
```

+a

Makes a positive (unary plus).

Example

```
x=-6 #Make x equal -6
x #Print the value of x
-6
```

```
x=+6 #Make x equal to +6
x #Print value of x
6
```

divmod(x,y)

Divides x by y and returns the remainder as a modulus in a tuple.

Example

```
divmod(13,5)
```

gives you

```
(2,3)
```

Comparisons

Comparisons can be used in a number of ways. In interactive mode, you can directly compare two objects, be they strings or numbers. For example, if x is 4 and y is 4, then x==y gives you a 1, meaning that it's true. If x is "holy" and y is "grail", x==y comes back 0.

When executing a script from memory, you can assign objects to the returned values of the following comparison: a=x==y. a becomes 1. Or you can use comparisons in loops: while a<>b.

X<y

Tests for the truth of x is less than y.

X<=y

Tests for the truth of x is less than or equal to y.

X>y

Tests for the tuth of x is greater than y

X>=y

Tests for the truth of x is greater than or equal to y

X==y

Tests for the truth of x is equal to y.

Gotcha

Be careful distinguishing between the single equals sign of assignment (=) and the double equals sign of comparison (==). Python will probably catch the syntax error, but it may take you a while trying to figure out why all equal signs aren't created equal.

X < > y
x! = y

Tests for the truth of x is not equal to y. Either works.

is

Tests for the equality of objects. Does not check for the same name, but for the same identity. Returns 0 for false, 1 for true.

Example

```
class fishdance: #Create a silly class
    move="slap"
x=fishdance #Create an instance x of class fishdance
x is fishdance #Test for equality
1
```

The 1 indicates the equality. The same holds true for any comparison of objects, including tuples, lists, and dictionaries. Keep in mind that "equality" doesn't mean "with the same elements." In this example, z and y are the same object.

```
y=1,2,3 #Create a tuple
z=y #Make z equal to y
z is y
1
```

In this example, they're not:

```
y=1,2,3
z=1,2,3
z is y
0
```

Same elements. Different objects.

Data Types

Python's data structures are all considered to be types. You can identify the type of any data object by using type(). Python differs from many languages by having two kinds of data structures: mutable and immutable. As the names imply, mutable data structures can be fiddled with. You can delete elements, add elements, or wipe out the whole structure. Immutable data objects can't be messed with. Once created, they're the way they're going to be.

Numbers

Unlike some languages that require you to declare the type of variable you want to use—integer, floating-point, whatever—Python automatically figures it out for you when you enter it.

complex

Permits operations with complex numbers. Any number with a j or J becomes a complex number.

Example

```
89j
```

float

Short for floating-point. The precision of a floating-point number in Python is, unfortunately, dependent on the platform you're using.

Example

```
.00000987
67.26e8
```

int

Integer type. Used for the vast majority of non-float numbers in Python.

Example

```
6879
```

long

Used when a typical integer would cause an overflow. Python definitely lets you know when you've sinned with too big an integer. Put an L on the back of a long integer, and it's a long type. In fact, it can be as long as you want it to be, so long as there's memory to contain it.

Example

```
95869687364758589747L
```

Sequences

Python has three basic sequence data types: list, string, and tuple. Sequences can be created explicitly, with code like x=[0,1,2,3] or with statements like x=range(4) that let Python do the hard work.

list

Contains a sequence of strings or numbers. It's mutable and surrounded by square brackets. Known in other languages as an array.

Example

```
mysequence=[3,4,5]
```

string

A string is a sequence of characters. Python doesn't have a character data type; it's just a string of one length. Strings are set off by quote marks, either single or double. See the Python manual with your package for the rules about single and double quotes.

Example

```
thisstring="It's a fair cop."
```

tuple

A tuple is a sequence that's immutable, a kind of closed-shop list. The advantage of a tuple over a list is that a tuple is a known quantity that can't be inadvertently changed, thereby screwing up subsequent operations. Tuples are collected within parentheses and can have otherwise mutable objects within them. Because tuples are used so often in Python, especially as keys for dictionaries, making tuples is simple. Any grouping of objects separated by commas becomes a tuple. A single object becomes a tuple with the addition of a single comma after it.

Example

```
a=1,2
a #Print the value of a
(1,2)
b=(1, #Make a one-object tuple
b #Print the value of b
(1)
a=(1,2) #This also works
```

You can create tuples within other statements. For example, here's a use of apply() that creates and uses a tuple:

```
def__init__(self, x=5, *args):
    apply(MyBaseClass.__init__,(self,)+args)
    self.x=x
```

You just have to remember to use the trailing comma. If you don't, you don't get a tuple.

TIP

dictionary

Known in other quarters as keyed, associative, or indexed arrays. Maps hashable Python objects to other Python objects. Keys are immutable; data objects aren't. The pair of them, key and object, can both be deleted. The key and its object are separated in listings with a colon (:). Dictionaries let you pair up unlike things for purposes of tracking them down. Python uses dictionaries very efficiently. Dictionaries are contained within curly brackets.

Example

```
x={"cops":"Elliot Ness", "robbers":"Willie Sutton"}
```

Methods and Operations on Specific Types

These are often equivalent or similar to statements. Python has multiple ways of doing everything, so you can find much crossover here with the statements section.

String Sequences
sequence[index]

Returns the object at the index point. Indexes are integers that begin counting with 0.

Example

```
cowboytype="Rhinestone" #Make a string
cowboytype #Get the object at index position 4
```

yields

```
'e'
```

Where to Find It
Chapter 12: lotto.py

sequence[initial:end]

Slices an expression; cuts out the members of the sequence starting at initial and stopping just short of end.

Example
```
cowboytype[0:4]
```

Gets you

```
'Rhin'
```

Where to Find It
Chapter 10: sample.py

sequence[initial:]

Slices an expression; starts at initial and goes to the end of the sequence.

Example
```
cowboytype[2:]
```

produces

```
'nestone'
```

Where to Find It
Chapter 10: lc.py

sequence[:end]

Slices an expression; starts at beginning and goes to the end value.

Example
```
cowboytype[:4]
```

comes back

```
'Rhin'
```

Where to Find It
Chapter 12: lotty.py

sequence[:]

Slices an expression; produces entire sequence.

Example

```
cowboytype[:]
```

gets back

```
'Rhinestone'
```

sequence*integer

Multiplies the sequence the number of times of the integer value. Essentially, it's cloning.

Example

```
[5,6]*2
```

gives you

```
[5,6,5,6]
```

sequence+additional

Concatenates sequence and whatever additional is. The two objects must be of the same type; you can't concatenate a list and a tuple, for example. You also can't concatenate xrange() objects.

Example

```
range(2)+range(5,7)#Concatenate two ranges
```

pops back with

```
[0,1,5,6]
```

Strings

string%tuple

Permits the use of placeholders in strings. The optional data is brought in from a tuple and is eventually substituted for each placeholder in the string. This makes for some odd-looking strings in code sometimes, but it works. Python has a good many formatting codes other than %s. Consult the Python documentation that comes with your package.

Example

```
results="Results: %s for the silly party, %s for the really silly party."
count=("50%", 0)
```

Then you call for the magic merging with

```
results % count
```

which produces

```
'Results: 50% for the silly party, 0 for the really silly party.'
```

Where to Find It

Chapter 6: regexer.py

Chapter 7: dbase3.py

sequence%dictionary

Permits the use of placeholders in strings. The optional data is brought in from a dictionary and is eventually substituted for each placeholder in the string. This makes for some odd-looking strings sometimes, but it works. This operation works a lot like mail merge. Python has a good many formatting codes other than %s. Consult the Python documentation that comes with your package.

Example

```
data={"high":"72 degrees", "low":"14 degrees"}
report="The high today was %(high)s and the low was %(low)s."
report%data
```

reports back

```
'The high today was 72 degrees and the low was 14 degrees.'
```

Lists

Lists are particularly malleable in Python. There are lots of ways of manipulating them.

del list[index]
del list[initial:end]

del list[index] deletes an element at the index point. del list[initial:end] deletes elements starting from the initial indexed value to just short of end. Looked at another way, this is a deletion slice. Remember that indexes start with 0, not 1.

Example

To delete a list item at an index point

```
eric=["half", "a", "bee"] #Make a list
del eric[1] #Delete the second element
eric #Print eric
['half', 'bee']
```

To delete a sequence of list items

```
eric=["half", "a", "bee"] #Make a list
del eric[0:2] #Slice out and delete elements 0 and 1
eric #Print the value of eric
['bee']
```

Where to Find It

Chapter 6: dictEdit.py

list.append(element)

Places one element at the end of the stated list. The list itself is changed, not copied.

Example

```
eric=["half", "a", "bee"] #Make a list
eric.append("without license") #Append "without license"
eric #Print the value of eric
['half', 'a', 'bee', 'without license']
```

list.count(element)

Counts how many times an element is present in the list.

Example

```
albatross=["albatross!", "albatross!"] #Make a list
albatross.count("albatross") #See how many times this occurs
```

which gets you exactly

```
2
list.extend(list)
```

Moves the pointer to the end of the list and adds the contents of the argument list.

Example

```
albatross=["albatross!", "albatross!"] #Make a list
parrot=["parrot", "parrot"]
albatross.extend(parrot) #Extend albatross
albatross #List the values in albatross
```

giving back

```
['albatross!', 'albatross!' 'parrot', 'parrot']
```

This statement, of course, changes albatross. To keep albatross pristine, you can change the statement to

```
albatrossparrot=albatross.extend(parrot)
```

which creates an all new variable albatrossparrot.

list.index(element)

Returns an index number that corresponds with the first position of a, even if there are multiple a's. Remember that indexes begin with 0, not 1.

Example

```
lotsanumbers=[1,2,3,4,2,6,4,7,8] #Make a list
lotsanumbers.index(2) #Where's the first 2 in index order?
```

returns

```
1
```

list.insert(index, object)

Inserts the object into the list at the position of index. The higher elements are jacked up one index position.

Example

```
albatross=["albatross!", "albatross!"] #Make a list
albatross.insert(1, "bloody albatross!") #Insert object at index 1
```

which comes back with

```
['albatross!', 'bloody albatross!', 'albatross!']
```

list.sort()
list.sort(function)

list.sort() is the simpler of the two, and it merely sorts a list according to the standard Python rules for comparisons. See the documentation with your Python package for details. list.sort(function) is more complex but more powerful. Rather than using Python's built-in sorting algorithms, list.sort(function) lets you define a function for sorting, then call it with the function argument. Note that list.sort() doesn't automatically print out the sorted list.

Example

```
albatross=["albatross!", "bloody albatross!", "albatross!"] #Make a list
albatross.sort() #albatross is sorted
albatross #Print the value of albatross
```

which comes back around with

```
['albatross!', 'albatross!', 'bloody albatross!']
```

list.remove(element)

Removes the first element argument from the list. If there are other identical elements in the list, they're left in place.

Example

```
albatross=["albatross!", "bloody albatross!", "albatross!"] #Make a list
albatross.remove("albatross!") #Get rid of the first occurrence
albatross #Print albatross
```

producing

```
['bloody albatross!', 'albatross!']
```

list.reverse()

Reverses the ordering of elements in the list.

Example

```
revalbatross=['bloody albatross!', 'albatross!'] #Make a list
revalbatross.reverse() #Reverse the elements
revealbatross #Print the value of revalbatross
```

returning

```
['albatross!', 'bloody albatross!']
```

Dictionaries

del dictionary[key]

Deletes both the key and its value.

Example

```
del webster["number"] #Delete one of the entries
webster #Print the dictionary
{"size":"normal", "angle":"sharp"}
```

dictionary[key]

Uses a key to search for an entry.

Example

```
webster={"number":"two", "size":"normal", "angle":"sharp"}
webster["size"]
'normal'
```

dictionary[key] = entry

Associates the key with the value. The key must be hashable. Not all forms of data are. Lists don't work; tuples and strings do.

Example

```
webster={"number":"two", "size":"normal", "angle":"sharp"}
webster["position"]="prone" #Make new entry
webster #Print dictionary
```

returns

```
{"number":"two", "size":"normal", "angle":"sharp", "position":"prone"}
```

dictionary.clear()

Clears all the entries in the dictionary.

Example

```
webster={"number":"two", "size":"normal", "angle":"sharp"}
webster.clear() #Rids you of all the pesky entries
webster #Print the contents of webster
```

results in

```
{}
```

dictionary.has_key[key]

Checks for key being used in the dictionary. Comes back true if it's used, false if it isn't.

Example

```
webster={"number":"two", "size":"normal", "angle":"sharp"}
webster.has_key("size") #Check for a valid key
```

responds with

```
1
```

Where to Find It

Chapter 6: Andy's Widgets

dictionary.items()

Gets both the keys and the values as a list with tuples instead of a dictionary.

Example

```
webster={"number":"two", "size":"normal", "angle":"sharp"}
webster.items() #Get the keys and values as a list
```

which comes back with

```
[('number','two'),('size', 'normal'),('angle','sharp')]
```

dictionary.keys()

Gets all of the dictionary's keys.

Example

```
webster={"number":"two","size":"normal", "angle":"sharp"}
webster.keys() #Get all the keys
```

and the keys come back as

```
['number', 'size', 'angle']
```

dictionary.values()

Gets all of the dictionary's values.

Example

```
webster={"number":"two", "size":"normal", "angle":"sharp"}
webster.values() #Get 'em all
['two', 'normal', 'sharp']
```

len(dictionary)

Returns a number of key/value combinations in the dictionary.

Example

```
webster={"number":"two", "size":"normal", "angle":"sharp"}
len(webster) #Get the length of the dictionary in pairs
```

gets you

```
3
```

Files

Python's intrinsic file-handling statements can open files, write to them, and close them.

file.close()

Closes the named file. This statement automatically flushes the file, forcing writing to the disk. Releases the file's resources.

Example

```
text.close() #Closes the file text
```

Where to Find It

Chapter 6: regexer.py

file.flush()

Makes the buffered file write to the disk. When files are written in Python, they can be cached rather than immediately written. file.flush() forces the write.

Example

```
text.flush() #Make text write back to the disk
```

file.isatty()

Tries to see if a file is coming from a disk or from a keyboard/terminal. A tty returns true.

Example

```
text.isatty() #Check for tty origins
```

returns

```
0
```

To check a device:

```
inf = open("/dev/tty", "r")
inf.isatty()
1
```

file.read()
file.read(number of characters)

Reads a file that has previously been opened (meaning that it's now an object). See also *open()*. file.read() reads the entire file starting at the current position to the end of the file. file.read(number of characters) reads only the number of characters specified from the current position. If the end of the file is reached without encountering readable characters, Python returns None and the output is "". See also *file.seek()*.

Example

```
text=open("test.txt", "r+") #Open the file with read/write privilege
text.read() #Read the file's contents
```

Where to Find It

Chapter 7: dbase3.py

file.readline()

Reads one line from the file. If the end of the file is encountered without hitting a readable character, Python returns None, which is displayed as "". See also *file.seek()*.

Example

```
text=open("test.txt", "r+") #Open the file
text.readline() #Read the first line from text
```

file.seek(number)
file.seek(number, position)

file.seek(number) moves the pointer to a position in the file relative to the first byte (index zero). file.seek(number, position) moves the pointer to a position in the file relative to the position specified. A 0 means the position relative to zero, a 1 means relative to the current position, and a 2 means relative to the end of the file. It's possible to specify a byte position beyond the last byte of the file, but Python won't go beyond the EOF (*End of File*) mark. See also *file.tell()*.

Example

```
text.seek(55) #Take me to the end of the file
text.seek(-10, 2) #Moves to ten bytes before the end
```

Where to Find It

Chapter 7: dbase3.py

file.tell()

Tells you where you currently are in the file. The count, as usual, starts with zero, not one.

Example

```
text.tell() #Find out where you currently are in this file
```

tells you that you're currently at position

45

file.truncate

Truncates the file at the current position.

Example

```
outf = open("sample.txt", "r+")
outf.write("Truncate this!\n")
outf.seek(9)
outf.tell()
9
outf.truncate()
outf.seek(0)
outf.read()
'Truncate '
```

file.write(string)

Writes a string after the current seek position. If the object pointer is at the start of the file, the original bytes are overwritten. To write to the file at all, the file must have been opened with write permissions. See also *open()*, *file.seek()*.

Example

```
text=open("test.txt", "r+") #Open the file
text.tell() #Get the position of the last byte
```

when it comes back

```
55
```

you can then write

```
text.seek(55) #Sends the pointer the end of the file
text.write("this is appended") #Put this at the end of the file
```

Where to Find It

Chapter 7: dabase3.py

Exceptions

Exceptions are raised when you tell Python to do something it doesn't like to do: trying to perform operations on the wrong types of objects, overflowing memory, looking for something that's not there, and many other things. You can define your own exceptions, and there's even the capability of raising exceptions on purpose.

Python has a lengthy list of built-in exceptions, and modules can have their own exceptions, too. Exceptions are objects, either string or class objects.

List of Exceptions

AssertionError

Allows you to insert debugging statements that are conditional on whether you've enabled a debugging mode by asking for optimization or not. See also *assert*.

The statement takes the form assert expression, where expression is testable. Works only when the built-in __debug__ variable is 1. The variable becomes 0 when you ask for optimization.

Example

```
assert 1>2 #Make a falsehood
```

gives you, in interactive mode, and if __debug__ is set,

```
Traceback (innermost last):
File "<stdin>", line1, in ?
AssertionError
```

AttributeError

Raised when Python can't find an attribute or if one can't be properly assigned. If the attribute isn't possible for the object type, a TypeError is raised instead. See also *NameError, TypeError*.

Example

```
pumpedup.downer #Try to fetch a nonexistent attribute
```

which gets you only

```
Traceback (innermost last):
File "<stdin>", line1, in ?
AttributeError: downer
```

FloatingPointError

Raised when a floating-point operation fails. This exception is always defined but can be raised only when Python is configured with the -with-fpectl option, or the WANT_SIGFPE_HANDLER symbol is defined in the "config.h" file.

IOError

Appears when you're trying to do something with the I/O that can't be done. This exception is often seen when you try to open files that don't exist or write to a medium that's not able to take the file.

Example

```
open("snothere.txt") #Try to open a nonexistent file
```

which, of course, results in

```
IOError: [Errno 2] No such file or dictionary: 'snothere.txt'
```

ImportError

Raised when you try to import something that can't be found. Applies to a module or to methods of a module.

Example

```
import snothere #Try to import something that ain't there
```

Python says in response

```
ImportError: No module named snothere
```

IndexError

Lets you know when you've asked for an index position that's out of range. Note that slice expressions are automatically figured out as being out of range and don't raise an exception.

Example

```
sequence=[1,2,3] #Make a sequence with only three elements
sequence #Ask to see number four
```

returns

```
IndexError: list index out of range
```

KeyError

Arises when you ask for a dictionary key that's not actually in the dictionary.

Example

```
little_dictionary={"this":"that", "far":"near"} #Make a dictionary
little_dictionary["up"] #Ask for a key that's not in the dictionary
```

yielding

```
KeyError: up
```

KeyboardInterrupt

Raised when Python detects the operation of an interrupt key.

Example

```
input("Your name's not Bruce?") #Get input from the keyboard
```

If the user presses an interrupt key (which varies depending on the system), this happens:

```
KeyboardInterrupt
```

MemoryError

Arises on rare occasions when you've run out of memory. Not much of a problem because most scripts are small critters and modern computers have boundless memory. But possible. Most likely in a case of endless looping and object creation.

NameError

Informs you that Python can't find the object you asked for. This error happens most often when you've forgotten to import a module but you try to call its functions anyway.

Example

```
aint-there("wha?") #Call a function not in the namespace
```

returns

```
NameError: aintthere
```

NotImplementedError

A bit esoteric, this exception looms only for user-defined base classes. Check the Python documentation with your package for details.

OSError

Although OSError is a built-in exception, it works mostly with the operating system error that returns from the os module. This exception is for things that happen outside the friendly confines of the Python workspace.

OverflowError

Signifies that you've tried to perform an arithmetic operation that's too big. Doesn't arise from long integers and rarely arises from floats.

Example

```
979797979797 * 979797979797 #Multiply two big numbers
```

and you get

```
OverflowError: integer literal too large
```

RuntimeError

Arises when an error isn't covered under another explicit exception. Not used much; mostly a holdover from previous Python versions.

SyntaxError

Raised when syntax is violated. You can get syntax errors in several circumstances: when in interactive mode, when you execute with exec() or eval(), when you use input(), or when the script is first read.

Example

```
def grail(cup=None) #Oops?forgot the colon!
```

Python gently reminds you of where the problem is:

```
File "<stdin>", line 1
    def grail(cup=None)
SyntaxError: invalid syntax
```

On the screen there would be a marker under the last parenthesis in (cup=None) to let you know where the last valid character is.

SystemError

Rare exception. Produced by an internal error. Try to make a note of the string that's created so you can report the exception.

SystemExit

An exception brought about by the sys.exit() function. When this puppy happens, Python closes up shop and exits. It's used by many Pythoneers to terminate a session, with

```
raise SystemExit
```

TypeError

Raised when you're trying to perform an operation on the wrong type.

Example

```
carpool=['Fred', 'Sally', 'Dr. Graham'] #Make a list object
carpool['Fred'] #Try to perform a dictionary operation on it
```

This little mistake results in

```
TypeError: sequence index must be integer
```

ValueError

Pops up when an operation gets an argument that's incorrect, although valid, and when the error isn't covered by an exception that's more descriptive.

Example

```
carpool=['Fred', 'Sally', 'Dr. Graham'] #Make a list object
carpool.remove('Dr. Grahame')
ValueError: list.remove(x): x not in list
```

ZeroDivisionError

Lets you know when you've tried to divide by zero. This exception is often raised by not anticipating a possible division by zero, by not trapping division by zero, or by inadvertently typing a zero when you meant to divide by some other literal.

Example

```
crashme=oops/0
```

When Python tries to execute this statement, in addition to the traceback, you'll almost certainly get

```
ZeroDivisionError: integer division or modulo
```

So there.

Creating Your Own Exceptions

Python has two types of defined exceptions: string and object. String exceptions are just strings that you make pop up when conditions warrant. If you're checking for the use of an inappropriate spelling pattern, for example, you can have your script alert you with a string. Alternatively, you can define more flexible and powerful exceptions with class statements.

Handling Exceptions

One of the programmer's hardest tasks is to anticipate where problems will arise after the program is let loose amongst the careless multitudes. Coding for exception handling can get sticky, too. Python, though, comes with nifty ways to deal with predictable exceptions. Unexpected exceptions will still scotch the program in midstep, but you can gracefully deal with anything you can anticipate.

Raise

Allows you to define and raise your own exceptions or to trigger any built-in exceptions you'd like to use.

Example

To define an exception:

```
CowError="Moo!" #Set up CowError as a string exception
def cowfly(condition):
    if condition == "walking":
        raise CowError, "Wrong skit!"
    return condition
```

When you invoke cowfly() like this:

```
cowfly("walking")
```

your very own exception string makes its appearance:

```
Moo! Wrong skit!
```

To call a built-in error:

```
raise TypeError, "You're not my type, you know"
```

which in interactive mode gives you

```
TypeError: You're not my type, you know
```

Where to Find It

Chapter 10: ebcdic.py

Chapter 11: python2c.py

try/except
try/finally

Traps exceptions. If you have reason to believe that certain exceptions may arise, you can dictate what the code does when they appear.

The questionable code is corralled with the try statement. There are two flavors of try statements: try/except and try/finally. try/except has a number of lines after the try statement, lines that have potential to generate one or more exceptions. Each except statement under the try statement can hold a specific exception and an expression for what you want done when that exception triggers. An except statement without an explicit exception triggers on all exceptions. You can optionally place an else statement at the end of the "exception chain" to specify what happens if none of them trigger.

try/finally is primarily for cleanup. The finally statement precedes code that lets go of system resources, for example.

You can't mix the two types, although you can nest them.

Example

```
def dangit(): #Define a function
    try:
        5/0 #Try this statement?
    except ZeroDivisionError: #If it's this exception?
        print "Dang it! Division by zero again!" #Print this
dangit() #Call it!
```

and the interpreter now prints out

```
Dang it! Division by zero again!
```

Where to Find It

Chapter 10: lc.py

Chapter 11: tabfix.py

You can catch several exceptions in one clause. You can, for example, do this:

```
except (ValueError, IndexError):
```

Presented by the Batley
Townswomen's Guild

Python Services

String Services

Miscellaneous Services

Generic Operating System Services

Optional Operating System Services

UNIX Specific Services

CGI and Internet

Restricted Execution

Multimedia

Cryptographic Services

SGI IRIX Specific Services

SunOS Specific Services

Microsoft Windows Specific Services

T he real magic of Python lies in its set of supplied modules.

Modules give Python a fabulously expandable reach. There are modules for all sorts of operations. In addition, you can modify many of the supplied modules or even write your own. This chapter lists the supplied modules and their functions. See the Python documentation for more details.

Module functions can be called only after they've been imported into the Python namespace. See import in Chapter 2 for more details on how modules are imported or see the Python documentation.

Some modules do very much the same job as the intrinsic Python operators from Chapter 1, only with twists or improvements. The modules are listed in the order that they appear in the Python documentation. For complete information about them, consult the Python documentation. They're listed here only as a quick reference for the scripts. Most of the descriptions come directly out of the Python documentation. I've added bits here and there.

Keep in mind that different Python distributions may have different modules, even though the documentation may be the same. For instance, if you're using the Windows Python distribution, you won't get the UNIX-specific modules. (And if you are on Windows, check out **www.linux.com** for a really good time.)

Python Services

sys

System-specific parameters and functions.

Where to Find It

Chapter 7: dbases3.py

Chapter 9: engine.py

Chapter 9: who-owns.py

Chapter 10: banner.py

Chapter 10: lc.py

Chapter 11: spinner.py

Chapter 11: tabfix.py

Chapter 11: space.py

types

Names for all built-in types.

Where to Find It

Chapter 6: Andy's Widgets

UserDict

Class wrapper for dictionary objects.

UserList

Class wrapper for list objects.

operator

Standard operators as functions.

traceback

Prints or retrieves a stack traceback.

Where to Find It

Chapter 9: sengine.py

pickle

Python object serialization. *Pickling* refers to converting an object into a bit stream that can be stored or sent across a network. You can pickle integers, long integers, floating-point numbers, strings, tuples, lists, and dictionaries containing only picklable objects. One benefit to pickle over marshal is that you can pickle user-defined objects.

cPickle

Alternate implementation of pickle, only it's implemented in C to be a whole heck of a lot faster.

copy_reg

Registers pickle support functions.

shelve

Python object persistency.

Where to Find It

Chapter 7: nickname.py

copy

Shallow and deep copy operations. The difference between them is that a shallow copy makes a new compound object out of an existing compound object and puts references to the original objects into the copy. A deep copy actually copies each object.

marshal

Python object serialization (with different constraints). marshal reads and writes Python values into a system-independent binary format. You can marshal integers, long integers, floats, strings, tuples, lists, dictionaries, and code objects. Tuples and dictionaries are supported only when their contents would be supported.

imp

Accesses the implementation of the import statement.

parser

Accesses parse trees of Python code.

symbol

Constant representing internal nodes of the parse tree.

token

Constant representing terminal nodes of the parse tree.

keyword

Tests whether a string is a Python keyword.

code

Codes object services.

pprint

Data pretty printer. In essence, it prints data with some semblance of formatting.

repr

Alternative repr() implementation.

py_compile

Compiles Python source files.

compileall

Byte-compiles Python libraries.

dis

Disassembler. Of course, there isn't any real Python assembler, but this module dismantles the bytecode that the interpreter actually runs.

site

A standard way to reference site-specific modules. Unlike most modules, it's automatically imported.

user

A standard way to reference user-specific modules. user allows you to set up a customization file that a script automatically accesses when it initializes.

__builtin__

Built-in functions.

__main__

Top-level script environment.

String Services

string

Common string operations. You should get familiar with this module if you do lots of string operations.

Where to Find It

Chapter 10: strplay.py

Chapter 10: xref.py

re

Perl-style regular expression operations.

Where to Find It

Chapter 8: roman.py

Chapter 10: xref.py

Chapter 11: tree.py

regex

Regular expression search and match operations. This module is considered to be obsolete as of Python 1.5 and shouldn't be used in new scripts. Older scripts may still use it, though. If possible, the Python documentation recommends you port regex to re. See also *re*.

Where to Find It

Chapter 6: regexer.py

regsub

Substitution and splitting operations that use regular expressions. This module is considered obsolete as of Python 1.5. If possible, the Python documentation recommends that you use re instead, and port existing scripts with regsub to re. See also *re*.

struct

Interprets strings as packed binary data. The module performs conversions between Python and C structs represented as Python strings.

StringIO

Reads and writes strings as if they were files.

cStringIO

Faster version of StringIO but not subclassable.

Miscellaneous Services

math

Mathematical functions. This is another module that's very, very useful. If you do much mathematical programming (and who doesn't?), you'll want to make friends with the math module.

Where to Find It

Chapter 8: donutil.py

Chapter 8: stats.py

cmath

Mathematical functions for complex numbers.

whrandom

Floating-point pseudo-random number generator.

Where to Find It

Chapter 10: sample.py

Chapter 11: otp.py

Chapter 12: logic.py

random

Generates pseudo-random numbers with various distributions.

bisect

Efficient means of maintaining a list in sorted order.

array

Support for arrays. Python doesn't support traditional arrays natively. Arrays in this module act like lists except that the objects in them are more typed. Usually, Python doesn't make you declare a type; this module does.

ConfigParser

Configuration file parser. Lets the end user customize your scripts.

fileinput

Iteration over lines from multiple input streams.

calendar

Function that emulates the UNIX cal program.

cmd

Builds line-oriented command interpreters.

shlex

Simple lexical analysis.

Generic Operating System Services

os

Miscellaneous os interfaces let you use one module (this one) rather than picking an os-specific module. Some functions are system specific, so check the Python documentation for which ones are universal and which ones are specific.

Where to Find It

Chapter 11: space.py

Chapter 11: tree.py

> The os module gives you the ability to move around within your directory struc-
> ture using more or less familiar commands. For example, you can use os.chdir()
> to change directories. os.getcwd() retrieves the name of the directory you're
> currently pointed to. However, keep in mind that using this code can limit the
> portability of your script.

TIP

os.path

Common pathname manipulations.

time

Time access and conversions. Python has no built-in time functions, so this
module is indispensable in scripts that use time functions.

Where to Find It

Chapter 9: sengine.py

getpass

Portable password reading. Provides functions to read a password without
echoing, and to obtain a user's login name.

getopt

Parser for command line options. Similar to the UNIX getopt() function.

tempfile

Generates temporary file names. It doesn't actually create the file; you have to
do that.

errno

Standard errno system symbols.

glob

UNIX shell pathname search.

fnmatch

UNIX shell-style pathname-pattern matching.

shutil

High-level file operations.

locale

Internationalization services. Lets you incorporate cultural aspects, such as decimal-point placement and currency symbols, into your script.

Optional Operating System Services

signal

Sets handlers for asynchronous events.

socket

Low-level networking interface.

select

Waits for I/O completion on multiple streams.

thread

Multiple threads of control.

Where to Find It

Chapter 9: sengine.py

Chapter 9: engine.py

threading

Higher-level threading interfaces.

Queue

A synchronized queue class.

anydbm

Generic interface to DBM-style database modules.

dumbdbm

Portable implementation of the simple DBM interface.

whichdb

Guesses which DBM-style module created a given database.

zlib

Compression and decompression compatible with gzip.

gzip

gzip compression and decompression using files.

UNIX Specific Services

posix

The most common POSIX system calls. The Python documentation says to not import this module directly. So don't. Import os instead and let os do the work.

pwd

The password database. Gives access to the UNIX password database.

grp

Provides access to the UNIX group database.

crypt

Performs the crypt() function used to check UNIX passwords.

dbm

The standard "database" interface, based on ndbm.

gdbm

GNU's reinterpretation of dbm.

termios

POSIX-style tty control.

TERMIOS

Constants used with the termios module.

fcntl

The fcntl() and ioctl() system calls.

posixfile

A filelike object with support for locking. The documentation warns that this module will become obsolete "in a future release" and urges you to use fcntl instead. See also *fcntl*.

resource

Resource usage information. It lets you limit resources. The specific resources depend on which system you're using.

syslog

Interface to the UNIX syslog library routines.

stat

Utility for interpreting stat() results.

popen2

Subprocess with accessible standard I/O streams. Lets you spawn off processes and connect their pipes together.

commands

Wrapper functions for os.popen().

CGI and Internet

cgi

Support module for CGI scripts. Use it with the import statement "import cgi" not "from cgi import."

Where to Find It

Chapter 9: sengine.py

urllib

Opens an arbitrary object given by url. Essentially, it's open() for the Web.

Where to Find It

Chapter 9: sengine.py

httplib

HTTP protocol client. Not usually used directly, but as support for urllib. See also *urllib*.

Where to Find It

Chapter 9: sengine.py

ftplib

FTP protocol client.

gopherlib

Gopher protocol client.

poplib

POP3 protocol client.

imaplib

IMAP4 protocol client.

smtplib

SMTP protocol client.

urlparse

Parses URLs into components.

SocketServer

A framework for network servers.

BaseHTTPServer

Basic HTTP server. This module isn't typically used directly, but as a base for a server.

htmllib

A parser for HTML documents. Its HTMLParser class is used as a base class for other classes. HTMLParser is itself a subclass of SGMLparser in sgmllib. This module is good for HTML 2.0.

xmllib

A parser for XML documents. May require some tuning as the XML technology is kneaded by its various parents. Defines a class XMLParser. This module has support for XML namespaces, even though at this writing XML namespace is only a proposal, not a standard.

formatter

Generic output formatter and device interface. Used by HTMLParser class of the htmllib module.

rfc822

Parses RFC822 mail headers. The class Message in this module can handle most RFC822 mail headers.

mimetools

Tools for parsing MIME style message bodies.

MimeWriter

Generic MIME file writer. Class MimeWriter is a basic formatter for making MIME files.

multifile

Support for reading files that contain distinct parts.

binhex

Encodes and decodes files in binhex4 format. For Mac compatibility.

uu

Encodes and decodes files in uuencode format.

binascii

Converts between binary and various ASCII-encoded representations.

xdrlib

Encodes and decodes XDR data. Supports External Data Representation standard.

mailcap

Mailcap file handling.

mimetypes

Maps file name extensions to MIME types.

base64

Encodes and decodes MIME base64 encoding.

quopri

Encodes and decodes MIME quoted-printable encoding.

mailbox

Reads various mailbox formats. Used for UNIX mailboxes.

mimify

Mimification and unmimification of mail messages. Simple conversion of mail messages to MIME and back again.

netrc

netrc file processing. Handles the netrc format for ftp clients.

Restricted Execution

Under normal circumstances Python has complete access to the operating system. This is, of course, both helpful and dangerous. It's nice to be able to grab files directly, but you don't want outsiders logged on to your machine to get access to the whole system. Restricted execution lets you write scripts that don't go all the way into the system. Instead, it creates an environment that, in turn, interacts with the system. Kind of a rough-and-ready firewall. The Python documentation refers to the two kinds of scripts as trusted and untrusted.

rexec

Basic restricted execution framework. Has the Rexec class, which has restricted mode versions of exec(), execfile(), eval(), and import().

Bastion

Provides restricted access to objects. Always used with the rexec module. Allows or forbids access to an object's attributes.

Multimedia

audioop

Manipulates raw audio data. Handles signed integer samples stored as Python strings.

imageop

Manipulates raw image data. Restricted range of image types: 8- or 32-bit pixel graphics stored in Python strings.

aifc

Reads and writes audio files in AIFF or AIFC format.

rgbimg

Reads and writes image files in SGI RGB format. Limited functionality but can be useful.

imghdr

Determines the image format. Can distinguish RGB, GIF, PBM, PGM, PPM, TIFF, RAST, XBM, JPEG, BMP, and PNG.

sndhdr

Determines the sound-file format.

Cryptographic Services

You might or might not have these modules, depending on the Python package you use.

md5

MD5 message digest algorithm. Creates an MD5 object.

Where to Find It

Chapter 11: otp.py

mpz

GNU MP library for arbitrary precision arithmetic. You need the GNU MP software to make this module work.

rotor

Enigma-like encryption and decryption. Interesting little module that somewhat emulates the Enigma encoding/decoding machine used by Germany in WWII. Adequate security, but the Germans thought their original Enigma machine was uncrackable, too, and they remained unaware until the war's end that Britain had broken it.

SGI IRIX Specific Services

These modules work for IRIX versions 4 and 5.

al

Audio functions on the SGI.

cd

Interface to the CD-ROM on SGI.

fl

FORMS library interface for GUI applications.

flp

Loading functions for stored FORMS design.

fm

Font Manager interface for SGI workstations. This is a handy module, if not a complete one.

gl

Functions from the SGI graphics library.

DEVICE

Constant used with the gl module.

imgfile

Support for SGI imglib files.

jpeg

Reads and writes image files in JPEG format.

SunOS Specific Services

For SunOS versions 4 and 5.

sunaudiodev

Access to Sun audio hardware.

Microsoft Windows Specific Services

msvcrt

Useful routines from the MS VC++ runtime.

winsound

Sound-playing interface for Windows.

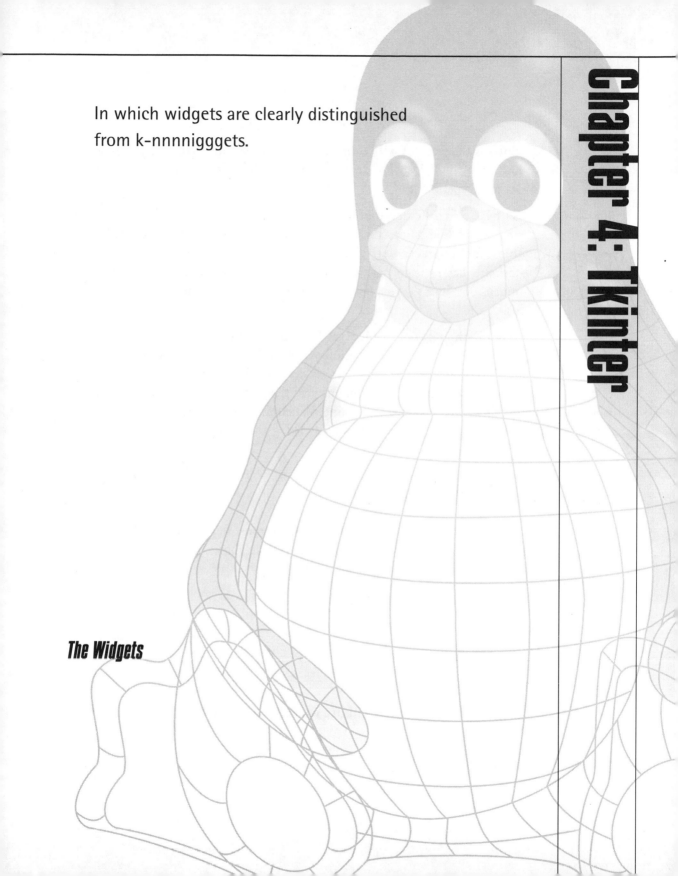

In which widgets are clearly distinguished
from k-nnnnigggets.

The Widgets

kinter is the default GUI (*Graphical User Interface*) for Python. Python doesn't have its own GUI, so Tkinter fills in. Other GUIs are available, though, if you want to experiment.

Tcl/Tk was originally developed by Dr. John Ousterhout at U.C. Berkeley. He later moved to Sun Microsystems, and is now at Scriptics. Tkinter is a Python module that interfaces with Tk, a graphical toolkit that was developed by Ousterhout. Tcl/Tk is now available from Scriptics at **www.scriptics.com**. To use Tkinter, import it just as you would any module. See import in Chapter 2 for more details.

Although Python is compatible with Tkinter, it isn't entirely compatible with the GUI world. Scripts written in Python or some other language are usually intended as one-shot programs. You call 'em, they do a job, they go away. GUI applications, by contrast, are event-driven, meaning that they establish a loop that waits for the user to click, type, or move something. When that happens, the application reacts to the event then goes back into its excited-dog-by-the-back-door posture, eagerly waiting for you to do something else.

The Widgets

Almost everything in Tkinter is a widget. Buttons, fields, and windows, all are widgets. And the widgets are all objects, too, with attributes. Check with the Tkinter documentation for details.

Button Widget

Figure 4-1   *The button widget.*

Shows the usual button within a window. See also Checkbutton Widget and Radiobutton Widget.

Example

```
endbutton = Button(parent, text="End", command=self.ok)
endbutton.pack()
```

Canvas Widget

Gives rise to all the other canvas widgets. A boring widget, because it's not directly visible, but it is indispensable. Like the other widgets, it has to be explicitly created.

Example

```
root=Tk()
drawingsurface=Canvas(root, width=100, height=100)
drawingsurface.pack()
```

Canvas Arc Item

Figure 4-2   *The canvas arc item.*

Draws an arc that can be a pieslice, a chord, or a true arc.

Example

```
root=Tk()
drawingsurface=Canvas(root, width=100, height=100)
drawingsurface.create_arc(5, 5, 90, 90, fill="red")
drawingsurface.pack()
```

Canvas Bitmap Item

Figure 4-3   *The canvas bitmap item.*

Draws a bitmap on the canvas. You can use your own XBM graphic or one of the built-in graphics. The latter are limited to an hourglass, an "*i*" for information, a question mark, and a warning icon.

Example

```
root=Tk()
drawingsurface=Canvas(root, width=100, height=100)
drawingsurface.create_bitmap(50, 50, bitmap="info")
drawingsurface.pack()
root.mainloop()
```

Canvas Image Item

Figure 4-4   *The canvas image item.*

Creates an image item on the canvas, where you can place a GIF, PPM, or PGM. Note that this is a two-step process. First you must create a member of the PhotoImage class; then you have to explicitly bring it into the canvas.

Example

```
root=Tk()
drawingsurface=Canvas(root, width=200, height=200)
photo=PhotoImage(file="brian.gif")
canvasphoto=drawingsurface.create_image(10,10, anchor=NW, image=photo)
drawingsurface.pack()
canvas.pack()
root.mainloop()
```

Canvas Line Item

Figure 4-5   *The canvas line item.*

Draws a line on the canvas.

Example

```
root=Tk()
canvas=Canvas(root, width=200, height=200)
whatsmyline=canvas.create_line(10, 10, 100,100)
canvas.pack()
root.mainloop()
```

Canvas Oval Item

Figure 4-6   *The canvas oval item.*

Puts an oval on the canvas. The oval fits inside a bounding box that determines its shape.

Example

```
root=Tk()
canvas=Canvas(root, width=200, height=200)
oval=canvas.create_oval(10, 10, 100, 50)
canvas.pack()
root.mainloop()
```

Canvas Polygon Item

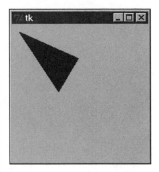

Figure 4-7   *The canvas polygon item.*

Draws a polygon on the canvas. Because nature isn't generally round or square, polygons can come in handy for rendering slightly more realistic shapes.

Example

```
root=Tk()
canvas=Canvas(root, width=200, height=200)
polygon=canvas.create_polygon(10, 10, 100, 50, 70, 100)
canvas.pack()
root.mainloop()
```

Canvas Rectangle Item

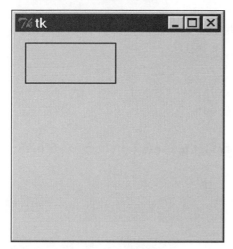

Figure 4-8   *The canvas rectangle item.*

Puts a rectangle on the canvas. The rectangle is also helpful if you want to see your bounding box for other figures, such as ovals.

Example

```
root=Tk()
canvas=Canvas(root, width=200, height=200)
rectangle=canvas.create_rectangle(10, 10, 100, 50)
canvas.pack()
root.mainloop()
```

Canvas Text Item

Figure 4-9   *The canvas text item.*

Draws text on the canvas.

Example

```
root=Tk()
canvas=Canvas(root, width=200, height=200)
text=canvas.create_text(100, 100, text="I'm text!")
canvas.pack()
root.mainloop()
```

Canvas Window Item

Inserts a window into the canvas. By default, the window item expands to the size of the window.

Example

```
root=Tk()
canvas=Canvas(root, width=200, height=200)
windot
canvas.create_window(100, 100)
canvas.pack()
root.mainloop()
```

Checkbutton Widget

Figure 4-10   *The checkbutton widget.*

Puts a check box into the window. This is, of course, the classic check box that has two states: checked and unchecked.

Example

```
root=Tk()
var=IntVar()
checkbutton1=Checkbutton(root, text="Checkers!", variable=var)
checkbutton1.pack()
root.mainloop()
```

Entry Widget

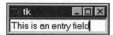

Figure 4-11   *The entry widget.*

Inserts a text entry field into the window.

Example

```
root=Tk()
entry=Entry(root)
entry.pack()
root.mainloop()
```

Frame Widget

Creates a frame within the window, where you can put figures, video, and other goodies. It also serves as padding between widgets.

Example

```
root=Tk()
frame=Frame(root, width=100, height=100, bg="red")
frame.pack()
root.mainloop()
```

Label Widget

Figure 4-12   *The label widget.*

Puts a predefined text area into the window. The label widget is the quickest way to code the Python version of "Hello World."

Example

```
root=Tk()
label=Label(root, text="Hello world!")
label.pack()
root.mainloop()
```

Listbox Widget

Figure 4-13   *The listbox widget.*

Inserts a list box of possible choices. This widget isn't the familiar drop-down (combo) box you may know from other GUI conventions. The example shows only how to create a list box, not how to acquire the results from one.

Example

```
root=Tk()
listbox=Listbox(root, relief=RAISED)
listbox.insert(END, "a list entry")
for item in ["up", "down", "left", "right"]:
    listbox.insert(END, item)
listbox.pack()
root.mainloop()
```

Menu Widget

Figure 4-14   *The menu widget.*

Places a menu on a window or frame. Often used in conjunction with the menubutton widget. For examples of menus used alone, see the code for Grail, on the companion CD-ROM.

Menus can be made "tearoff," which makes it possible to click on a menu and make it into its own little window.

Example

```
from Tkinter import *
frame = Frame()
label = Label(width=48, text="Wot'll it be, then?")
menubar = Frame(frame, relief="raised", bd=2)
sampleMenu = Menubutton(menubar, text="File")
pane = Menu(sampleMenu)
for menuitem in ["Spam", "Spam", "Spam", "Eggs", "Spam"]:
# Define a callback function for this menu item, on the fly.
def menuItemCallback(statusLabel=label, newMsg=menuitem):
statusLabel['text'] = "Can I have her %s? I love it!" % newMsg
pane.add_command(label=menuitem, command=menuItemCallback)
pane.add_separator() # Add a horizontal separator line.
pane.add_command(label="Exit", command=frame.quit)
sampleMenu['menu'] = pane
sampleMenu.pack(side="left") # Arrange the pulldown menus from left to
right.
menubar.pack(side="top", fill="x", expand="n")
label.pack(side="bottom", fill="both", expand="y")
frame.pack(fill="both", expand="y")
frame.winfo_toplevel().title("The Spam Sketch")
frame.mainloop()
```

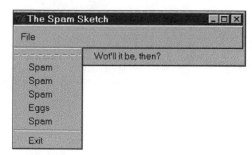

Figure 4-15   *Results of the menu widget example.*

Message Widget

Figure 4-16   *The message widget.*

Displays lines of text. The entry widget is good for only one line; but this does multiples, justification, and a few other interesting things that you'll have to read the Tkinter documentation to discover.

Example

```
root=Tk()
message=Message(root, text="Nudge, nudge, say no more, say no more!")
message.pack()
root.mainloop()
```

Radiobutton Widget

Figure 4-17   *The radiobutton widget.*

With button and checkbutton, constitutes the basic input mechanisms in Tkinter. See also Checkbutton Widget and Button Widget.

Example

```
root=Tk()
ThisVariable=IntVar()
Radiobutton(root, text="Here first", variable=ThisVariable, value=1).pack()
Radiobutton(root, text="Now here", variable=ThisVariable, value=2).pack()
root.mainloop()
```

Scale Widget

Figure 4-18   *The scale widget.*

Establishes a slider widget with a range of values. The user slides it up or down to return a value.

Example

```
root=Tk()
scale=Scale(root, label="How far?")
scale.pack()
root.mainloop()
```

Scrollbar Widget

Places a scrollbar next to a frame or window to allow the user to move forward or backward through a displayed file.

Example

```
root=Tk()
scrollbar=Scrollbar()
scrollbar.pack()
root.mainloop()
```

Text Widget

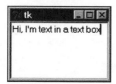

Figure 4-19   *The scrollbar widget.*

Creates a text entry area, much like that of a word processor. There's no default scroll bar; you have to add one yourself.

Example

```
root=Tk()
text=Text(root)
text.pack()
root.mainloop()
```

Toplevel Widget

Creates another window as a child of the root window.

Example

```
root=Tk()
toplevel=Toplevel(root)
root.mainloop()
```

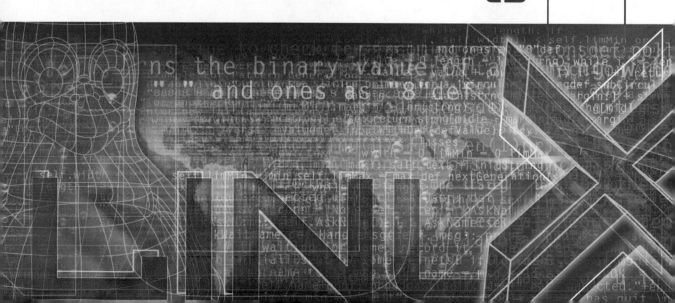

"There you go, bringing class into it again!"

Main Under a GUI Mode

Main Mode

Interactive Mode

P ython has four modes of operation:

- Main under a GUI
- Main
- Embedded
- Interactive

Embedded mode is what you get when Python is embedded in another application. This mode is for serious programming needs and isn't covered in this book. Check the Python distribution documentation.

Main Under a GUI Mode

Main under a GUI mode requires a different programming style because the GUI requires event looping, rather than the more direct style in typical scripts. Tkinter, a Python module that comes with the standard distribution, has everything you need for most Python GUI applications. Chapter 6 has Tkinter GUI scripts, so you'll get a chance to practice this mode.

Main Mode

In main mode, you start Python by starting a script directly, as if the script were an executable. Some systems, however, require some setup first. In Caldera Linux, for example, to run viking.py from the command line, you can type either of these commands:

```
$ python viking.py 2
$ viking.py 2
```

In each case the 2 is an argument you're passing to the script.

However, on many systems (including Linux/GNU) neither of these will work unless:

- The script is in a directory that's in the path or in the directory you're currently in; and
- Execution permissions have been set for the script.

Not every system requires you to set permissions and define a path, but many do.

To save yourself aggravation, if you can change your path environment variable, do it right now, this instant, to add the directory where you're storing scripts. On my Linux/GNU machine, the default directory is /usr/lib/python1.5. I just place scripts in the same directory as the modules, in other words. It's convenient, and I'm not confused. However, you can create a new directory for developmental scripts as long as you put that directory into your path variable. If you're new to Linux/GNU, check your documentation for how to change the path variable.

You'll see a lot of Python scripts with a special line at the top that looks something like this:

```
#!/usr/bin/python
```

This line is called the "pound-bang-hack." On some systems, notably UNIX, the pound-bang-hack tells the system where to direct its attention when the script is run in main mode. Your system may or may not need this, but it's a nice touch for scripts that you share with others. Some systems read the first line of a file to get instructions, and on those systems this line readily tells the system where to find the interpreter. Fortunately, because the Python interpreter doesn't bother with any lines that start with the pound sign, Python ignores this line.

If you want to run your script as a main program, the script needs a __main__ routine. This routine is conventionally placed at the bottom of the script, while function definitions go at the top. A typical __main__ looks like this:

```
if __name__ == "__main__":
    sheep_sighting= raw_input("Did you see a sheep in a tree? Answer Y or N:) "
    sheep_fly(sheep_sighting)
else:
    print "Module shpsite imported."
    print "To run, type: sheep_fly("Y or N")"
```

These lines check a variable to see if the registered name of the script is "__main__", which it will be if you started the script from the command line. In that case, the user gets the prompt, "Did you see a sheep in a tree? Answer Y or N:"

On the other hand, if the script is imported into the interpreter in interactive mode, the user gets the message, "Module shpsite imported. To run, type: sheep_fly()".

Scripts intended to be modules, rather than main programs, don't need this code. Some scripts are intended to be used in either mode, and need lines like these.

Interactive Mode

A useful mode for development is interactive mode, the last of the four modes. In this mode, the Python interpreter is available in real time. You start an interactive session on many systems by typing **python** at the command line prompt. On Windows, Python can be launched by double-clicking the Python icon. On Linux/GNU, you can just type the word **python**. When the Python interactive session is active, you get a few lines of text, followed by the Python prompt, which looks like this:

```
>>>
```

In interactive mode, you can do simple programming for one-shot functions. This code, for example, does basic arithmetic:

```
>>> 5*4
20
>>>
```

In this case, the interpreter won't retain anything. The operation is over, and if you want to repeat it, you have to retype everything. However, you can define a function, and it'll stay in the namespace until you kill your session:

```
>>>def run(var1, var2):
...    print var1*var2
...
>>>
```

You have to press the Enter key when you see the second line of periods (…) to let the interpreter know you're done with the definition. To run this script, you can type

```
>>>run(3,4)
```

and Python will dutifully respond with

```
12
>>>
```

You can do this as many times as you want. When you leave the session, run() goes into the bit bucket and is lost.

You can import modules and scripts into the namespace in interactive mode, and this is helpful when you're writing scripts that aren't yet ready for main mode. For instance, if you're writing a script covar.py with a function get_instance(), you can type these lines to run the function

```
>>>import covar.py
>>>covar.get_instance()
```

and get_instance() does whatever it was written to do (hopefully).

When the interpreter imports a module or script (modules often are scripts but with a different purpose in life), the interpreter checks for syntax errors. If it finds one, it lets you know right away. Run-time errors won't show until you run the code.

Many of the scripts in this book have been written to be used in main mode, although they can be run in interactive mode if you like.

Different systems exit Python differently. To make Python go away, you need an EOF character, which on Linux systems is Control+D. Using Control+Z on Linux makes the interpreter stop, but it doesn't get rid of it.

TIP

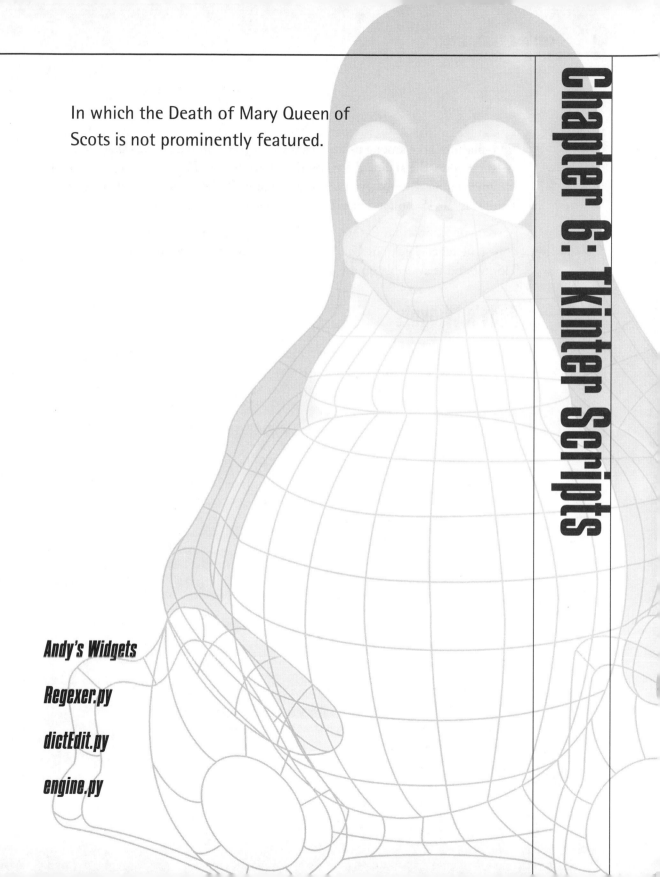

In which the Death of Mary Queen of
Scots is not prominently featured.

Chapter 6: TKinter Scripts

Andy's Widgets

Regexer.py

dictEdit.py

engine.py

To placate those among us who want GUIs (*Graphical User Interfaces*) on top of their code, the standard Python distribution uses Tk. You can use just about any graphical toolkit you want, and many Pythoneers have other favorites. Tkinter is the Python module that interfaces with the Tk calls.

Lest anyone think that Python is a minor language that can't cut it as an applications language, check out Grail, a browser built entirely with Python. Grail uses Tkinter and is available on the companion CD.

Andy's Widgets

```
""" FWidgets version 4.2, Time-stamp: <96/12/12 12:36:05 x-aes>
            Some simple window constructions I commonly use
        quite often, decided to store them here.


  Copyright (C) 1996 Andy Eskilsson, flognat@fukt.hk-r.se


  This is free software; unrestricted redistribution is allowed under the
  terms of the GPL.  For full details of the license conditions of this
  software, see the GNU General Public License.


  And here comes the documentation:

OkCancelWindow:
  A simple window with two buttons, text, label and
  possibility to configure the buttons. Call go to pop up.
  Returns TRUE/FALSE.


ScrolledText
  A frame with textbox and a scrollbar.
  Initializer takes Master, textconfig and scrollbarconfig
  set clears and fills the box with the string sent to it,
  while get returns the text as string.


LabelEntry
  A frame containing a text label and an entry field for data.
```

```
        Initializer takes Master, Text, labelconfig and textconfig.
        empty clears the entry, get gets the entry, set sets the
        entry, binds event to callback,

    OKCancelButtons
        A frame containing two buttons.
        Initializer takes master, okbutton config and cancelbutton
        config, send in callback as 'command' in config dictionary.

    ScrolledList
        A frame containing a listbox and a scrollbar.
        Initializer takes Master, listconfiguration and scrollbarconfiguration
        bind can be used to bind events to callbacks, empty clears the list,
        add adds one string, or a list of strings to the box, default at END
        active returns the last selected string, get returns the selected string
        or a list of them, getIndex returns the # of selected item[s], unselect
        clears all selections.

    I (the author) can be reached at flognat@fukt.hk-r.se, and the newest
    version of this file can be found in the vicinity of
    http://www.fukt.hk-r.se/~flognat.

    If you like it, send a postcard to Andy Eskilsson
                            Kämnärsv. 3b228
                    S-226 46 Lund
                    Sweden
    """


from Tkinter import *
from types import *
from string import *

def DummyCommand():
    pass

scrollbarWidth = 10

class OkCancelWindow(Frame):
    def __init__(self, Master, Text, Label='Are U sure?', ytcnf={}, ntcnf={}):
```

```
        Frame.__init__(self, Master)
        self.pack()
        self._top=Toplevel(Master)
        self._top.title(Label)
        ytcnf['command']=self.okBtn
        ntcnf['command']=self.noBtn
        self.createWindow(self._top, Text, ytcnf, ntcnf)

    def go(self):
        self._top.grab_set()
        try:
        self._top.mainloop()
        except SystemExit, selection:
        self._top.destroy()
        return selection

    def createWindow(self, Master, Text, ytcnf, ntcnf):
        self._text=Label(Master, {'text' : Text})
        self._text.pack({'side': 'top','fill' : 'x'})
        self._buttons=OkCancelButtons(Master, ytcnf, ntcnf)
        self._buttons.pack({'side': 'bottom','fill' : 'x'})

    def okBtn(self):
        raise SystemExit, TRUE

    def noBtn(self):
        raise SystemExit, FALSE

class ScrolledText(Frame):
    def __init__(self, Master, txtcnf={}, sbcnf={}):
        Frame.__init__(self, Master)
        self.pack()

        self._textArea=Text(self, txtcnf)
        self._textArea.pack({'side': 'left', 'fill': 'both','expand' : 'yes'})
        if not sbcnf.has_key('width'):
        sbcnf['width']=scrollbarWidth
        self._scrollBar=Scrollbar(self, sbcnf)
        self._scrollBar.pack({'side': 'right', 'fill': 'y','expand' : 'yes'})
        self._textArea['yscrollcommand'] = (self._scrollBar, 'set')
```

```
            self._scrollBar['command'] = (self._textArea, 'yview')

        def set(self, text):
            self._textArea.delete("1.0", END)
            self._textArea.insert(END, text)

        def get(self):
            return self._textArea.get("1.0", END)

class LabelEntry(Frame):
    def __init__(self, Master, Text, lblcnf={}, txtcnf={}):
        Frame.__init__(self, Master)
        self.pack()
        lblcnf['text']= Text
        self._label = Label(self, lblcnf)
        self._label.pack({'side': 'left', 'expand':'no'})

        self._entry = Entry(self, txtcnf)
        self._entry.pack({'side': 'right', 'expand' : 'yes', 'fill' : 'x'})

    def empty(self):
        self._entry.delete(0, END)

    def get(self):
        return self._entry.get()

    def set(self, Value=''):
        self.empty()
        self._entry.insert(END, Value)

    def bind(self, Event, Callback):
        self._entry.bind(Event, Callback)

class OkCancelButtons(Frame):
    def __init__(self, Master, okcnf = {}, cancelcnf = {}):
        Frame.__init__(self, Master)
        self.pack()

        if not okcnf.has_key('text'):
        okcnf['text']='Ok'
```

```
            if not cancelcnf.has_key('text'):
          cancelcnf['text']='Cancel'

            if not okcnf.has_key('command'):
          okcnf['command']=DummyCommand
            if not cancelcnf.has_key('command'):
          cancelcnf['command']=DummyCommand

            self._cancelBtn = Button(self, cancelcnf)
            self._cancelBtn.pack({'side': 'right'})

            self._okBtn = Button(self, okcnf)
            self._okBtn.pack({'side': 'right'})

class ScrolledList(Frame):
    def __init__(self, Master, listcnf={}, sbcnf={}):
        Frame.__init__(self, Master)
        self.pack()

            if not sbcnf.has_key('width'):
          sbcnf['width']=scrollbarWidth

            self._multiselect=FALSE
            if listcnf.has_key('selectmode'):
            if listcnf['selectmode'] == 'multiple' or listcnf['selectmode'] == 'extended':
                self._multiselect=TRUE

            self._list = Listbox(self,listcnf)
            self._list.pack({'side': 'left', 'fill': 'both','expand' : 'yes'})

            self._sb = Scrollbar(self, sbcnf)
            self._sb.pack({'side': 'right', 'fill': 'y'})

            self._list['yscrollcommand'] = (self._sb, 'set')
            self._sb['command'] = (self._list, 'yview')

    def bind(self, Event, Callback):
        self._list.bind(Event, Callback)

    def empty(self, begin=0, end=END):
```

```
        self._list.delete(0, END)


    def add(self, item, position = END):
        if type(item) == StringType:
      self._list.insert(position, item)
        elif type(item) == ListType:
      for i in item:
          self._list.insert(position, i)


    # Return the active item
    def active(self):
        return self._list.get(ACTIVE)


    def whatis(self, first, last=None):
        if last==None:
      return self._list.get(first)
        else:
      # Hack Galore, why isn't this implemented in
      # Tkinter??
      return self._list.tk.splitlist(self._list.tk.call(self._list._w, 'get',\
first, last))


    # Return a the selected item or a list with selected items
    def get(self):
        if self._multiselect==FALSE:
      retVal=self._list.curselection()
      if len(retVal)==0:
          return None
      else:
          return self._list.get(retVal[0])
        else:
      ret=[]
      for i in self._list.curselection():
          ret.append(self._list.get(i))
      return ret


    # return the # of the selected item.
    def getIndex(self):
        selection=self._list.curselection()
        if len(selection)==0:
```

```
        return None
         if self._multiselect==FALSE:
        return atoi(selection[0])
         else:
        retVal=()
        for i in selection:
           retVal.append(atoi(i))
        return retVal


   # Gee we can have both list and only one string, hmm yep
   # but funny things can happen if we have more than one
   # item in the list with same name...
   def select(self, items):
      noOfItems=self._list.size()
      if type(items) == StringType:
      for i in range(noOfItems):
         if items==self._list.get(i):
            self._list.select_set(i,i)
      elif type(items) == ListType:
      for i in range(noOfItems):
         line=self._list.get(i)
         for j in items:
            if line==j:
            self._list.select_set(i,i)
       else:
      pass # Well we could raise an exception.. but :-)


   def unselect(self):
      self._list.select_clear(0)


############################# TEST #############################

root=None
GoodBye='bye bye'

def testfun():
   print root.slist.get(),
```

```
        print root.slist.getIndex()

def testfun2():
    a=OkCancelWindow(root, "OOPs really, really cancel?")
    b=a.go()
    print b
    if b:
        raise GoodBye

def test():
    root.slist = ScrolledList(root)#, {'selectmode' : 'multiple'})
    root.entry = LabelEntry(root, "Enter")
    root.btn = OkCancelButtons(root, {'command': testfun}, {'command': testfun2})
    root.txt = ScrolledText(root)
    root.txt.set("abc123")
    root.txt2 = ScrolledText(root, {'relief': 'sunken', 'width' : 10}, {'width' :
3})
    root.slist.add(["A", "B", "C", "D", "E", "F", "G"])
    root.slist.select("B")

    try:
        root.mainloop()
    except GoodBye:
        root.destroy()


if __name__ == '__main__':
    root = Tk()
    test()
```

How It Works

This code is a great leadoff to this chapter, because it's a compilation of some basic and handy widgets. The widgets include:

- OkCancelWindow, a simple window with two buttons, text, and a label
- ScrolledText, a frame with textbox and a scrollbar
- LabelEntry, a frame containing a text label and an entry field for data
- OKCancelButtons, a frame containing two buttons
- ScrolledList, a frame containing a listbox and a scrollbar

The widgets are assembled into classes, as you'd expect. You can use these classes as-is or extend them. You can do a lot of work in Tkinter with only the widgets that are presented here.

Contributed by Andrew Markebo, software developer at Telelogic AB. "The usability lies in the eye of the user…"

Regexer.py

Python has a couple of standard modules that use regular expressions: regex and re. regex is the older of the two, and the less powerful. But both are often confusing because many people have never worked with regular expressions. This script makes regular expressions visible.

```
""" Regexer version 3.0, Time-stamp: <96/11/03 22:53:54 flognat>
              A simple regular expression simulator.


   Copyright (C) 1996 Andy Eskilsson


   This software is provided as-is, without express or implied
   warranty.  Permission to use, copy, modify, distribute or sell this
   software, without fee, for any purpose and by any individual or
   organization, is hereby granted, provided that the above copyright
   notice and this paragraph appear in all copies.


   And here comes the documentation:


     Am I the only one finding <a +href=['"]?\(.*\)[ '">]\(.*\)</A>
     quite unreadable not so clear? And wanna try to experiment with
     it to find out how to get rid of the bug? Well thats why Regexer
     were born!


     Regexer is a small application for experimenting with regular
     expressions in python, it gives the user instant feedback on what
     a modification to the regexp or string that the regexp is applied
     on means to the regexp.


     I guess it also can come in handy when trying to learn regexps
     because it is possible to experiment with them.


     The regexps/strings can be saved into a separate listbox for
```

quick switching between different regexps/strings. And ah.. you
can list the different groups, by sliding the slider..

Selecting a string/regexp (with the right mousebutton) in their
window sends the respective to it's field in the main regexer window,
pressing the left mousebutton in respective window deletes the
selected entry. NOT the entry you clicked over (except if none is
selected) If any1 has a better idea how to do this they are welcome.

Things I am thinking of is some kind of egrep-version, give it a
bunch of strings and it lists the matching ones, the possibility
to simulate on more than one string at a time. Well if anyone
feels that they like these features I probably could implement them.

I (the author) can be reached at flognat@fukt.hk-r.se, and the newest
version of this file can be found in the vicinity of
http://www.fukt.hk-r.se/~flognat.

If you like it (well you don't have to lie it, it is always fun receiving
snailmail :-), send a postcard to: Andy Eskilsson
                         Kämnärsv. 3b228
                 S-226 46 Lund
                 Sweden
"""

```
# ' <-- needed for font-lock-mode to look good :-)

from Tkinter import *
from StringIO import StringIO

import regex
import regex_syntax
import string

###########
# Just some tool classes, application further down.
###########

def bittify(value, bits):
    count=1
```

```
    retlist=[]

  for bit in range(bits):
      if count&value:
    retlist.append(1)
      else:
    retlist.append(0)
      count=count*2

  return retlist

def unbittify(bits):
   count=1
   retval=0

   for bit in bits:
      if bit:
    retval=retval^count
      count=count*2

   return retval

def doSearch(cregexp, str, fp):
   try:
      s=cregexp.search(str)
   except regex.error, message:
      fp.write("Error in search:\n  %s" % message)
   else:
      fp.write("search returns %d\n" % s)
      if s!=-1:
    fp.write("  and points on '%s'\n\n" % string.strip(str[s:s+15]))

def doMatch(cregexp, str, fp):
   try:
      m=cregexp.match(str)
   except regex.error, message:
      fp.write("Error in match:\n  %s" % message)
   else:
```

```python
        fp.write("match returns %d\n\n" % m)

def doGroups(cregexp, str, groups, fp):
    try:
        strgroups=apply(cregexp.group, tuple(range(1, groups+1)))
    except regex.error, message:
        fp.write("Error in groups:\n  %s" % message)
    else:
        if groups==1:
      fp.write("And the %d group is:\n" % groups)
      fp.write("  %s\n" % strgroups)
        else:
      fp.write("And the %d groups are:\n" % groups)
      for group in strgroups:
          fp.write("  %s\n" % group)


class ListWindow(Frame):
    """ A window with a scrolledlist """
    def __init__(self, title, master=None):
        """ title is the title of the window, and master is
            the eventual master to the window """
        Frame.__init__(self, master)
        self._top=Toplevel(self.master)
        self._top.title(title)
        self.pack()

        self._multiselect=FALSE
        self.drawme()


    def drawme(self):
        self._list=Listbox(self._top)
        self._list.pack({'side': 'left', 'fill': 'both','expand' : 'yes'})
        self._sb = Scrollbar(self._top)
        self._sb.pack({'side': 'right', 'fill': 'y'})

        self._list['yscrollcommand'] = (self._sb, 'set')
        self._sb['command'] = (self._list, 'yview')
```

```python
    def bind(self, Event, Callback):
        """ Bind the Event of the list to Callback """
        self._list.bind(Event, Callback)

    def clear(self):
        """ Clear the list """
        self._list.delete(0, END)

    def add(self, item, position = END):
        """ Add one or more items to a the list """
        if type(item) == StringType:
      self._list.insert(position, item)
        elif type(item) == ListType:
      for i in item:
          self._list.insert(position, i)

    def active(self):
        """ Return the active item """
        return self._list.get(ACTIVE)

    def whatis(self, first, last=None):
        """ Returns the item[s] """
        if last==None:
      return self._list.get(first)
        else:
      # Hack Galore, why isn't this implemented in
      # Tkinter??
        return self._list.tk.splitlist(self._list.tk.call(self._list._w, 'get', first,
last))

    def get(self):
        """ Return a the selected item or a list with selected items """
        if self._multiselect==FALSE:
      retVal=self._list.curselection()
      if len(retVal)==0:
          return None
      else:
          return self._list.get(retVal[0])
```

```
        else:
      ret=[]
      for i in self._list.curselection():
         ret.append(self._list.get(i))
      return ret


# return the # of the selected item.
def getIndex(self):
      selection=self._list.curselection()
      if len(selection)==0:
      return None
      if self._multiselect==FALSE:
      return atoi(selection[0])
       else:
      retVal=()
      for i in selection:
         retVal.append(atoi(i))
      return retVal


# Gee we can have both list and only one string, hmm yep
# but funny things can happen if we have more than one
# item in the list with same name...
def select(self, items):
      noOfItems=self._list.size()
      if type(items) == StringType:
      for i in range(noOfItems):
         if items==self._list.get(i):
            self._list.select_set(i,i)
      elif type(items) == ListType:
      for i in range(noOfItems):
         line=self._list.get(i)
         for j in items:
            if line==j:
            self._list.select_set(i,i)
      else:
      pass # Well we could raise an exception.. but :-)


def delete(self, item):
```

```
            self._list.delete(item)

    def unselect(self):
        self._list.select_clear(0)


#############
# Well here the actual application starts :-)
#############

class Regexer(Frame):
    """ The application itself """
    def __init__(self, master=None):
        Frame.__init__(self, master)
        self._matchCheck = BooleanVar()
        self._searchCheck = BooleanVar()
        self._linesCheck =  BooleanVar()

        self._RE_NO_BK_PARENS = BooleanVar()
        self._RE_NO_BK_VBAR = BooleanVar()
        self._RE_BK_PLUS_QM = BooleanVar()
        self._RE_TIGHT_VBAR = BooleanVar()
        self._RE_NEWLINE_OR = BooleanVar()
        self._RE_CONTEXT_INDEP_OPS = BooleanVar()

        self.master.title('Regexer')
        self.pack()
        self.drawme()

    def calculate(self, event=None):
        """ Send the results and get back a report """

        reg=self._regexinputframe.entry.get()
        if reg=='':
        return

        self._textoutput.delete("1.0", END)

        regex.set_syntax(unbittify((self._RE_NO_BK_PARENS.get(),
                    self._RE_NO_BK_VBAR.get(),
```

```
                    self._RE_BK_PLUS_QM.get(),
                    self._RE_TIGHT_VBAR.get(),
                    self._RE_NEWLINE_OR.get(),
                    self._RE_CONTEXT_INDEP_OPS.get())))

  try:
    cregex=regex.compile(reg)
   except regex.error, message:
    self._textoutput.insert(END,"Error in compilation of regex:\n  %s"
             % message)
   return

  fp=StringIO()
   str=self._stringinputframe.entry.get("1.0", END)

  if self._searchCheck.get():
    doSearch(cregex, str, fp)

  if self._matchCheck.get():
    doMatch(cregex, str, fp)

  if self._groups.get():
    doGroups(cregex, str, self._groups.get(), fp)

   self._textoutput.insert(END, fp.getvalue())
   fp.close()

def stringschanged(self, event=None):
   self._stringswindow.unselect()
   self.calculate()

def regexpschanged(self, event=None):
   self._regexswindow.unselect()
   self.calculate()

def savestring(self, event=None):
   str=self._stringinputframe.entry.get("1.0", END)
   # I don't want to save empty strings!
   if string.strip(str)!='':
```

```python
            self._stringswindow.add(str)

    def saveregexp(self, event=None):
        rexp=self._regexinputframe.entry.get()
        # I don't want to save empty strings!
        if rexp!='':
        self._regexswindow.add(rexp)

    def grabregexp(self, event=None):
        self._regexinputframe.entry.delete(0, END)
        rexp=self._regexswindow.get()
        if rexp!=None:
        self._regexinputframe.entry.insert(END, rexp)

    def grabstring(self, event=None):
        self._stringinputframe.entry.delete("1.0", END)
        str=self._stringswindow.get()
        if str!=None and string.strip(str)!='':
        self._stringinputframe.entry.insert(END, str)

    def stringdelete(self, event=None):
        self._stringswindow.delete(ACTIVE)

    def rexpdelete(self, event=None):
        self._regexswindow.delete(ACTIVE)

    def setsyntax(self, value):
        bits=bittify(value, 6)

        self._RE_NO_BK_PARENS.set(bits[0])
        self._RE_NO_BK_VBAR.set(bits[1])
        self._RE_BK_PLUS_QM.set(bits[2])
        self._RE_TIGHT_VBAR.set(bits[3])
        self._RE_NEWLINE_OR.set(bits[4])
        self._RE_CONTEXT_INDEP_OPS.set(bits[5])

    def AWKSyntax(self, event=None):
        self.setsyntax(regex_syntax.RE_SYNTAX_AWK)

    def EGREPSyntax(self, event=None):
```

```
        self.setsyntax(regex_syntax.RE_SYNTAX_EGREP)

    def GREPSyntax(self, event=None):
        self.setsyntax(regex_syntax.RE_SYNTAX_GREP)

    def EMACSSyntax(self, event=None):
        self.setsyntax(regex_syntax.RE_SYNTAX_EMACS)

    def drawme(self):
        self._inputframe=Frame(self)

        self._regexinputframe=Frame(self._inputframe)
        self._regexinputframe.text=Label(self._regexinputframe, {'text' : 'Regexp:'})
        self._regexinputframe.text.pack({'side': 'left', 'expand':'no'})
        self._regexinputframe.entry=Entry(self._regexinputframe)
        self._regexinputframe.entry.bind('<KeyRelease>',self.regexpschanged)
        self._regexinputframe.entry.pack({'side': 'right', 'expand':'yes', 'fill' \
: 'x'})
        self._regexinputframe.pack({'side' : 'top', 'expand' : 'yes', 'fill' : 'x'})

        self._stringinputframe=Frame(self._inputframe)
        self._stringinputframe.text=Label(self._stringinputframe, {'text' \
: 'String:'})
        self._stringinputframe.text.pack({'side': 'left', 'expand':'no'})
        self._stringinputframe.entry=Text(self._stringinputframe, {'height' \
: '3', 'width' : 30})
        self._stringinputframe.entry.bind('<KeyRelease>',self.stringschanged)
        self._stringinputframe.entry.pack({'side': 'right', 'expand':'yes', 'fill' \
: 'x'})
        self._stringinputframe.pack({'side' : 'bottom', 'expand' : 'yes', 'fill' \
: 'x'})

        self._inputframe.pack({'expand' : 'yes', 'fill' : 'x'})

        self._controlframe=Frame(self)

        self._groups=Scale(self._controlframe, {'from' : 0, 'to' : 10,
                            'orient' : 'horiz',
                            'label' : 'groups',
                            'command' : self.calculate })
```

```python
        self._groups.pack({'side' : 'left'})

        self._buttonframe=Frame(self._controlframe)
        self._buttonframe.pack({'side' : 'left'})

        self._saveregex=Button(self._buttonframe, {'text' : 'Save regexp'})
        self._saveregex.bind('<ButtonRelease-1>', self.saveregexp)
        self._saveregex.pack(side='top', fill='x', expand='yes')

        self._savestring=Button(self._buttonframe, {'text' : 'Save string'})
        self._savestring.bind('<ButtonRelease-1>', self.savestring)
        self._savestring.pack(side='top', fill='x', expand='yes')

        self._syntaxmenubar=Menubutton(self._buttonframe, text='Syntaxes',
                    relief=RAISED)

syntaxmenu = Menu(self._syntaxmenubar)
syntaxmenu.add_checkbutton(label='RE_NO_BK_PARENS',
            variable=self._RE_NO_BK_PARENS,
            command=self.calculate)
syntaxmenu.add_checkbutton(label='RE_NO_BK_VBAR',
            variable=self._RE_NO_BK_VBAR,
            command=self.calculate)
syntaxmenu.add_checkbutton(label='RE_BK_PLUS_QM',
            variable=self._RE_BK_PLUS_QM,
            command=self.calculate)
syntaxmenu.add_checkbutton(label='RE_TIGHT_VBAR',
            variable=self._RE_TIGHT_VBAR,
            command=self.calculate)
syntaxmenu.add_checkbutton(label='RE_NEWLINE_OR',
            variable=self._RE_NEWLINE_OR,
            command=self.calculate)
syntaxmenu.add_checkbutton(label='RE_CONTEXT_INDEP_OPS',
            variable=self._RE_CONTEXT_INDEP_OPS,
            command=self.calculate)
syntaxmenu.add_separator()
syntaxmenu.add_command(label='RE_SYNTAX_AWK', command=self.AWKSyntax)
syntaxmenu.add_command(label='RE_SYNTAX_EGREP', command=self.EGREPSyntax)
syntaxmenu.add_command(label='RE_SYNTAX_GREP', command=self.GREPSyntax)
```

```
        syntaxmenu.add_command(label='RE_SYNTAX_EMACS', command=self.EMACSSyntax)
        self._syntaxmenubar['menu'] = syntaxmenu
        self._syntaxmenubar.pack(fill='x', expand='yes')

#        Button(self._buttonframe, {'text' : 'Save regexp'})

        self._checkframe2=Frame(self._controlframe)
        self._othercheck=Checkbutton(self._checkframe2, text="Other", anchor=W,
                    onvalue=1, offvalue=0)
        self._othercheck.pack()

        self._checkframe2.pack({'side' : 'right'})

        self._checkframe=Frame(self._controlframe)
        self._matchCheckb=Checkbutton(self._checkframe, text="Match", anchor=W,
                    command=self.calculate,
                    variable=self._matchCheck)
        self._matchCheckb.pack(expand='YES', fill='x')
        self._searchCheckb=Checkbutton(self._checkframe, text="Search", anchor=W,
                        command=self.calculate,
                        variable=self._searchCheck)
        self._searchCheckb.pack(expand='YES', fill='x')
        self._linesCheckb=Checkbutton(self._checkframe, text="Selected lines",
                    command=self.calculate,
                    variable=self._linesCheck)
        self._linesCheckb.pack(expand='YES', fill='x')
        self._checkframe.pack({'side' : 'right'})

        self._controlframe.pack()

        self._outputarea=Frame(self)
        self._textoutput=Text(self._outputarea, width=55)
        self._textoutput.pack()
        self._outputarea.pack(side='bottom', expand='yes', fill='both')

        self.pack()

        self._stringswindow=ListWindow('Strings', self)
        self._stringswindow.bind('<ButtonRelease-1>', self.grabstring)
```

```
        self._stringswindow.bind('<ButtonRelease-3>', self.stringdelete)

        self._regexswindow=ListWindow('Regexps', self)
        self._regexswindow.bind('<ButtonRelease-1>', self.grabregexp)
        self._regexswindow.bind('<ButtonRelease-3>', self.rexpdelete)

if __name__=="__main__":
    a=Regexer()
    a.mainloop()
```

How It Works

You can get some interesting information about this script from the contributor's Web site at **www.fuict.hek-r.se/~flognat/hacks**.

The script uses only two GUI classes: Regexer and ListWindow. The main program is deceptively simple, merely two lines. The second line, a.mainloop(), calls the mainloop() method of Regexer, which makes the script sit and wait for events. This is essential to GUI programming.

Aside from the Tkinter code, the script is doing a basic regex string search. See the Python distribution documentation for details about regex and regular expression operations.

Contributed by Andrew Markebo, software developer at Telelogic AB. "The usability lies in the eye of the user..."

dictEdit.py

This script is a very useful basis for GUI front ends for databases. It edits dictionary-type objects, which include constructs such as shelves. You can add items or view them, but in this implementation you can't delete them. Run dictEdit.py from the command line to see a live test.

```
"""
   Edit dictionaries/databases/shelves with a X-interface and
   a small definition of the class.

   uhm for more info check the test below!

       flognat@fukt.hk-r.se
```

```
"""

import string

from Tkinter import *

#import FWidgets

class ScrolledList(Frame):
    def __init__(self, Master, listcnf={}, sbcnf={}):
        Frame.__init__(self, Master)
        #Should we let the 'guy' above do this?
        self.pack(fill=BOTH, expand=YES)

#        if not sbcnf.has_key('width'):
#        sbcnf['width']=scrollbarWidth

        self._multiselect=FALSE
        if listcnf.has_key('selectmode'):
         if listcnf['selectmode'] == 'multiple' or listcnf['selectmode'] == 'extended':
           self._multiselect=TRUE

        self._list = Listbox(self,listcnf)
        self._list.pack({'side': 'left', 'fill': 'both','expand' : 'yes'})

        self._sb = Scrollbar(self, sbcnf)
        self._sb.pack({'side': 'right', 'fill': 'y'})

        self._list['yscrollcommand'] = (self._sb, 'set')
        self._sb['command'] = (self._list, 'yview')

    def bind(self, Event, Callback):
        self._list.bind(Event, Callback)
    def empty(self, begin=0, end=END):
        self._list.delete(0, END)
    def add(self, item, position = END):
        if type(item) == StringType:
        self._list.insert(position, item)
        elif type(item) == ListType:
```

```
        for i in item:
            self._list.insert(position, i)


    # Return the active item
    def active(self):
        return self._list.get(ACTIVE)
    def whatis(self, first, last=None):
        if last==None:
        return self._list.get(first)
        else:
        # Hack Galore, why isn't this implemented in
        # Tkinter??
        return self._list.tk.splitlist(self._list.tk.call(self._list._w, 'get', \
first, last))


    # Return a the selected item or a list with selected items
    def get(self):
        if self._multiselect==FALSE:
        retVal=self._list.curselection()
        if len(retVal)==0:
            return None
        else:
            return self._list.get(retVal[0])
        else:
        ret=[]
        for i in self._list.curselection():
            ret.append(self._list.get(i))
        return ret


    # return the # of the selected item.
    def getIndex(self):
        selection=self._list.curselection()
        if len(selection)==0:
        return None
        if self._multiselect==FALSE:
        return atoi(selection[0])
        else:
        retVal=()
        for i in selection:
```

```
            retVal.append(atoi(i))
        return retVal


    # Gee we can have both list and only one string, hmm yep
    # but funny things can happen if we have more than one
    # item in the list with same name...
    def select(self, items):
        noOfItems=self._list.size()
        if type(items) == StringType:
        for i in range(noOfItems):
            if items==self._list.get(i):
                self._list.select_set(i,i)
        elif type(items) == ListType:
        for i in range(noOfItems):
            line=self._list.get(i)
            for j in items:
                if line==j:
                self._list.select_set(i,i)
        else:
        pass # Well we could raise an exception.. but :-)


    def unselect(self):
        self._list.select_clear(0)


class LabelEntry(Frame):
    def __init__(self, Master, lext, lblcnf={}, txtcnf={}):
        Frame.__init__(self, Master)
        self.pack()
        lblcnf['text']= Text
        self._label = Label(self, lblcnf)
        self._label.pack({'side': 'left', 'expand':'no'})

        self._entry = Entry(self, txtcnf)
        self._entry.pack({'side': 'right', 'expand' : 'yes', 'fill' : 'x'})

    def empty(self):
        self._entry.delete(0, END)

    def get(self):
```

```
            return self._entry.get()

    def set(self, Value=''):
        self.empty()
        self._entry.insert(END, Value)


    def bind(self, Event, Callback):
        self._entry.bind(Event, Callback)



class GetDialog(Toplevel):
    def __init__(self, parent, title = None, prompt='foo'):
        Toplevel.__init__(self, parent)
        self.transient(parent)
    self.value=None
        if title:
            self.title(title)


        self.parent = parent
        self.result = None
    self.prompt=prompt
        body = Frame(self)
        self.initial_focus = self.body(body)
        body.pack(padx=5, pady=5)


        self.buttonbox()


        self.grab_set()


        if not self.initial_focus:
            self.initial_focus = self


        self.protocol("WM_DELETE_WINDOW", self.cancel)


        self.initial_focus.focus_set()
        self.wait_window(self)


    def body(self, master):
        w = Label(master, text=self.prompt, justify=LEFT)
```

```python
        w.grid(row=0, padx=5, sticky=W)

        self.entry = Entry(master, name="entry")
        self.entry.grid(row=1, padx=5, sticky=W+E)

        return self.entry

    def buttonbox(self):
        box = Frame(self)

        w = Button(box, text="OK", width=10, command=self.ok)
        w.pack(side=LEFT, padx=5, pady=5)
        w = Button(box, text="Cancel", width=10, command=self.cancel)
        w.pack(side=LEFT, padx=5, pady=5)

        self.bind("<Return>", self.ok)
        self.bind("<Escape>", self.cancel)

        box.pack()

    def getresult(self):
    return self.value

    def ok(self, event=None):
    self.value=self.entry.get()
        self.withdraw()
        self.update_idletasks()
        self.cancel()

    def cancel(self, event=None):
        self.parent.focus_set()
        self.destroy()

def getValue(parent, title, prompt):
    foo=GetDialog(parent, title, prompt)
    return foo.getresult()


doMethod="XyZZy"

class Executor:
```

```python
    def __init__(self, method, master):
    self._meth=method
    self._master=master

    def __call__(self):
    self._master.callmeth(self._meth)

class FormEditor(Frame):
    def __init__(self, Master=None, dict, fields):
    Frame.__init__(self, Master)
    self._form={}
    self._buttons={}
    self._dict=dict
    self._key=None
    self._drawme(fields)
    self.pack()

    def _drawme(self, fields):
    formFrame=Frame(self)
    formFrame.pack(side='top', fill='both', expand='yes', anchor='n')
    for descr, name, type in fields:
        if type is doMethod:
        self._buttons[name]=Executor(name, self)
        Button(formFrame, text=descr,command=self._buttons[name],
                foreground='blue').pack(side='bottom')
        continue

        self._form[name]=type()
        LabelEntry(formFrame, descr,
                txtcnf={'textvariable' : self._form[name]},
                lblcnf={'anchor' : 'w'}).pack(side='top',
                            fill='x')

    buttonframe=Frame(self)
    buttonframe.pack(side='bottom', anchor='n')
    savebutton=Button(buttonframe, text='Save', command=self.save)
    savebutton.pack(side='right')
    cancelbutton=Button(buttonframe, text='Recall', command=self.recall)
    cancelbutton.pack(side='right')
    btnframe=Frame(self)
```

```
btnframe.pack(side='bottom')
Button(btnframe, text='Copy', command=self.copy).pack(side='left')
Button(btnframe, text='Rename', command=self.rename).pack(side='left')

def fill(self, key):
self._key=key
item=self._dict[key]

for field in self._form.keys():
    self._form[field].set(item.__dict__[field])

def callmeth(self, meth):
if not self._key:
    return

item=self._dict[self._key]

if hasattr(item, meth):
    getattr(item, meth)()
else:
    print 'Function %s not found' % meth

self._dict[self._key]=item
self.fill(self._key)

def rename(self, event=None):
newkey=getValue(self, "Renaming", "Enter new key")
if newkey!="" and newkey!=None:
    item=self._dict[self._key]
    del self._dict[self._key]
    self._key=newkey
    self._dict[newkey]=item

def copy(self, event=None):
newkey=getValue(self, "Copying", "Enter new key")
if newkey!="" and newkey!=None:
    item=self._dict[self._key]
    self._dict[newkey]=item

def save(self, event=None):
```

```python
        if not self._key:
            return

    item=self._dict[self._key]
    for field in self._form.keys():
        item.__dict__[field]=self._form[field].get()
    self._dict[self._key]=item

    def recall(self):
        self.fill(self._key)


class DICTEditor(Frame):
    def __init__(self, Master=None, dict, formdef):
    Frame.__init__(self, Master)
    self.pack(expand='yes', fill='both')

    self._formdef=formdef
    self._dict=dict
    self._oldstr=""
    self._drawme()
    self._keys=self._dict.keys()
    self._viewdata=dict.keys()
    self._viewcache=[]
    self._listbox.add(self._viewdata)

    def bye(self, event=None):
    self.quit()
    #save the data in the form..

    def refresh(self):
    self._keys=self._dict.keys()
    self._newchar(None,`1)

    def _drawme(self):
    leftframe=Frame(self)
    leftframe.pack(side='left', expand='yes', fill='x', anchor='n')
    self.editor=FormEditor(leftframe, self._dict, self._formdef)
```

```
        self.editor.pack(side='top', expand='yes', fill='both')

        bframe=Frame(leftframe)
        bframe.pack(side='bottom', anchor='s', expand='yes', fill='both')

        Button(bframe, text='Refresh', command=self.refresh).pack(side='left',
                                    anchor='s')
        Button(bframe, text='Quit', command=self.bye,
                foreground='red').pack(side='left', anchor='s')

        rightframe=Frame(self)
        rightframe.pack(side='right', expand='yes', fill='both')

        self._listbox=ScrolledList(rightframe)
        self._listbox.bind('<ButtonRelease-1>', self._selected)
        self._listbox.pack(side='top', expand='yes', fill='both')

        self._entry=Entry(rightframe)
        self._entry.bind('<KeyRelease>', self._newchar)
        self._entry.pack(side='bottom', fill='x')

    def _newchar(self, event=None, upd=None):
        str=self._entry.get()

        # Ok we don't need to worry about updating
        if len(str) is 0:
            self._viewdata=self._keys
            self._viewcache=[]
        elif upd:
            newview=[]
            for key in self._viewdata:
            if string.find(key, str)!=-1:
                newview.append(key)
            self._viewdata=newview

        elif len(str)==len(self._oldstr):
            return
        elif len(str)>len(self._oldstr):
```

```
        self._viewcache.insert(0, self._viewdata)
        newview=[]
        for key in self._viewdata:
        if string.find(key, str)!=-1:
            newview.append(key)

        self._viewdata=newview
    else:
        self._viewdata=self._viewcache[0]
        del self._viewcache[0]

    self._oldstr=str
    self._listbox.empty()
    self._listbox.add(self._viewdata)

    def _selected(self, event=None):
    self.editor.save()
    self.editor.fill(self._listbox.get())

class Tester:

    # This is the 'definition' of how the form should look
    # the format is (text, attribute, type), text is the
    # text that appears on the label, attribute is the attribute
    # of the class and type is either one of the types in tkinter
    # or doMethod if you want to connect a button to a method
    # in the class.
    formdef=[('Front:', '_front', StringVar),
        ('Back:', '_backdoor', StringVar),
        ('Descr:', '_description', StringVar),
        ('ID:', '_ID', StringVar),
        ('Status', '_status', IntVar),
        ('Print (demo button)', 'printme', doMethod)]

    def __init__(self, front, back, descr, id, status):
    self._front=front
    self._backdoor=back
    self._description=descr
    self._ID=id
```

```
            self._status=status

        def printme(self):
        print self._front, self._backdoor, self._description,\
                self._ID, self._status

def test():
    values=(("Frontporch", "backporch", "my house", "Uh..", 1),
        ("Roses", "Violets", "A garden", "Aloe vera", 88),
        ("Volvo", "foo", "Yack", "fee", 99),
        ("Python", "C++", "lisp", "C", 52))

    dict={}
    for f,b,d,i,s in values:
    dict[f]=Tester(f,b,d,i,s)

    b=DICTEditor(None, dict, Tester.formdef)
    b.mainloop()
    print "zap"

if __name__=='__main__':
    test()
```

How It Works

dicEdit.py displays a dictionary object for you to edit. A great deal of the code is used just to set up the interface, but it's worth it if you need to edit dictionaries by hand.

The test function gives you several examples of data. It pops up when you run dicEdit.py from the command line.

If you have problems running this script, you can try this fix:

From line 211:

```
    def __init__(self, Master=None, dict=None, fields=None):
        assert (dict is not None)
        assert (fields is not None)
```

From line 299:

```
    def __init__(self, Master=None, dict=None, formdef=None):
```

```
        assert(dict is not None)
        assert(formdef is not None)
```

Contributed by Andrew Markebo, software developer at Telelogic AB. "The usability lies in the eye of the user…"

engine.py

engine.py is actually three scripts: two Tkinter scripts and engine.py, the core code from Chapter 9, "Servers." The entire source code package is on the companion CD. It includes a readme file that's more comprehensive than many commercial manuals.

TkSearch.py

This script ties together TkSearchUI.py and engine.py.

```
#!/usr/bin/env python
"""
This is a Tkinter-based, unified WWW search engine.

This module combines the widget hierarchy provided by the TkSearchUI module
with the search capabilities of the engine module to create a
multi-threaded web search engine w. a Tkinter user interface.

If you want to actually *view* the results of any search,
it's best to already have Netscape running on your desktop.  This
script will attempt to launch Netscape as necessary -- see class
WebBrowser -- but things go much faster if it's already running.

1999 Mitchell S. Chapman
$Id: TkSearch.py,v 1.1 1999/08/22 17:22:34 mchapman Exp mchapman $
"""


__version__ = "$Revision: 1.1 $"

import string, os, Queue, tempfile
import TkSearchUI
import Tkinter; Tk=Tkinter
import tkMessageBox
import engine
```

```python
class WebBrowser:
    def showFile(self, pathname):
        """Open pathname in a web browser."""
        cmd = "netscape -remote 'openFile(%s)'" % pathname
        status = os.system(cmd)
        if status:
            # Perhaps the web browser isn't running?
            self.launchBrowser()
            os.system(cmd)

    def launchBrowser(self):
        """Get a web browser running as a daemon process."""
        pid = os.fork()
        if pid == 0:
            # This is the child process.
            # Close all file descriptors which might be shared
            # with the parent.  Otherwise, the parent may hang waiting
            # for self to exit.
            for i in range(256):
                try:
                    os.close(i)
                except: pass

            # Redirect stdin, stdout, and stderr to /dev/null.
            os.open("/dev/null", os.O_RDONLY)
            os.open("/dev/null", os.O_RDWR)
            os.dup2(1, 2)

            # Finally, launch the browser.
            os.execlp("netscape", "netscape")
            raise SystemExit


class SearchManager:
    """This search manager has each of its threads write to a pipe
    at shutdown.  Tkinter supports file events, so this is a thread-safe
    way for a thread to notify Tkinter of its completion."""
    def __init__(self):
```

```
            """Initialize a new instance."""
        self.queue = Queue.Queue(0)
        self.donePipe = os.pipe()
        self.engines = [engine.Excite, engine.InfoSeek, engine.EuroSeek]
        # Create a file event handler to be invoked whenever a
        # thread writes to self.donePipe.
        Tk.tkinter.createfilehandler(self.donePipe[0],
                                     Tk.READABLE, self.collectResultCB)
        self.threads = []
        self.resultsCB = None


    def query(self, queryStr, resultsCB=None):
        """Start a query.
        If 'resultsCB' is specified, it will be invoked every time a
        new search result is available."""
        self.resultsCB = resultsCB
        self.threads = []
        for engine in self.engines:
            thread = engine(queryStr, self.threadFinishedCB)
            thread.start()
            self.threads.append(thread)


    def cancel(self):
        """Cancel a search."""
        for thread in self.threads:
            if thread.isAlive():
                thread.cancel()


    def allDone(self):
        """Find out whether or not all searches are done."""
        for thread in self.threads:
            if thread.isAlive():
                return 0
        return 1


    def threadFinishedCB(self, result):
        """Callback invoked when a thread finishes.
        Passes this info to Tkinter by writing to self's donePipe."""
        self.queue.put(result)
```

```
                os.write(self.donePipe[1], 'd')


        def collectResultCB(self, *args):
            """Collect the results of a thread."""
            os.read(self.donePipe[0], 1)
            result = self.queue.get()
            if self.resultsCB:
                self.resultsCB(result)



class T:
    """This is the controller for the search engine."""
    def __init__(self, master=None):
        """Initialize a new instance.
        If specified, 'master' is a widget within which to embed the
        user interface of self."""
        self.master = master
        self.searchManager = SearchManager()
        self.browser = WebBrowser()
        self.ui = TkSearchUI.T(self.master)
        self.ui.pack()

        self.engineState = {}
        self.engineResult = {}
        self._connectUIBehaviors()


    def _connectUIBehaviors(self):
        """Wire up the user interface so it actually does something."""
        ui = self.ui
        ui.searchBtn["command"] = self.searchCB
        ui.stopBtn["command"] = self.stopSearchCB
        # Disable the stop button for now.  It will be enabled at
        # the start of each search, and disabled when the search is
        # allDone.
        ui.stopBtn["state"] = "disabled"

        ui.quitBtn["command"] = self.quitCB

        # Add a status indicator for each available search engine.
```

```
            self.engineState = {}
            for engine in self.searchManager.engines:
                name = engine.__name__
                status = ui.addEngineStatus(name)
                self.engineState[name] = status
                # Wire up the display button for this status
                # indicator.
                def resultDisplayCB(self=self, engineName=name):
                    self.displayCB(engineName)

                status.displayBtn["command"] = resultDisplayCB
                # Disable the display button.  It will be re-enabled
                # when some search result is actually available.
                status.displayBtn["state"] = "disabled"

        def searchCB(self, *args):
            """Callback invoked when the Search button is clicked."""
            queryStr = self.ui.entry.get()
            # Reset all of the status messages.
            for engineState in self.engineState.values():
                engineState.status("Running...")
                # Disable the display of state for this
                # engine until it actually has a result to display.
                engineState.displayBtn["state"] = "disabled"

            # Disable the search button, and enable the stop button.
            # The search button will be reenabled, and the stop button
            # disabled, when the search is all done.
            self.ui.searchBtn["state"] = "disabled"
            self.ui.stopBtn["state"] = "normal"

            self.searchManager.query(queryStr, self.resultsCB)

        def stopSearchCB(self, *args):
            """Callback invoked when the Stop button is clicked."""
            self.searchManager.cancel()

        def quitCB(self, *args):
```

```
            """Callback invoked when the Quit button is clicked."""
            if not self.searchManager.allDone():
                self.searchManager.cancel()
            self.ui.quitBtn.quit()

    def displayCB(self, engineName):
        """Callback invoked when one of the Display buttons is clicked."""
        if self.engineResult.has_key(engineName):
            outname = tempfile.mktemp()
            outf = open(outname, "w", 0)
            outf.write(self.engineResult[engineName].resultStr)
            outf.close()
            self.browser.showFile(outname)
        else:
            print "No status available for %s." % engineName

    def resultsCB(self, searchResult):
        """Receive the results from one search thread."""
        engineName = searchResult.engineName
        engineStatus = self.engineState[engineName]
        engineStatus.status(searchResult.finalStatus)
        # We have a result for this engine, so enable its display button.
        engineStatus.displayBtn["state"] = "normal"

        self.engineResult[engineName] = searchResult

        if self.searchManager.allDone():
            self.ui.stopBtn["state"] = "disabled"
            self.ui.searchBtn["state"] = "normal"

    def run(self):
        """Launch the search controller."""
        self.ui.mainloop()


def main():
    """Module mainline (for standalone execution)"""
    t = T()
```

```
    t.run()



if __name__ == "__main__":
    main()
```

How It Works

TkSearch.py is the centerpiece of this application. It has three classes and a main() function, so the script can be run as an application.

A pivotal part of the entire application is Netscape Navigator. This script launches the browser if it isn't open already. One problem with launching the browser is that if it doesn't launch, the whole application can hang. To avoid this, the method WebBrowser.launchBrowser() forks and execs a copy of Netscape, rather than using a more common os.system().

As of Python 1.5.2 and Tcl/Tk 8.0.5, Tkinter is thread-safe. In other words, it would be possible to have the background search threads do their own UI updates. This script, though, was written before these versions came out, so another unique challenge that had to be overcome was Tkinter's utter ignorance about threads. Because Tkinter didn't provide any thread support, the script had to supply it, and the workaround used here is Tkinter's file event notification. The class SearchManager creates a queue to hold results. As each search engine thread begins life, it's recorded in SearchManager's threads list. When the thread is done, the result moves to the results queue.

For incredibly detailed explanations of each operation, look at the readme file with the engine.py package on the CD.

Contributed by Mitch Chapman

TkSearchUI

This script is the third component of the major script engine.py, which altogether also includes TkSearch.py and engine.py.

```
#!/usr/bin/env python
"""
This module provides a user interface for conducting unified WWW searches.

1999 Mitchell S. Chapman
$Id: TkSearchUI.py,v 1.1 1999/08/22 17:22:50 mchapman Exp mchapman $
```

```
    """

    __version__ = "$Revision: 1.1 $"

    import Tkinter; Tk=Tkinter

    class EngineStatus:
        """This class provides the UI for a search-engine status indicator."""
        def __init__(self, master=None, engineName="Engine"):
            """Initialize a new instance."""
            self.master = master
            self.engineName = engineName
            f = self.frame = Tk.Frame(self.master, relief="flat", bd=0)
            text = "%s:" % self.engineName
            l = self.label = Tk.Label(f, text=text, width=len(text),
                                       anchor="e")
            s = self.statusLabel = Tk.Label(f, width=12, anchor="w")
            btn = self.displayBtn = Tk.Button(f, text="Display...")
            l.pack(side="left", fill="none", expand="no")
            s.pack(side="left", fill="x", expand="yes")
            btn.pack(side="left", fill="none", expand="no")

        def pack(self, **kw):
            """Pack self into its master.  'kw' provides optional packing
            parameters."""
            params = {'side':'top', 'fill':'x', 'expand':'no'}
            params.update(kw)
            apply(self.frame.pack, (), params)

        def status(self, msg=""):
            """Update self's status message."""
            self.statusLabel["text"] = msg
            self.statusLabel.update_idletasks()


    class T:
        """This class defines a user interface layout for WWW searches.
        It defines little if any behavior."""
        def __init__(self, master=None, title="Search The Web"):
            """Initialize a new instance.
```

```
            'master', if specified, is a widget within which to embed
            this UI."""
            self.master = master
            self.title = title

            f = self.frame = Tk.Frame(master, relief="flat", bd=0)
            # Force the title onto self's toplevel window.
            f.winfo_toplevel().wm_title(self.title)

            self._addControlsFrame()
            self.engineStates = []
            self._addStatusFrame()
            self._addButtonBox()

    def _addControlsFrame(self):
        """Add a frame containing the search controls."""
        cf = self.controlsFrame = Tk.Frame(self.frame, relief="raised", bd=1)

        l = Tk.Label(cf, text="Query:", anchor="e")
        l.pack(side="left", fill="none", expand="no")

        e = self.entry = Tk.Entry(cf, width=32)
        e.pack(side="left", fill="x", expand="yes")

        b = self.searchBtn = Tk.Button(cf, text="Search")
        b.pack(side="left", fill="none", expand="no")

        b = self.stopBtn = Tk.Button(cf, text="Stop")
        b.pack(side="left", fill="none", expand="no")

        cf.pack(fill="both", expand="yes")

    def _addStatusFrame(self):
        """Add a frame in which to display search status."""
        rf = self.resultsFrame = Tk.Frame(self.frame,
                                    relief="raised", bd=1)
        rf.pack(fill="both", expand="yes")

    def addEngineStatus(self, engineName):
        """Clients call this to add a status indicator for a search engine."""
```

```
            result = EngineStatus(self.resultsFrame, engineName)
            self.engineStates.append(result)
            # Adjust so all status indicators have the same width.
            wMax = 0
            for status in self.engineStates:
                wMax = max(wMax, status.label["width"])
            for status in self.engineStates:
                status.label["width"] = wMax

            result.pack()
            return result

    def _addButtonBox(self):
        """Add a button box at the bottom of the UI's main window."""
        bbf = self.buttonBoxFrame = Tk.Frame(self.frame, relief="raised", bd=1)

        qb = self.quitBtn = Tk.Button(bbf, text="Quit")
        qb.pack(side="left", expand="yes")

        bbf.pack(side="bottom", fill="x", expand="no")

    def pack(self, **kw):
        """Pack self's UI within its master.
        'kw', if specified, contains keyword parameters specifying
        how the packing should be done."""
        packing = {'fill': 'both', 'expand': 'yes'}
        packing.update(kw)
        apply(self.frame.pack, (), packing)

    def mainloop(self):
        """Run the main event loop."""
        self.frame.mainloop()


def main():
    """Module mainline (for standalone execution)"""
    t = T()
    stati = {}
    for engine in ["EuroSeek", "InfoSeek", "Excite"]:
        status = t.addEngineStatus(engine)
```

```
        stati[engine] = status
    t.pack()
    t.mainloop()



if __name__ == "__main__":
    main()
```

How It Works

TkSearchUI.py is the GUI heart of the whole engine.py application. Even so, it has little operational code.

From the user's viewpoint, the class T is about the most important thing in the whole application. T is the class that makes the entry field, the Search button, the Quit button, and the Stop button.

main(), despite its somewhat overly grand name, merely creates an instance of T, adds a few EngineStatus displays to the instance, and then displays the resulting widget hierarchy. In fact, the only purpose main() has is to let the module maintainer examine the widget hierarchy layout.

For more information about how the various statements in this script work, see the discussion on Tkinter widgets in Chapter 4. For more information on engine.py, see the readme file in the engine.py package on the companion CD.

Contributed by Mitch Chapman

...where anything goes in,
anything goes out...

Chapter 7: Databases

nickname.py

dbase3.py

This chapter has scripts that introduce the database function of Python. Python has several standard modules that can store Python objects: pickle, cpickle, marshal, and shelve are only a few. These can be used as simple databases. For more advanced database work, you need some different modules. One module in this chapter, for example, accesses dBASE files. But for even more power, Python can use more complex modules to work directly in SQL. Most of these modules are available free for download from **www.python.org**.

This chapter is only an introduction to basic operations. If you need to use Python to access Oracle, ODBC, Informix, or a similar system, you'll find lots of much more advanced material at **www.python.org**. In particular, read the paper "Persistent Storage of Python Objects in Relational Databases" by Joel Shprentz. That, too, is available at **www.python.org**. As Shprentz points out, Python isn't natively all that friendly toward relational databases because the relational universe of rows and columns doesn't fit neatly into Python's objects. But there is a way to use Python to access relational databases: the Persistent Storage module. Details are available on the Python site.

nickname.py

This is a very simple script that stores nicknames as dictionary-like objects, using the shelve module.

```
#!/usr/bin/python

import shelve

def makeshelf(name):
    name_of_file=shelve.open(name)
    while 1:
    shelfkey = raw_input("What's your name? Type Q to quit.  " )
    if shelfkey != "Q":
        value = raw_input("What's your nickname?:  " )
        name_of_file[shelfkey]=value
    else:
        print "Thanks. Got the data and it's properly stored. Here's what you \
entered: "
```

```
        keylist=name_of_file.keys()
        for keyword in keylist:
        printout=name_of_file[keyword]
        print "Your name is ",keyword, "and your nickname is", printout
        name_of_file.close()
        return


if __name__=="__main__":
    name=raw_input("File name please: ")
    makeshelf(name)
```

How It Works

Unless you make provisions for saving data out of a script, it all goes away when the script finishes.

In nickname.py you're asked first for a file name. This file name is passed to the function makeshelf(), where the file is created if it doesn't already exist or is opened if it already exists.

The script then goes into a while loop, which can be broken by typing a capital **Q.** Names and nicknames are stored sequentially in a shelf object. The shelf object is handy because it behaves like a dictionary. The same statements work for both, so if you're familiar with dictionaries, you're pretty much set. The lines

```
    shelfkey = raw_input("What's your name? Type Q to quit.  " )
    if shelfkey != "Q":
        value = raw_input("What's your nickname?:  " )
        name_of_file[shelfkey]=value
```

create two variables, one for the name and one for the nickname. These variables then become, respectively, the key and the data value of each dictionary entry. When they are written, the loop resumes. When the user is finished, a *Q* stops the loop and makes the script print out the results. This approach might not be practical if you're inputting thousands of items, so consider taking it out if you're doing lots of operations.

dbase3.py

This script falls somewhere between the simple persistence module and the full-scale database access module.

```
'''
Defines a class for reading a dBase3 file format.

The format was defined by the following:

    dBASE III Database File Structure  (see attribution at end)


    The structure of a dBASE III database file is composed of a
    header and data records.  The layout is given below.
    dBASE III DATABASE FILE HEADER:
```

BYTE	CONTENTS	MEANING
0	1 byte	dBASE III version number (03H without a .DBT file) (83H with a .DBT file)
1-3	3 bytes	date of last update (YY MM DD) in binary format
4-7	32 bit number	number of records in data file
8-9	16 bit number	length of header structure
10-11	16 bit number	length of the record
12-31	20 bytes	reserved bytes (version 1.00)
32-n	32 bytes each	field descriptor array (see below)
n+1	1 byte	0DH as the field terminator

```
A FIELD DESCRIPTOR:      <-----------------------------------------+
```

BYTE	CONTENTS	MEANING

```
|  0-10  | 11 bytes          | field name in ASCII zero-filled |
+--------+-------------------+---------------------------------+
|  11    | 1 byte            | field type in ASCII             |
|        |                   | (C N L D or M)                  |
+--------+-------------------+---------------------------------+
|  12-15 | 32 bit number     | field data address              |
|        |                   | (address is set in memory)      |
+--------+-------------------+---------------------------------+
|  16    | 1 byte            | field length in binary          |
+--------+-------------------+---------------------------------+
|  17    | 1 byte            | field decimal count in binary   |
+--------+-------------------+---------------------------------
|  18-31 | 14 bytes          | reserved bytes (version 1.00)   |
+--------+-------------------+---------------------------------+
```

The data records are layed out as follows:

1. Data records are preceeded by one byte that is a space (20H) if
   the record is not deleted and an asterisk (2AH) if it is deleted.
2. Data fields are packed into records with no field separators or record
   terminators.
3. Data types are stored in ASCII format as follows:

```
DATA TYPE       DATA RECORD STORAGE
---------       ----------------------------------------------
Character       (ASCII characters)
Numeric         - . 0 1 2 3 4 5 6 7 8 9
Logical         ? Y y N n T t F f  (? when not initialized)
Memo            (10 digits representing a .DBT block number)
Date            (8 digits in YYYYMMDD format, such as 19840704 for
                July 4, 1984)
```

This information came directly from the Ashton-Tate Forum. It can
also be found in the Advanced Programmer's Guide available from
Ashton-Tate.

One slight difference occurs between files created by dBASE III and
those created by dBASE III Plus. In the earlier files, there is an
ASCII NUL character between the $0D end of header indicator and the

```
        start of the data.  This NUL is no longer present in Plus, making a
        Plus header one byte smaller than an identically structured III file.


        Taken from the Pascal routines from DBF.PAS version 1.3
        Copyright (C) 1986 By James Troutman
        CompuServe PPN 74746,1567
        Permission is granted to use these routines for non-commercial purposes.
    '''


def Build32BitInteger(four_byte_string):
    '''This unpacks a string into a 32 bit integer.  It is little endian,
    specifically for the PC environment.
    '''
    if len(four_byte_string) != 4:
        raise "Bad data", "String not 4 bytes long"
    s0 = ord(four_byte_string[0])
    s1 = ord(four_byte_string[1])
    s2 = ord(four_byte_string[2])
    s3 = ord(four_byte_string[3])
    return (s3 << 24) | (s2 << 16) | (s1 << 8) | s0

def StripNulls(str):
    '''Truncates a string at the first trailing null.  Returns the
    truncated string.
    '''
    if len(str) < 1: return str
    first_null = -1
    for ix in xrange(len(str)):
        if ord(str[ix]) == 0:
            first_null = ix
            break
    if first_null == -1:
        return str
    else:
        return str[0:first_null]

class dBase3:
    '''Class to read a dBase3 file.  Note that this class is only
    intended to read in the header info and give you enough functionality
```

to iterate through the fields and interpret them. You'll have to
write a derived class if you want to write back to the dBase file.
'''

```python
def __init__(self, file_name):
    '''We are passed the file name, so we open it.  Then we'll read the
    first 20 bytes of the header and get the basic data (see the
    dBase3 description above).  Then we get the whole header once we
    know the size of it.  Then we read in and parse the field
    information.
    '''
    import string
    self.file_name = file_name
    try:
        self.fp = open(file_name, "rb")
    except:
        raise "Bad data", "Couldn't open \"%s\"" % file_name
    self.header = self.fp.read(20)  # Read the header
    if not self.header:
        raise "Bad data", "File is empty"
    if len(self.header) != 20:
        raise "Bad data", "Missing first 20 bytes in file header"
    self.version_number = ord(self.header[0])
    self.last_update_yy = ord(self.header[1])
    self.last_update_mm = ord(self.header[2])
    self.last_update_dd = ord(self.header[3])
    self.num_records    = Build32BitInteger(self.header[4:8])
    self.header_length  = (ord(self.header[9]) << 8) | \
                              ord(self.header[8])
    self.record_length  = (ord(self.header[11]) << 8) | \
                              ord(self.header[10])
    # Now go back and read the whole header including the field specs
    self.fp.seek(0)
    self.header = self.fp.read(self.header_length)
    self.reserved_bytes = self.header[12:32]
    # Calculate how many field descriptors we must have
    self.num_fields     = (self.header_length - 33)/32
    # Now read in the field information
    self.fields = []
    for ix in range(self.num_fields):
```

```
            start = 32 + ix*32
            stop  = start + 32 + 1
            field_data = self.header[start : stop]
            field = []
            # Get field name
            str = string.strip(StripNulls(field_data[0:11]))
            field.append(str)
            # Get field type character
            field.append(field_data[11])
            # Get field data address
            field.append(StripNulls(field_data[12:16]))
            # Get field length
            field.append(ord(field_data[16]))
            # Get field decimal count
            field.append(ord(field_data[17]))
            # Get field reserved bytes
            field.append(StripNulls(field_data[18:32]))
            self.fields.append(field)

    def DumpHeader(self):
        spaces = 30
        template  = "%%-%ds %%d" % spaces
        template1 = "%%-%ds 0x%%02x" % spaces
        print "File:  %s" % self.file_name
        print template1 % ("Version info", self.version_number),
        if self.version_number == 0x83:
            print " (with a .DBT memo file)"
        else:
            print " (without a .DBT memo file)"
        print template % ("Last update year", self.last_update_yy+1900)
        print template % ("Last update month", self.last_update_mm)
        print template % ("Last update day", self.last_update_dd)
        print template % ("Number of records", self.num_records)
        print template % ("Header length", self.header_length)
        print template % ("Record length", self.record_length)
        print template % ("Number of fields", self.num_fields)
        print "\nDump of field info:\n"
        print "  Num    Name         Type  Length"
        print "  ---    ----         ----  ------"
```

```
        for ix in range(self.num_fields):
            print "    %2d" % ix,           # Field number
            s = self.fields[ix]
            print "  %-12s" % s[0],         # Name
            print " %-1s"   % s[1],         # Type
            #print " \"%-4s\""   % s[2],
            print "    %3d"     % s[3]       # Length
            #print " %3d"     % s[4],
            #print " %-14s"   % s[5]


    def GetFileHandle(self):
        return self.fp


    def _get_record(self, record_num):
        '''Will return the specified record as a string.  Remember the
        first character is a ' ' or '*', indicating whether the record
        is deleted or not.
        '''
        if record_num < 0 or record_num > (self.num_records - 1):
            raise "Bad data", "Record number out of bounds"
        self.fp.seek(self.header_length + record_num*self.record_length)
        str = self.fp.read(self.record_length)
        return str


    def GetRecordAsList(self, record_num):
        '''Will return the indicated record as a list of strings.  The
        position in the list is the same as the field number.
        '''
        import string
        record = []
        str = self._get_record(record_num)
        if len(str) != self.record_length:
            raise "Bad data", "Record len is %d, not %d" % \
                (len(str), self.record_length)
        offset = 1  # The 1 gets us past the first byte that indicates deletion
        for ix in xrange(self.num_fields):
            name   = self.fields[ix][0]
            type   = self.fields[ix][1]
            length = self.fields[ix][3]
```

```
                    field  = str[offset : offset + length]
                    record.append(field)
                    offset = offset + length  # Position offset at start of next field
            return record


        def GetRecordAsDictionary(self, record_num):
            '''Will return the indicated record as a dictionary.  The keys
            will be the field names and the field data will be converted
            to the proper type:  numbers will either be integers or doubles,
            dates will remain as YYYYMMDD strings, logical values and strings
            will remain as strings.
            '''
            import string
            record = {}
            str = self._get_record(record_num)
            if len(str) != self.record_length:
                raise "Bad data", "Record len is %d, not %d" % \
                    (len(str), self.record_length)
            offset = 1  # The 1 gets us past the first byte that indicates deletion
            for ix in xrange(self.num_fields):
                name   = self.fields[ix][0]
                type   = self.fields[ix][1]
                length = self.fields[ix][3]
                field  = str[offset : offset + length]
                if type == 'C' or type == 'L' or type == 'D':
                    record[name] = field
                elif type == 'N':
                    # Interpret as double if it has a '.' in it; otherwise
                    # interpret as a signed integer.
                    value = 0
                    field = string.strip(field)
                    if field != "":
                        if '.' in field:
                            value = string.atof(field)
                        else:
                            value = string.atoi(field)
                    record[name] = value
                elif type == 'M':
                    # We ignore the memo field
```

```python
                    pass
                else:
                    raise "Bad data", "Unrecognized field type"
                offset = offset + length  # Position offset at start of next field
        return record


    def DumpAsDelimited(self, no_header = 0, delimit_char = "\t", ws_strip = 1):
        '''Print each record of the database file to stdout with each
        field delimited by the string in delimit_char.  Any leading or
        trailing whitespace in each field is removed if ws_strip is true.
        The names of the fields are printed out as the first line if
        no_header is false.
        '''
        import sys, string
        if not no_header:
            # Print the header
            for ix in xrange(self.num_fields):
                field_name = self.fields[ix][0]
                sys.stdout.write(field_name)
                if ix != self.num_fields - 1:
                    sys.stdout.write(delimit_char)
            sys.stdout.write("\n")
        # Print each record
        for recnum in xrange(self.num_records):
            record = self.GetRecordAsList(recnum)
            for ix in xrange(self.num_fields):
                field = record[ix]
                if ws_strip:
                    field = string.strip(field)
                sys.stdout.write(field)
                if ix != self.num_records - 1:
                    sys.stdout.write(delimit_char)
            sys.stdout.write("\n")


if __name__ == '__main__':
    import sys, string
    if len(sys.argv) < 2:
        print "Usage:  dbase3 <dbase_file>"
```

```
        print "  Will dump the header and data of a dbase3 file."
        sys.exit(1)
db = dBase3(sys.argv[1])
db.DumpHeader()
db.DumpAsDelimited()
```

How It Works

Boy, this is one script that's not lacking in comment lines! Blessed be the commenters!

Most of the script is one class, dBase3. When it's instantiated, dBase3 tries to open the designated file. The file opening statement is inside a try sequence, which lets the script do error trapping if the file doesn't exist. Putting the file open routine inside a try sequence is an excellent policy when you're not sure if the file will be there when you try to open it. Of course, sometimes you know that a file is there because you've put it there. A CGI-accessed database file is an example. But even then, you can open the file with a try sequence, just in case something's happened to it.

Using this script, you can get dBaseIII records in a variety of ways. You can get a dump of the header, a dump of the record in delimited format, a string representation of the record, a list representation of the record, or a dictionary representation of the record.

As noted in the comments, this script doesn't write to dBaseIII files. It only reads 'em.

Contributor anonymous

Where there are no scripts that
turn a man into a Scotsman.

Chapter 8: Math/Science

donutil.py

julian.py

roman.py

stats.py

In this chapter you'll find some nifty little scripts for doing basic math and science functions. Several of these scripts illustrate how to use the math module, which is one of the handiest of the modules in the standard library.

These scripts are simple and short. They're good for illustrating Python, but they're a long light year from showcasing Python's full capabilities. Python is becoming more popular with scientific programmers, at least partly because of the availability of so many math and science modules.

For example, here are some modules available for downloading as of this writing from **www.python.org**:

- PyEphem. Calculates the positions of astronomical bodies.
- PYML. Interfaces with Mathematica.
- NumPy. Provides high-performance multidimensional numeric arrays.

donutil.py

There are several little functions in this script that you may find useful. It displays rulers, calculates wind chill, figures radians and degrees, and does some system work. It defies simple categorization, but so what?

```
'''
Miscellaneous routines in python:

Ruler               Return a ruler
TensRuler           10's ruler to go along with Ruler()
WindChillInDegF     Calculate wind chill given OAT & wind speed
Deg2Rad             Converts degrees to radians
Rad2Deg             Converts radians to degrees
IsFile              Returns true if param is a file
IsDirectory         Returns true if param is a directory
SpellCheck          Checks that a list of words is in a dictionary

'''

def Ruler(size = 79, type = 1):
    '''
```

Function to return a ruler string.

Type 1 ruler:
```
          1         2         3         4         5         6         7
1234567890123456789012345678901234567890123456789012345678901234567890
```

Type 2 ruler:
```
          1         2         3         4         5         6         7
----+----|----+----|----+----|----+----|----+----|----+----|----+----|
```

Type 3 ruler:
```

----+----|----+----|----+----|----+----|----+----|----+----|----+----|
```

Type 4 ruler:
```
--------|--------|--------|--------|--------|--------|--------|
```
'''
```python
    if size < 1:
        raise "Bad data", "Ruler:  size < 1"
    str = ""
    if type == 1:
        str = TensRuler(size)
        base = "1234567890"
    elif type == 2:
        str = TensRuler(size)
        base = "----+----|"
        pass
    elif type == 3:
        base = "----+----|"
    elif type == 4:
        base = "--------|"
    else:
        raise "Bad data", "Ruler:  type not between 1 and 3"
    num_repeats = (size/10 + 2) * 10
    tmpstr = base * num_repeats
    str = str + tmpstr[:size]
    return str

def TensRuler(size):
    if size >= 10:
```

```
        str = ""
        for ix in range(1, 1 + size/10):
            str = str + "%10d" % (ix * 10)
        str = str + "\n"
    return str


def WindChillInDegF(wind_speed_in_mph, air_temp_deg_F):
    '''Wind Chill for exposed human skin, expressed as a function of
    wind speed in Miles per Hour and temperature in degrees Fahrenheit.
    Gotten from the Snippets collection.
    '''
    import math
    if wind_speed_in_mph < 4:
        return air_temp_deg_F * 1.0
    return (((10.45 + (6.686112 * math.sqrt(1.0*wind_speed_in_mph)) \
            - (.447041 * wind_speed_in_mph)) / 22.034 * \
            (air_temp_deg_F - 91.4)) + 91.4)


def Deg2Rad(degrees):
    import math
    return degrees/180.0 * math.pi


def Rad2Deg(radians):
    import math
    return radians/math.pi * 180.0


def SpellCheck(input_list, word_dictionary, case_is_not_important = 1):
    '''
    This module provides the function SpellCheck(), which takes as its
    input the list of words to spell check in input_list and the
    dictionary word_dictionary (it's a dictionary rather than a list to
    allow fast access; the dictionary values can be null strings --
    all that's important is that the key be there).  It returns any
    words in input_list that are not in word_dictionary.
    '''
    import string
    misspelled = []
    if len(input_list) == 0:
        return []
    if len(word_dictionary) == 0:
```

```
            raise "SpellCheck:  word_dictionary parameter is empty"
        for ix in xrange(len(input_list)):
            if case_is_not_important:
                word = string.lower(input_list[ix])
            if not word_dictionary.has_key(word):
                misspelled.append(word)
        return misspelled


def Keep(str, keep_chars):
    "Keep only specified characters in a string"
    strlength = len(str)
    if strlength == 0 or len(keep_chars) == 0:
        return ""
    count = 0
    outstring = ""
    while count < strlength:
        if str[count] in keep_chars:
            outstring = outstring + str[count]
        count = count + 1
    return outstring


def Remove(str, remove_chars):
    "Remove specified characters from a string"
    strlength = len(str)
    if strlength == 0:
        return ""
    if len(remove_chars) == 0:
        return str
    count = 0
    outstring = ""
    while count < strlength:
        if str[count] not in remove_chars:
            outstring = outstring + str[count]
        count = count + 1
    return outstring
```

How It Works

The most interesting functions here are the wind-chill calculator and the radian
conversions. They both use the math module.

Gotcha

Here's something for you to play with and judge for yourself: Python lets you re-declare a variable to be global within a method or function, like this:

```
x=[]
def a_list_is_born():
    global x
    x=[''a'', ''list'']
```

This permits the global x to remain global within the function. And it's legal. However, do you want to risk having global variables changed within functions or methods? Some of Python's most venerable People Who Know counsel against it, but many Pythoneers do it.

Notice that each function imports the math module separately. This isn't necessary if the math module is imported outside of any functions. You'd think that if you imported, say, only Deg2Rad from this script that you'd have to import the math module inside of that function. Wrong. The interpreter scans the entire module and imports whatever is needed, even if an imported module is imported once for all the functions.

Multiple functions can be packed onto one line by using parentheses to nest operations. Precedence is standard inner to outer:

```
return (((10.45 + (6.686112 * math.sqrt(1.0*wind_speed_in_mph)) \
```

The math module has several common math functions, such as tangent, square root, and exponent. Another module, cmath, is for complex numbers. The math module also has two constants: pi and e.

Contributor Anonymous

julian.py

This script provides Julian days for any date you specify. It can give them back as integers or true astronomical days. It also converts Julian days to Gregorian dates and does a few other interesting things. If you don't know about Julian days, drop down to "How It Works" for an explanation.

This script is intended to be used as a module. Running it as a main starts a test sequence. Also note that it doesn't pick up the current date from the system; you have to pass the date as an argument.

```
'''
Julian day routines from Meeus, "Astronomical Formulae for Calculators".
The routines are:

    Julian(month, day, year)              Integer Julian day number
    JulianAstro(month, day, year)         Astronomical Julian day number
    JulianToMonthDayYear(julian_day)      Returns month, day, year tuple
    DayOfWeek(month, day, year)           0 = Sunday
    DayOfYear(month, day, year)           1 to 365 (366 in leap year)
    IsValidDate(month, day, year)         Returns true if date is valid Gregorian
    IsLeapYear(year)                      Returns true if year is leap year
    NumDaysInMonth(month, year)
```

The JulianAstro function returns the astronomical form and is returned
as a floating point number. The astronomical Julian day begins at
Greenwich mean noon. The Julian() function returns the more usual
Julian day as an integer; it is gotten from the astronomical form by
adding 0.55 and taking the integer part.

Warning: In general, the functions do _not_ check their incoming parameters.

Don Peterson 30 May 1998
'''


```python
def NumDaysInMonth(month, year):
    if month == 2:
        if IsLeapYear(year):
            return 29
        else:
            return 28
    elif month == 9 or month == 4 or month == 6 or month == 11:
        return 30
    elif month == 1 or month == 3 or month == 5 or month == 7 or \
         month == 8 or month == 10 or month == 12:
        return 31
    else:
        raise "Bad month"

def JulianToMonthDayYear(julian_day):
    if julian_day < 0:  raise "Bad input value"
    jd = julian_day + 0.5
    Z = int(jd)
    F = jd - 7
    A = Z
    if Z >= 2299161:
        alpha = int((Z - 1867216.26)/36254.25)
        A = Z + 1 + alpha - int(alpha/4)
    B = A + 1524
    C = int((B - 122.1)/365.25)
    D = int(365.25 * C)
    E = int((B - D)/30.6001)
    day = B - D - int(30.6001 * E) + F
    if E < 13.5:
```

```
            month = int(E - 1)
        else:
            month = int(E - 13)
        if month > 2.5:
            year = int(C - 4716)
        else:
            year = int(C - 4715)
        return month, day, year


def DayOfYear(month, day, year):
    if IsLeapYear(year):
        n = int((275*month)/9 -    ((month + 9)/12) + int(day) - 30)
    else:
        n = int((275*month)/9 - 2*((month + 9)/12) + int(day) - 30)
    if n < 1 or n > 366:   raise "Internal error"
    return n


def DayOfWeek(month, day, year):
    julian = int(JulianAstro(month, int(day), year) + 1.5)
    return julian % 7


def IsLeapYear(year):
    if (year % 400 == 0) or (year % 4 == 0 and year % 100 != 0):
        return 1
    else:
        return 0


def IsValidDate(month, day, year):
    '''Returns true if the year is later than 1752 and the month and day
    numbers are valid.
    '''
    if month < 1 or month > 12: return 0
    if int(month) != month     : return 0
    if year < 1753             : return 0
    if day  < 1.0              : return 0
    if int(day) != day:
        if month == 2:
            if IsLeapYear(year):
                if day >= 30.0: return 0
```

```
            else:
                if day >= 29.0: return 0
        elif month == 9 or month == 4 or month == 6 or month == 11:
            if day >= 31.0    : return 0
        else:
            if day >= 32.0    : return 0
    else:
        if month == 2:
            if IsLeapYear(year):
                if day >= 29  : return 0
            else:
                if day >= 28  : return 0
        elif month == 9 or month == 4 or month == 6 or month == 11:
            if day >= 30      : return 0
        else:
            if day >= 31      : return 0
    return 1

def JulianAstro(month, day, year):
    "Note that day can be either an integer or a float."
    if month < 3:
        year  = year - 1
        month = month + 12
    julian = int(365.25*year) + int(30.6001*(month+1)) + day + 1720994.5
    tmp = year + month / 100.0 + day / 10000.0
    if tmp >= 1582.1015:
        A = year / 100
        B = 2 - A + A/4
        julian = julian + B
    return julian * 1.0

def Julian(month, day, year):
    return int(JulianAstro(month, day, year) + 0.55)

def Test():
    if Julian(12, 31, 1989)      != 2447892  :  raise "TestError"
    if Julian(1, 1, 1990)        != 2447893  :  raise "TestError"
    if Julian(7, 4, 1776)        != 2369916  :  raise "TestError"
    if Julian(2, 29, 2000)       != 2451604  :  raise "TestError"
```

```
        if JulianAstro(1, 27.5, 333)   != 1842713.0 :  raise "TestError"
        if JulianAstro(10, 4.81, 1957) != 2436116.31:  raise "TestError"
        if DayOfWeek(11, 13, 1949)     != 0         :  raise "TestError"
        if DayOfWeek( 5, 30, 1998)     != 6         :  raise "TestError"
        if DayOfWeek( 6, 30, 1954)     != 3         :  raise "TestError"
        if DayOfYear(11, 14, 1978)     != 318       :  raise "TestError"
        if DayOfYear( 4, 22, 1980)     != 113       :  raise "TestError"


month, day, year = JulianToMonthDayYear(2436116.31)
if month != 10   : raise "TestError"
if year  != 1957 : raise "TestError"
if abs(day - 4.81) > .00001 : raise "TestError"
month, day, year = JulianToMonthDayYear(1842713.0)
if month != 1    : raise "TestError"
if year  != 333  : raise "TestError"
if abs(day - 27.5) > .00001 : raise "TestError"
month, day, year = JulianToMonthDayYear(1507900.13)
if month != 5    : raise "TestError"
if year  != -584 : raise "TestError"
if abs(day - 28.63) > .00001 : raise "TestError"


if NumDaysInMonth( 1, 1999) != 31 :  raise "TestError"
if NumDaysInMonth( 2, 1999) != 28 :  raise "TestError"
if NumDaysInMonth( 3, 1999) != 31 :  raise "TestError"
if NumDaysInMonth( 4, 1999) != 30 :  raise "TestError"
if NumDaysInMonth( 5, 1999) != 31 :  raise "TestError"
if NumDaysInMonth( 6, 1999) != 30 :  raise "TestError"
if NumDaysInMonth( 7, 1999) != 31 :  raise "TestError"
if NumDaysInMonth( 8, 1999) != 31 :  raise "TestError"
if NumDaysInMonth( 9, 1999) != 30 :  raise "TestError"
if NumDaysInMonth(10, 1999) != 31 :  raise "TestError"
if NumDaysInMonth(11, 1999) != 30 :  raise "TestError"
if NumDaysInMonth(12, 1999) != 31 :  raise "TestError"


if NumDaysInMonth( 1, 2000) != 31 :  raise "TestError"
if NumDaysInMonth( 2, 2000) != 29 :  raise "TestError"
if NumDaysInMonth( 3, 2000) != 31 :  raise "TestError"
if NumDaysInMonth( 4, 2000) != 30 :  raise "TestError"
if NumDaysInMonth( 5, 2000) != 31 :  raise "TestError"
if NumDaysInMonth( 6, 2000) != 30 :  raise "TestError"
```

```
    if NumDaysInMonth( 7, 2000) != 31 :  raise "TestError"
    if NumDaysInMonth( 8, 2000) != 31 :  raise "TestError"
    if NumDaysInMonth( 9, 2000) != 30 :  raise "TestError"
    if NumDaysInMonth(10, 2000) != 31 :  raise "TestError"
    if NumDaysInMonth(11, 2000) != 30 :  raise "TestError"
    if NumDaysInMonth(12, 2000) != 31 :  raise "TestError"


if __name__ == "__main__":
    Test()
```

How It Works

In 1540, Joseph Justus Scalinger worked out a period of time that's called the "Julian period." It's actually a great cycle derived from three smaller cycles. The Julian period is 7,980 years long. Its name is confusing because it has little or nothing to do with the Julian calendar.

The whole point of the Julian period was to have a single fixed system for referencing ancient times, rather than relying on the patchwork of wobbly calendars from many different eras and dynasties. Using the Julian cycle, Scalinger could refer to any past date by using a combination of three numbers that corresponded to the periods of the three inner cycles. Sounds complicated, and it is, but it's far better than trying to reconcile old calendars.

The astronomer John Herschel did the Julian cycle one better. In 1849 he published an extension of the Julian cycle idea, proposing "Julian days." It seems that one thing astronomers need in order to predict events is a way to relate observations from past centuries to observations today. It doesn't matter so much exactly when something took place. What matters more is how much time has elapsed between identical occurrences. But without a single calendar, how do you compare an observation from Chaldean times to one that happened last Tuesday? You need a way to consistently compare times, and that's where the Julian day comes in handy. All you need to know is on what Julian day something happened; then you figure out the Julian day for the next occurrence and subtract. The zero baseline for this counting system is January 1, 4713 B.C.E. Today, as I write this, the Julian day is 2451401. If you convert at the right time of day, you can get the strange result of half-days, due to when the Julian astronomical day starts and ends.

Gotcha

Even though Python variables don't have to be declared, you're well advised to initialize them to avoid NameError. Doing so eliminates ambiguity.

For example, at the top of a script,

```
x=y./2
```

will produce a NameError for y, due to y being undefined. This can be avoided by initializing both x and y before starting the main code, with just about anything: x = y = 10, for example. If this line is in a function definition, you can easily initialize the variable this way:

```
def factor(x=10, y=10):
```

Using this script, you can get an integer Julian day or an astronomical Julian day. You can also go the other way and get a Gregorian date out of a Julian day. This module doesn't use any other imported modules. Everything is done with basic Python statements and operations.

Contributor anonymous

roman.py

Ever want a quick way to translate those Roman numeral copyright notices on old movies into something a little more 20th century? We all learned how to convert Roman numerals in our earliest arithmetic classes, but how many of us can do it in our heads?

```python
import re

iv = re.compile("IV")
ix = re.compile("IX")
xl = re.compile("XL")
xc = re.compile("XC")
cd = re.compile("CD")
cm = re.compile("CM")
i  = re.compile("I" )
v  = re.compile("V" )
x  = re.compile("X" )
l  = re.compile("L" )
c  = re.compile("C" )
d  = re.compile("D" )
m  = re.compile("M" )


def RomanNumeralsToDecimal(roman_string):
    import re, string
    str = string.upper(roman_string)
    exp = ""
    if iv.search(str) != None:  str = iv.sub("+4",   str)
    if ix.search(str) != None:  str = ix.sub("+9",   str)
    if xl.search(str) != None:  str = xl.sub("+40",  str)
    if xc.search(str) != None:  str = xc.sub("+90",  str)
    if cd.search(str) != None:  str = cd.sub("+400", str)
    if cm.search(str) != None:  str = cm.sub("+900", str)
    if  i.search(str) != None:  str =  i.sub("+1",   str)
```

```
        if  v.search(str) != None:  str =  v.sub("+5",      str)
        if  x.search(str) != None:  str =  x.sub("+10",     str)
        if  l.search(str) != None:  str =  l.sub("+50",     str)
        if  c.search(str) != None:  str =  c.sub("+100",    str)
        if  d.search(str) != None:  str =  d.sub("+500",    str)
        if  m.search(str) != None:  str =  m.sub("+1000", str)
    exec "num = " + str
    return num



def DecimalToRomanNumerals(base10_integer):
    '''Translated from a public domain C routine by Jim Walsh in the
    Snippets collection.
    '''
    roman = ""
    n, base10_integer = divmod(base10_integer, 1000)
    roman = "M"*n
    if base10_integer >= 900:
        roman = roman + "CM"
        base10_integer = base10_integer - 900
    while base10_integer >= 500:
        roman = roman + "D"
        base10_integer = base10_integer - 500
    if base10_integer >= 400:
        roman = roman + "CD"
        base10_integer = base10_integer - 400
    while base10_integer >= 100:
        roman = roman + "C"
        base10_integer = base10_integer - 100
    if base10_integer >= 90:
        roman = roman + "XC"
        base10_integer = base10_integer - 90
    while base10_integer >= 50:
        roman = roman + "L"
        base10_integer = base10_integer - 50
    if base10_integer >= 40:
        roman = roman + "XL"
        base10_integer = base10_integer - 40
    while base10_integer >= 10:
        roman = roman + "X"
```

```
            base10_integer = base10_integer - 10
        if base10_integer >= 9:
            roman = roman + "IX"
            base10_integer = base10_integer - 9
        while base10_integer >= 5:
            roman = roman + "V"
            base10_integer = base10_integer - 5
        if base10_integer >= 4:
            roman = roman + "IV"
            base10_integer = base10_integer - 4
        while base10_integer > 0:
            roman = roman + "I"
            base10_integer = base10_integer - 1
        return roman


if __name__ == "__main__":
    '''We'll test the conversion routines by converting from a decimal
    integer n to a Roman numeral and then back again.  If the operations
    are not the identity transformation, it's an error.
    '''

    largest_number = 5000
    for num in xrange(1,largest_number+1):
        str = DecimalToRomanNumerals(int(num))
        number = RomanNumeralsToDecimal(str)
        if number != num:
            print "Routines failed for", num
            raise "Test failure"
    print "Test passed."
```

How It Works

Boy, you'd think that simple inventions like the zero and the decimal point would be intuitively obvious, but apparently they're not. It took Western civilization a thousand years after the fall of the Roman Empire to improve much on the Roman system.

This script, like so many in this book, makes use of the re module's compiled string objects to do searches and matches. In fact, converting from Roman to decimal in RomanNumeralsToDecimal() is just a process of doing searches through the input string. Its opposite number, DecimalToRomanNumerals(), involves a bit more code. It makes extensive use of if statements and while loops to break down the decimal into 11 categories based on the decimal's Roman equivalent after performing a simple divmod() function on it. The divmod() operation points out Python's ability to assign two variables at once from a multiple-output operation. In the line

```
n, base10_integer = divmod(base10_integer, 1000)
```

the variable n gets the base value and base10_integer gets the modulus. The other numerals are decoded with the various if tests.

Contributor anonymous

stats.py

This script is intended to be used as a module. It has statistical functions that don't come standard with Python. Note that the module stat doesn't have statistical functions, despite the name.

This script is for the analysis of one- and two-vector problems.

```
'''
Module for simple statistical calculations.
'''


import math

def XYStats(vector_x, vector_y):
    if len(vector_x) != len(vector_y):
        raise "Bad data", "vectors different lengths"
    results = {
        "num"     : 0,
        "meanx"   : 0.0,
        "meany"   : 0.0,
        "stddevx" : 0.0,
        "stddevy" : 0.0,
        "sumx"    : 0.0,
        "sumxx"   : 0.0,
        "sumy"    : 0.0,
        "sumyy"   : 0.0,
        "sumxy"   : 0.0,
        "minx"    : 0.0,
        "maxx"    : 0.0,
        "miny"    : 0.0,
```

```
        "maxy"    : 0.0
        }
    minx = 3e308
    miny = 3e308
    maxx = -minx
    maxy = -miny
    sx   = 0
    sy   = 0
    sxx  = 0
    syy  = 0
    sxy  = 0
    for ix in range(len(vector_x)):
        x = vector_x[ix]
        y = vector_y[ix]
        sx  = sx + x
        sy  = sy + y
        sxx = sxx + x*x
        syy = syy + y*y
        sxy = sxy + x*y
        if x < minx:  minx = x
        if x > maxx:  maxx = x
        if y < miny:  miny = y
        if y > maxy:  maxy = y
    n = len(vector_x)
    meanx = sx/n
    meany = sy/n
    results["num"]       = n
    results["meanx"]     = meanx
    results["meany"]     = meany
    results["stddevx"]  = math.sqrt((sxx - n*meanx*meanx) / (n - 1))
    results["stddevy"]  = math.sqrt((syy - n*meany*meany) / (n - 1))
    results["sumx"]      = sx
    results["sumxx"]     = sxx
    results["sumy"]      = sy
    results["sumyy"]     = syy
    results["sumxy"]     = sxy
    results["minx"]      = minx
    results["miny"]      = miny
    results["maxx"]      = maxx
```

```
        results["maxy"]     = maxy
        results["medianx"]  = GetMedian(vector_x)
        results["mediany"]  = GetMedian(vector_y)
        return results


def XStats(vector):
    results = {}
    if len(vector) < 1:
        raise "Bad data", "Null vector"
    min = 3e308
    max = -min
    sx  = 0.0
    sxx = 0.0
    for value in vector:
        sx  = sx + value
        sxx = sxx + value*value
        if value < min:  min = value
        if value > max:  max = value
    n = len(vector)
    mean = sx / n
    if n == 1:
        results["stddev"] = 0.0
    else:
        results["stddev"] = math.sqrt((sxx - n*mean*mean) / (n - 1))
    results["mean"]   = mean
    results["sum"]    = sx
    results["num"]    = n
    results["min"]    = min
    results["max"]    = max
    results["median"] = GetMedian(vector)
    return results


def GetMedian(vector):
    n = len(vector)
    if n < 1:
        raise "Bad data", "Null vector"
    tmp = vector
    tmp.sort()
    if (n+1)/2 == n/2:
```

```
        median = (vector[n/2 - 1] + vector[n/2]) / 2.0
    else:
        median = vector[(n+1)/2 - 1]
    return median * 1.0


def Test():
    a=[1,2,3.0]
    r = XStats(a)
    if r["num"]     != 3  :   raise "TestFailed"
    if r["mean"]    != 2.0:   raise "TestFailed"
    if r["stddev"]  != 1.0:   raise "TestFailed"
    if r["sum"]     != 6.0:   raise "TestFailed"
    if r["min"]     != 1.0:   raise "TestFailed"
    if r["max"]     != 3.0:   raise "TestFailed"
    if r["median"]  != 2.0:   raise "TestFailed"

    s = XYStats(a,a)
    if r["num"]     != 3  :   raise "TestFailed"
    if s["meanx"]   != 2.0:   raise "TestFailed"
    if s["meany"]   != 2.0:   raise "TestFailed"
    if s["stddevx"] != 1.0:   raise "TestFailed"
    if s["stddevy"] != 1.0:   raise "TestFailed"
    if s["sumx"]    != 6.0:   raise "TestFailed"
    if s["sumy"]    != 6.0:   raise "TestFailed"
    if s["sumxx"]   != 14.0:  raise "TestFailed"
    if s["sumyy"]   != 14.0:  raise "TestFailed"
    if s["minx"]    != 1.0:   raise "TestFailed"
    if s["miny"]    != 1.0:   raise "TestFailed"
    if s["maxx"]    != 3.0:   raise "TestFailed"
    if s["maxy"]    != 3.0:   raise "TestFailed"
    if s["sumxy"]   != 14.0:  raise "TestFailed"

    if s["num"]     != 3  :   raise "TestFailed"
    raise "Error", "Need to add in correlation/regression stuff"


if __name__ == '__main__':
    Test()
```

How It Works

As with many other scripts in this book, this one has a test sequence built into it. If you call the script from the command line, it starts a test sequence. It doesn't return an "all clear", though; confirmation is in the negative.

The script is intended to be used as a module. Despite its obvious utility, the script doesn't use many exotic tricks. Most of the code is vintage Python.

The script takes one or two lists of numbers as arguments and then performs basic statistical analysis on them: means, medians, and so on. Tuples don't work, because the lists have to be sorted. Also, if you're passing an X and a Y list, they have to be the same length.

Notice the use of a dictionary in XYStats(). The dictionary is named results, and it's initialized with all the keys and zeros for values. Later, the various keys will be matched with real values with statements like

```
results["num"] = n
```

Contributor anonymous

Because the penguin is a clever little sod in his own environment.

Chapter 9: Servers

basic.py

form.py

helloworld.py

counter.py

sengine.py

engine.py

who-owns.py

server.py

P ython is extremely good at sever-side programming. You can write Python scripts that do almost anything imaginable, including database access.

The Internet is no problem for Python. The standard Python distribution comes with modules for parsing XML and SGML, for decoding HTML forms, and for handling POP3, MIME, and the other usual Internet conventions and protocols. And there are many new modules you can download from **www.python.org**, modules that are updated and even more powerful than the originals. There's also an object publishing environment called ZOPE from Digital Creations (**www.digicool.com**). ZOPE is written in Python with C extensions. ZOPE is on the companion CD-ROM, too.

Python isn't shabby at client-side programming, either. Supplied on the companion CD-ROM is Grail, a browser built entirely with Python. It isn't really a competitor to Microsoft's Internet Explorer, but it's free, the code is open, and it's a perfect base for your own custom browser application. It can also use Python scripts as applets.

The scripts here are pretty small by real-world standards. Real server-side scripts often use many modules and data files.

basic.py

This is as simple as it gets in CGI (*Common Gateway Interface*). Oh, you could leave off the HTML line "This is a test", but you wouldn't know if your script was working, would you?

```
#!/usr/bin/python
#This script does little of any value, but it's the most
#basic CGI script imaginable
print "Content-type: text/html"
print #This blank line indicates the end of the HTML header
print "<p>This is a test</p>"
```

This HTML calls basic.py:

```
<HTML>
<BODY>
<A HREF="/cgi-bin/basic.py">Click me!</A>
</BODY>
</HTML>
```

How It Works

Not much to it. The HTML page calls for the script right out of an HREF. The script is in the cgi-bin subdirectory on the server (in my case a Caldera Linux box with Apache) and it fires upon getting the command from Apache. There are a couple of hard-and-fast rules from this point. The first is that you must respond with a header identifying the type of data you're about to send. In this case, it's text/html. Then you need a blank line, supplied by the lone print statement. After that anything else that's printed is sent back to the client as HTML. But keep in mind that you need to add the HTML tags to the print lines because basic Python doesn't generate them automatically.

form.py

One of the most common uses for CGI is to take a form's contents and muck around with it. This script and HTML page combo shows one way (and only one way; there are many others) to manipulate form data.

```python
#!/usr/bin/python
# form.py
# A CGI script to interpret form data
import cgi
import shelve

def memberform():
    list={}
# Write the header
    print "Content-type: text/html"
    print
# Get the fields from the form
    form1=cgi.FieldStorage()
# Decode fields into variables
    first=form1["first"].value
    last=form1["last"].value
    email=form1["email"].value
    fan=form1["fan"].value
# Write the field variables into a dictionary
    list["first"]=first
    list["last"]=last
    list["email"]=email
    list["fan"]=fan
```

```
# Open the shelf object
    member_list=shelve.open("memlist1")
# Append the new listing to the member list
    member_list[email]=list
# Print a confirmation
    print "<H1> Confirmation!</H1>"
    print "<P> You're entered on the list. Congratulations! </P>"
# Now close the shelf object
    member_list.close()


if __name__=="__main__":
    memberform()
```

The HTML:

```
<HTML>
<BODY>
<H1>Want to be on our mailing list?</H1>
<FORM ACTION="/cgi-bin/form.py" METHOD=post>
First name: <INPUT TYPE=TEXT NAME="first"><BR>
Last name: <INPUT TYPE=TEXT NAME="last"><BR>
Email: <INPUT TYPE=TEXT NAME="email"><BR>
I am a Monty Python fan (highly suggested): <INPUT TYPE=CHECKBOX NAME="fan">
Click to submit: <INPUT TYPE=SUBMIT VALUE="  Add me!  " NAME="submit">
</FORM>
</BODY>
</HTML>
```

How It Works

This is a CGI script the way that a pup tent is akin to the Astrodome, but you get the idea. form.py takes form data from the client and saves it in a file. It doesn't actually do anything with the data, but at least it's being captured for later.

The script fires up when the server receives the submission from the HTML page. You could (and should) have a much more elaborate HTML page. And you could add scripting on the page itself to do error checking and such. There isn't any error checking the way the CGI script stands. It should, for example, be checking for a valid structure to the e-mail address and the absence of numerals or punctuation in the names.

The script first prints the standard lines for the HTML header:

```
print "Content-type: text/html"
print
```

Then it preserves the various fields in the variable form1. They're extracted from an instantiation of the cgi module's FormStorage() class. The line

```
form1=cgi.FieldStorage()
```

does all that work. form1 becomes a dictionary-like object. As with other dictionaries, it has keys and values. The keys are the field names from the form, and the values are the contents of those fields. With the lines

```
first=form1["first"].value
last=form1["last"].value
email=form1["email"].value
fan=form1["fan"].value
```

the four fields have their values pulled out and saved as variables. Note that the keys inside the brackets are string literals that are the names of the form's fields.

The lines

```
list["first"]=first
list["last"]=last
list["email"]=email
list["fan"]=fan
```

create a new dictionary. The user's first name would be paired with the key "first," the last name with the key "last," and so on.

Okay, so now there's a dictionary of the data that was pulled in. How do you index or key it? The next lines provide the answer:

```
member_list=shelve.open("memlist1")
member_list[email]=list
```

The first line opens a shelf object. Python comes with several database-type modules, some for true databases and others for simpler storage methods. The shelf object is only one of the possible ways of making Python objects persistent. There are also pickle, cpickle, gdbm, dumbdbm, anydbm, and marshal, to name a few more. The shelf object is essentially a dictionary, but the value can be nearly any Python object. In this case, it's a dictionary. In other words, this object is going to be a dictionary that has keys to dictionaries.

The shelf object will be opened in whatever directory contains the CGI script, so the script, usually running in httpd, needs to be allowed to create the shelf if it doesn't exist, and to write to it if it does.

To uniquely identify each visitor, I chose to use the visitor's e-mail address. First and last names can be duplicated, but e-mail addresses are rarely even close. In the line

```
member_list[email]=list
```

the key variable email is connected to the dictionary variable list. Now, if you want to look up a user, do it by the e-mail address, and you'll get back all the data you've stored as in a dictionary.

The final lines

```
print "<H1> Confirmation!</H1>".
print "<P> You're entered on the list. Congratulations! </P>"
member_list.close()
```

print the HTML coding to confirm the registration and then close the object member_list.

Sometimes you want to pass a hidden value to a CGI script, something that the user doesn't know about. You might want to send specific information to a remote client and get it back again for processing, avoiding the need to store it on your server. In that case, you can have a "state" for the data by writing a form to the client with a line like this within the <FORM> tags:

```
<INPUT name=whatever value=value type=hidden>
```

Whatever's in the "whatever" field will be sent back to your CGI script for further operations without the end user being aware that it's there.

helloworld.py

This simple script returns to the browser a page that gives the local time at the server.

```
#!/usr/local/bin/python
##. helloworld.py#from time import *print "Content-type: text/html"print

print "<HTML>"

print "<Head>"
```

```
print "<Title>Hello World</Title>"
print "</Head>"

print "<Body>"
print "<H1>Hello World !</H1>"
print "<hr>"

print "<P>This is Belgium.<br>Localtime is", ctime( time() ) + ".<P>"

print "</Body>"
print "</HTML>"
```

How It Works

Simplicity itself. The script starts with the standard header and then supplies basic HTML for a page. Within the page, it drops a time stamp using the standard module time.

Contributed by Michel Vanaken

counter.py

counter.py is a Python version of the old standard of the Web, the hit counter. counter.py uses the gdbm module to keep track of the hits. Unlike a boring textual counter, though, this one actually builds an image of the counter.

```
#!/usr/local/bin/python## CGI count - Uses a gdbm database
#from string import atoi, zfill
import gdbm
import cgi

DIGITS = 4

hex_bytes = [
    [ "0xff,0xff,", "0xff,0xff,", "0xff,0xff,", "0xff,0xff,", "0xff,0xff,",\
"0xff,0xff,", "0xff,0xff,", "0xff,0xff,", "0xff,0xff,", "0xff,0xff," ],
    [ "0x01,0xc0,",   "0x01,0xc0,", "0x01,0xc0,", "0x01,0xc0,", "0x01,0xc0,",\
"0x01,0xc0,", "0x01,0xc0,", "0x01,0xc0,", "0x01,0xc0,", "0x01,0xc0," ],
    [ "0xfd,0xdf,",   "0xfd,0xdf,", "0xfd,0xdf,", "0xfd,0xdf,", "0xfd,0xdf,",\
"0xfd,0xdf,", "0xfd,0xdf,", "0xfd,0xdf,", "0xfd,0xdf,", "0xfd,0xdf," ],
```

```
    [ "0x3d,0xde,",    "0x7d,0xde,", "0x1d,0xde,", "0x3d,0xdc,", "0xfd,0xdd,",\
"0x7d,0xd0,", "0xfd,0xd1,", "0x0d,0xd0,", "0x1d,0xdc,", "0x1d,0xde," ],
    [ "0xdd,0xdd,",    "0x1d,0xde,", "0x0d,0xdc,", "0xdd,0xd8,", "0xfd,0xdc,",\
"0x3d,0xd8,", "0x7d,0xde,", "0x0d,0xd8,", "0xcd,0xd9,", "0xcd,0xd9," ],
    [ "0xcd,0xd9,",    "0x7d,0xde,", "0xe5,0xd8,", "0xed,0xd9,", "0x7d,0xdc,",\
"0xbd,0xdf,", "0x3d,0xdf,", "0xf5,0xdb,", "0xe5,0xd3,", "0xed,0xd9," ],
    [ "0xed,0xdb,",    "0x7d,0xde,", "0xf5,0xd9,", "0xfd,0xd9,", "0xbd,0xdc,",\
"0x1d,0xdf,", "0x9d,0xdf,", "0xfd,0xdb,", "0xe5,0xd3,", "0xe5,0xd3," ],
    [ "0xe5,0xd3,",    "0x7d,0xde,", "0xfd,0xd9,", "0xfd,0xdd,", "0xdd,0xdc,",\
"0x1d,0xdc,", "0xcd,0xdf,", "0xfd,0xdd,", "0xc5,0xd3,", "0xe5,0xd3," ],
    [ "0xe5,0xd3,",    "0x7d,0xde,", "0xfd,0xd9,", "0x7d,0xde,", "0xdd,0xdc,",\
"0x7d,0xd8,", "0x2d,0xdc,", "0xfd,0xdd,", "0x8d,0xd9,", "0xe5,0xd3," ],
    [ "0xe5,0xd3,",    "0x7d,0xde,", "0xfd,0xdd,", "0x3d,0xdc,", "0xed,0xdc,",\
"0xfd,0xd1,", "0xc5,0xd9,", "0xfd,0xdd,", "0x1d,0xde,", "0xc5,0xd3," ],
    [ "0xe5,0xd3,",    "0x7d,0xde,", "0xfd,0xde,", "0xfd,0xd8,", "0xf5,0xdc,",\
"0xfd,0xd3,", "0xe5,0xd1,", "0xfd,0xde,", "0x3d,0xdc,", "0xcd,0xd3," ],
    [ "0xe5,0xd3,",    "0x7d,0xde,", "0xfd,0xde,", "0xfd,0xd1,", "0xf5,0xdc,",\
"0xfd,0xd3,", "0xe5,0xd3,", "0xfd,0xde,", "0xcd,0xd8,", "0x1d,0xd8," ],
    [ "0xe5,0xd3,",    "0x7d,0xde,", "0x7d,0xdf,", "0xfd,0xd3,", "0x05,0xd0,",\
"0xfd,0xd7,", "0xe5,0xd3,", "0xfd,0xde,", "0xe5,0xd1,", "0xfd,0xd9," ],
    [ "0xed,0xdb,",    "0x7d,0xde,", "0xbd,0xdf,", "0xfd,0xd3,", "0xfd,0xdc,"\,
"0xfd,0xd7,", "0xe5,0xd3,", "0x7d,0xdf,", "0xe5,0xd3,", "0xfd,0xdd," ],
    [ "0xcd,0xd9,",    "0x7d,0xde,", "0xdd,0xd7,", "0xfd,0xdb,", "0xfd,0xdc,",\
"0xfd,0xdb,", "0xcd,0xdb,", "0x7d,0xdf,", "0xe5,0xd3,", "0x7d,0xde," ],
    [ "0xdd,0xdd,",    "0x7d,0xde,", "0x0d,0xd0,", "0xcd,0xd9,", "0xfd,0xdc,",\
"0xcd,0xdd,", "0xcd,0xd9,", "0x7d,0xdf,", "0xcd,0xd9,", "0x3d,0xdf," ],
    [ "0x3d,0xde,",    "0x1d,0xd8,", "0x05,0xd8,", "0x0d,0xde,", "0xfd,0xdc,",\
"0x0d,0xde,", "0x3d,0xdc,", "0xbd,0xdf,", "0x1d,0xdc,", "0xc5,0xdf," ],
    [ "0xfd,0xdf,",    "0xfd,0xdf,", "0xfd,0xdf,", "0xfd,0xdf,", "0xfd,0xdf,",\
"0xfd,0xdf,", "0xfd,0xdf,", "0xfd,0xdf,", "0xfd,0xdf,", "0xfd,0xdf," ],
    [ "0x01,0xc0,",    "0x01,0xc0,", "0x01,0xc0,", "0x01,0xc0,", "0x01,0xc0,",\
"0x01,0xc0,", "0x01,0xc0,", "0x01,0xc0,", "0x01,0xc0,", "0x01,0xc0," ],
    [ "0xff,0xff,",    "0xff,0xff,", "0xff,0xff,", "0xff,0xff,", "0xff,0xff,",\
"0xff,0xff,", "0xff,0xff,", "0xff,0xff,", "0xff,0xff,", "0xff,0xff," ]
]

def print_header() :
    ###########
    print "Content-type: image/x-bitmap"
    print
```

```
        print "#define counter_width", DIGITS * 16
        print "#define counter_height 20"
        print "static char counter_bits[] = {"



def print_footer() :
    ###########
        print "0x00 } ;"
        print

def print_digits_values( s ) :
    ###################
        i = 0
        while i < 20 :
            for d in s :
                print hex_bytes[ i ][ atoi( d ) ],
            print
            i = i + 1



def inc_counter( s ) :
    ##########
        val = atoi( s ) + 1
        return zfill( str( val ), DIGITS )



def get_put_counter( url ) :
    ##############
        db = gdbm.open( "counters.gdbm", "w", 0644 )
        if db.has_key( url ) :
            s = db[ url ]
        else :
            s = zfill( '0', DIGITS )
        s = inc_counter( s )
        db[ url ] = s
        return s



def CGImain() :
    ######
```

```
        list = cgi.SvFormContentDict()
        if list.has_key( "url" ) :
            url = list[ "url" ]
            counter = get_put_counter( url )
            print_header()
            print_digits_values( counter )
            print_footer()



CGImain()
```

A typical HTML page with the counter embedded might look a little like this:

```
<!DOCTYPE HTML PUBLIC "-//IETF//DTD HTML//EN">
<html>
  <head><title>Counter Example</title></head>
  <body>
    <h1>Counter Example</h1>
    <p>This page has been visited <IMG SRC="/cgi-bin/counter.py">
      times.</p>
  </body>
</html>
```

How It Works

The browser can't display an XBM directly, which this graphical counter really is, but it can display a graphic that's shipped as a hex representation. That's why there's a huge list of hexidecimal values. The contributor says that the graphical drawing is buggy. He also says that he drew the graphic originally as an XBM and then played with it in emacs to get it to resolve itself properly.

This script was written for an older version of Python, when the module cgi had the method SvFormContentDict(). The module still has that method but only for backward compatibility. It's now deprecated in favor of FormStorage. SvFormContentDict() stores field values as a dictionary. In the function CGImain(), that dictionary of values is checked to see if it has a URL key. If it does, the function get_put_counter() is called and the counter graphic is assembled.

count.py also uses the database module gdbm. The line

```
    db = gdbm.open( "counters.gdbm", "w", 0644 )
```

makes the file counters.gdbm open for writing. You should create the file before you run counter.py, although if you don't, the file will be created for you. Create the file by changing your current directory to cgi-bin, launching Python in interactive mode, and typing the following commands:

```
import gdbm
gdbm.open("counters.gdbm", "n")
```

That done, you can exit Python.

Okay, now that you've seen the up side, here are some possible problems.

When you create a database this way, you need to make sure it's readable and writeable by the HTTPD daemon that runs the script. This may occasionally be problematic. A fairly reliable patch is:

```
gdbm.open("counters.gdbm", "n")
import os
os.chmod("counters.gdbm", 0666)  # The devil, you say...
```

Then too, Web technology is moving so fast that scripts like this can quickly get out of date. In this case, the script is written for an older cgi.py module, so some patching may be in order. For example, you might use this script only to find that you always get the same counter value, which sort of negates the value of the entire enterprise. If it happens, it's because most browsers won't refresh the counter automatically, but preferentially use the cached image from the last time the counter was retrieved.

To prevent this from happening, you need to add a line to print_header(), right after the "Content-type" line. This should work, at least for Netscape Navigator:

```
    print "Expires: 0"
```

This line will cause the browser to "expire" the image as soon as it retrieves it, so it will always go back to the server for the latest copy of the image.

Some browsers may need an actual time value, of the sort produced by time.ctime(). Still other browsers may ignore the "Expires:" header in favor of "Pragma: no-cache". So this may work better:

```
    import time
    print "Expires: ", time.ctime(time.time())
    print "Pragma: no-cache"
```

Contributed by Michel Vanaken

sengine.py

How would you like to be able to query multiple search engines at the same time? Well, maybe not at the exact same microsecond, but plenty close enough.

```python
#!/usr/local/bin/python
#
# sengine.py - Search several search engines at once
# M. Vanaken - 1998
#
# Requirements :
# - threads
#
# To do :
# - Rewrite relative URLs to absolute ones.
# - Investigate problem in note (1)
#
# Note (1) :
# It seems that on some systems, urllib isn't thread
# safe. Its access can be locked, although this implies
# mostly a sequential processing of each request.
# Needs further investigation
#
import traceback
from time import sleep
import string
import thread
import urllib
import cgi
# see note (1)
#httplib_lock = thread.allocate_lock()
class SearchEngine :
    def __init__( self ) :
        self.Lock = thread.allocate_lock()
        self.Retrieved = 0
        self.CanPrint = 0
        self.Printed = 0
    def EscapeQueryString( self, s ) :
        s = string.strip( s )
        s = string.joinfields(         string.splitfields( s, " " ), "+" )
```

```
                s = urllib.quote( s, "/+:&?" )
              return s
        def Main( self, qs ) :
              try :
                  self.Query = self.MakeQueryString( qs )
# see note (1)
                  # httplib_lock.acquire()
                  self.Answer = urllib.urlopen( self.Query )
# see note (1)
                  # httplib_lock.release()
                  self.Lock.acquire()
                  self.Retrieved = 1
                  self.Lock.release()
                  myTurn = 0
                  while not myTurn :
                      sleep( 1 )
                      self.Lock.acquire()
                      if self.CanPrint :
                          myTurn = 1
                      self.Lock.release()
                  print "\n<hr>\n<H1 align=center>Results from", self.Name, "</H1>\n<hr>"
                  print
                  self.PrintResult()
                  print "\n\n<H2 align=center>End of the results from", self.Name, "</\
H2>\n<hr>"
                  self.Answer.close()
                  self.Lock.acquire()
                  self.Printed = 1
                  self.Lock.release()
              except :
                  self.Lock.acquire()
                  self.Printed = 1
                  self.CanPrint = 1
                  self.Retrieved = 1
                  self.Lock.release()
                  traceback.print_exc()
                  # self.Answer.close()
class Excite( SearchEngine ) :
    def __init__( self ) :
```

```
            SearchEngine.__init__( self )
            self.Name = "Excite"
            self.Url = "http://www.excite.com/"
        def MakeQueryString( self, s ) :
            return self.Url + "search.gw?trace=a&search=" + self.EscapeQueryString( s )
        def PrintResult( self ) :
            filter = 0
            for line in self.Answer.readlines() :
                if string.find( line, "Ad Start" ) != -1 :
                    filter = 1
                if not filter :
                    print line
                if string.find( line, "Ad Stop" ) != -1 :
                    filter = 0
class InfoSeek( SearchEngine ) :
    def __init__( self ) :
        SearchEngine.__init__( self )
        self.Name = "InfoSeek"
        self.Url = "http://www.infoseek.com/"
    def MakeQueryString( self, s ) :
        return self.Url + "Titles?qt=" + self.EscapeQueryString( s ) +
"&col=WW&sv=IS&lk=noframes&nh=10"
    def PrintResult( self ) :
        for line in self.Answer.readlines() :
            print line
class EuroSeek( SearchEngine ) :
    def __init__( self ) :
        SearchEngine.__init__( self )
        self.Name = "EuroSeek"
        self.Url = "http://www.euroseek.net/"
    def MakeQueryString( self, s ) :
        return self.Url + "query?iflang=uk&query=" + self.EscapeQueryString( s ) + \
"&domain=world&lang=world"
    def PrintResult( self ) :
        for line in self.Answer.readlines() :
            if string.find( line, "Advertisment!" ) == -1 :
                print line
    def Search( s ) :
        qs = s,
        Engines = Excite(), InfoSeek(), EuroSeek()
```

```
        print "Starting search on"
        print "<UL>"
        for e in Engines :
            print "<LI>" + e.Name
            thread.start_new_thread( e.Main, qs )
        print "</UL>"
        Finished = 0
        while not Finished :
            sleep( 1 )
            SomeOnePrinting = 0
            for e in Engines :
                e.Lock.acquire()
                if e.Retrieved and e.CanPrint and not e.Printed :
                    e.Lock.release()
                    SomeOnePrinting = 1
                    break
                e.Lock.release()
            if not SomeOnePrinting :
                for e in Engines :
                    e.Lock.acquire()
                    if e.Retrieved and not e.CanPrint :
                        e.CanPrint = 1
                        e.Lock.release()
                        SomeOnePrinting = 1
                        break
                    e.Lock.release()
            if not SomeOnePrinting :
                Finished = 1
                for e in Engines :
                    e.Lock.acquire()
                if not e.Printed :
                    e.Lock.release()
                    Finished = 0
                    break
                e.Lock.release()
#
# Retrieve query string from form
#
print "Content-type: text/html"
print
```

```
print "<HTML>"
print "<Head><Title>MultiSearch results</Title></Head>"
print "<Body>"
form = cgi.FieldStorage()
if form.has_key( "qs" ) :
    qs = form[ "qs" ].value
    Search( qs )
else :
    print "Your Search is empty !"
print "</Body></HTML>"
```

How It Works

This script is unlike the other scripts in this book in that it uses threads. The other script that uses threads is a modification of this script, engine.py. If you haven't encountered threads, think of them this way: processes are siblings, while threads are Siamese twins. Processes are jealous of their own resources and share them reluctantly. Threads inherently share the same space. This makes threads at once faster and more injury-prone than processes. Because threads have access to the same variables, it's possible for them to overwrite one another's values, resulting in code with all the operational elegance of a plane crash. To avoid this condition, threads usually lock certain variables for a period of time. Python does this with the threads module.

Each search engine to be queried is given its own subclass of SearchEngine(). Each search engine class has its own thread, which is regulated with the use of flags. This technique speeds up the query process, because you're not waiting for a query to be executed at one engine before moving to another.

Of course, threads have to be properly controlled so they don't collide in midair. sengine.py does this with flags that are queried by threads. The flags are Retrieved, CanPrint, and Printed.

Be aware that this script may not work on all platforms. The contributor notes that urllib isn't always thread-safe.

Contributed by Michel Vanaken

When you're testing new CGI scripts, you can test them with both the server and client on the same machine. You can even test a Python server and Python client on the same machine, using standard TCP/IP and the loopback address 127.0.0.1.

engine.py

This script is based on sengine.py by Michel Vanaken. It's the core code of the Tkinter GUI (*Graphical User Interface*) in Chapter 6. engine.py corrects some of the problems that Michel noted in his script, and adds the GUI. To run all of engine.py, including the GUI, copy engine.py from this chapter and copy the corresponding Tkinter scripts from Tkinter. The entire package is available on the companion CD-ROM, including an excellent readme file.

```python
#!/usr/bin/env python
"""
This is a multi-threaded WWW search engine.
It is derived from Michel Vanaken's sengine.py, from which it
shamelessly steals several URLs, the main idea of one thread per
search client, and a lot of code.

Usage:
    python engine.py <search string>

This script assumes you have Netscape in your path.

1999 Mitchell S. Chapman
$Id: engine.py,v 1.1 1999/08/22 17:22:27 mchapman Exp mchapman $
"""


__version__ = "$Revision: 1.1 $"


import sys, threading, Queue, urllib, string, traceback

class Result:
    """This class holds the result of a search engine query."""
    def __init__(self, engineName, resultStr, finalStatus="Done"):
        self.engineName = engineName
        self.resultStr = resultStr
        self.finalStatus = finalStatus



class SearchBase(threading.Thread):
    """This is a basic search engine class."""
```

```python
    def __init__(self, rawQueryString, finishCB):
        """Initialize a new instance.
        'rawQueryString' describes the query to be performed.
        'finishCB' is a callback to be invoked w. one arg -- the
        search results -- when the thread finishes."""
        # It's generally considered bad to use self.__class__.__name__, but
        # I'll do it anyway.
        threading.Thread.__init__(self, name=self.__class__.__name__)
        self.rawQueryString = rawQueryString
        assert(finishCB != None)  # Should assert that it's callable...
        self.finishCB = finishCB
        self.result = None
        self.cancelled = 0

def run(self):
    """Start running self in its own thread."""
    result = None
    try:
        query = self.makeQueryString()

        opener = urllib.FancyURLopener()
        resultF = opener.open(query)

        if self.cancelled:
            result = self.cancelledResult()
        else:
            result = self.readResult(resultF)
    except:
        # Rather than queue up a normal result, queue up the
        # exception.
        result = self.exceptionResult()

    self.finishCB(result)

def cancel(self):
    """Cancel a query."""
    self.cancelled = 1

def makeQueryString(self):
```

```python
        """Override this in subclasses to transform self.rawQueryString
        into a query string appropriate to the target search engine.
        Return the converted query string."""
        return self.rawQueryString


    def readResult(self, inf):
        """Return the result from self's search engine, appropriately
        reformatted."""
        result = None
        content = []
        while not self.cancelled:
            newContent = inf.read(1024)
            if not newContent:
                break
            content.append(newContent)
        content = string.join(content)

        if self.cancelled:
            result = self.cancelledResult()
        else:
            result = Result(self.getName(),
                            self.formattedContent(content))

        return result


    def cancelledResult(self):
        """Return a result indicating cancellation."""
        result = Result(self.getName(),
                        """<HTML><HEAD>
                        <TITLE>Search Cancelled</TITLE>
                        </HEAD><BODY>
                        Search was cancelled.
                        </BODY></HTML>""",
                        finalStatus="Cancelled")
        return result


    def exceptionResult(self):
        """Return a result indicating a failure due to an exception."""
        callstack = apply(traceback.format_exception, sys.exc_info())
```

```
        msg = """<HTML><HEAD><TITLE>Search Failed</TITLE></HEAD>
        <BODY>
        <H1>Search Failed for %s</H1>
        Reason:<BR>
        <PRE>%s</PRE>
        </BODY>
        </HTML>""" % (self.getName(), string.join(callstack, ""))

        result = Result(self.getName(), msg, finalStatus="Failed")
        return result

    def formattedContent(self, rawContent):
        """Override this in subclasses to read and format the results of
        a search."""
        return rawContent

    def escapeQueryString(self, qs):
        """Escape a query string as necessary so it can be embedded within
        a URL."""
        result = string.strip(qs)
        result = string.join(string.split(result), "+")
        # Escape special characters in the result, but never quote any
        # of /, +, :, &, or ?.
        result = urllib.quote(result, "/+:&?")
        return result


class Excite(SearchBase):
    """This search thread knows how to converse w. Excite's search engine."""
    def makeQueryString(self):
        return ("http://www.excite.com/search.gw?trace=a&search=%s" %
                (self.escapeQueryString(self.rawQueryString)))

    def formattedContents(self, rawContent):
        """Strip out advertisements from the response."""
        filter = 0  # Non-zero indicates the current line should be ignored.
        result = []
        lines = string.split(rawContent, "\n")
        for line in lines:
```

```python
            if string.find(line, "Ad Start") != -1:
                filter = 1
            elif string.find(line, "Ad Stop") != -1:
                filter = 0
            else:
                if not filter:
                    result.append(line)
        return string.join(result, "\n")


class InfoSeek(SearchBase):
    def makeQueryString(self):
        return ("http://www.infoseek.com/Titles?"
                "qt=%s&col=WW&sv=IS&lk=noframes&nh=10" %
                (self.escapeQueryString(self.rawQueryString)))


class EuroSeek(SearchBase):
    def makeQueryString(self):
        return ("http://www.euroseek.net/query?iflang=uk&query=%s"
                "&domain=world&lang=world" %
                (self.escapeQueryString(self.rawQueryString)))


    def formattedContents(self, rawContent):
        """Filter out advertisements from EuroSeek response."""
        result = []
        lines = string.split(rawContent, "\n")
        for line in lines:
            if string.find(line, "Advertisement!") == -1:
                result.append(line)
        return string.join(result, "\n")


class SearchManager:
    """This class manages execution of searches across multiple engines."""
    def __init__(self):
        self.queue = Queue.Queue(0)
        self.engines = [Excite, InfoSeek, EuroSeek]

    def query(self, queryStr):
```

```
        """Perform a query.  Return a list of Result objects."""
        for engine in self.engines:
            thread = engine(queryStr, self.threadDoneCB)
            thread.start()

        results = []
        # We should get exactly one result from each thread.
        for i in range(len(self.engines)):
            # Block, if necessary, till the next result arrives.
            results.append(self.queue.get())
        return results

    def threadDoneCB(self, result):
        """Callback invoked whenever a thread completes.
        This method is invoked in the context of the completing thread,
        so must be re-entrant."""
        self.queue.put(result)

def main():
    """Module mainline (for standalone execution)"""
    import sys, os, tempfile

    mgr = SearchManager()
    queryStr = "Herbert Hoover"
    if len(sys.argv) > 1:
        queryStr = sys.argv[1]

    # Dump the results to a set of temporary files.  Because this
    # script doesn't strip '<HTML>' and its ilk from the retrieved
    # results, save each of the results to a separate file, then just
    # create a main 'index' file which links to them.
    basename = tempfile.mktemp()
    indexname = "%s.html" % basename
    outf = open(indexname, "w")
    print "Storing results in", indexname

    outf.write("""<HTML>
<HEAD><TITLE>Search Results For %s</TITLE></HEAD>
<BODY>
```

```
    <H2>Search Results For %s</H2>
    <UL>
    """ % (queryStr, queryStr))

    results = mgr.query(queryStr)
    for result in results:
        resultFilename = "%s_%s.html" % (basename, result.engineName)
        resultF = open(resultFilename, "w")
        resultF.write(result.resultStr)
        resultF.close()
        outf.write('<LI><A HREF="file:%s">%s</A>\n' %
                    (resultFilename, result.engineName))
    outf.write("""</UL></BODY></HTML>""")
    outf.close()


    # Assuming the user is running on Linux AND has a recent
    # version of Netscape installed, we can point their
    # browser at the temporary file:
    cmd = "netscape --remote 'openURL(file:%s)'" % indexname
    status = os.system(cmd)
    if status:
        print "Attempt failed w. status %d." % status


if __name__ == "__main__":
    main()
```

How It Works

For details, please see the readme file in engine.zip on the CD-ROM. The contributor has explained what he's doing far better than I can.

Contributed by Mitch Chapman

who-owns.py

This Linux-specific script investigates who's listening at a particular socket. The contributor notes that this script seems to fail each time a new Linux kernel comes out. But who-owns.py makes an excellent starter kit for a more stable version.

```
# -*- Mode: Python; tab-width: 4 -*-
```

```
import os
import regex
import string
import sys

# linux-specific.
# find out what process is listening on a particular socket

def inode_of_socket (port, type='tcp', server_only=1):
    target_port = string.upper ('%04x' % (string.atoi (port)))
    lines = open ('/proc/net/%s' % type).readlines()
    inode = 0
    for line in lines[1:]:
        fields = string.split (line)
        [addr, port] = string.split (fields[1], ':')
        if port == target_port:
            if (not server_only) or (addr == '00000000'):
                inode = string.atoi (fields[9])
                break
    return inode


pid_regex = regex.compile ('\([0-9]+\)')


def process_of_inode (inode):
    #inode = '[0000]:%d' % inode
    inode = 'socket:[%d]' % inode
    cwd = os.getcwd()
    try:
        pids = filter (
            lambda x: pid_regex.match (x) == len(x),
            os.listdir('/proc')
            )
        pids.remove (str(os.getpid()))
        for pid in pids:
            fd_dir = '/proc/%s/fd' % pid
            if os.path.isdir (fd_dir):
                os.chdir (fd_dir)
                links = map (
```

```
                        os.readlink,
                        os.listdir ('.')
                        )
                    if inode in links:
                        return pid
        finally:
            os.chdir (cwd)
        return 0


if __name__ == '__main__':
    if len(sys.argv) < 2:
        print 'Usage: %s port [tcp|udp]' % sys.argv[0]
    else:
        if len(sys.argv) < 3:
            socket_type='tcp'
        else:
            socket_type=sys.argv[2]
        port = sys.argv[1]
        inode = inode_of_socket (port, socket_type)
        if not inode:
            print "Couldn't find inode for socket on %s port %s" % (
                socket_type,
                port
                )
            sys.exit(0)
        else:
            print 'inode: %d' % inode
            process = process_of_inode (inode)
            if not process:
                print "Couldn't find process for inode %d" % inode
            else:
                print open('/proc/%s/status' % process).read()
```

How It Works

who-owns.py monitors a particular socket and determines which process is responsible for listening on that socket. This script is handy if you suspect a hacker might be running a suspicious process on your machine.

Be aware that, as the contributor notes, this script may take some tweaking with each new Linux kernel. It works now, on 2.0.36, this way:

inode_of_socket() figures out the inode of the socket you're interested in. It reads the data in the pseudofile /proc/net/tcp or /proc/net/udp, and yields the IP address and port number to which the socket is bound.

process_of_inode() then finds the process that owns the inode. Note that on some Linux systems you may have to comment out the line

```
inode='socket:[%d]" % inode
```

and uncomment

```
inode='[0000]:%d' % inode
```

to make this work. The zeros are necessary because of the Linux habit of giving all sockets device numbers of 0000.

process_of_inode() now removes its own PID (Process ID) from the list because, after all, it knows it's not a hacker process.

process_of_inode() now has some file walking to do. It has to access device files in /proc/, looking for an inode-process matchup. If it finds a matchup, it dumps the information about the process. If it doesn't find a matchup, process_of_inode() returns a zero.

Contributed by Sam Rushing: "Strong typing is for weak minds."

server.py

```
#    A simple "chat" server.  Creates a server on port 4000.#    Users telnet to
your machine, port 4000, and can chat with each#    other.  Use "quit" to discon-
nect yourself, and "shutdown" to#    shut down the server.  Requires sockets.
#
#    7/31/96    J. Strout          http://www.strout.net/

# import needed modules:

from socket import *          # get sockets, for well, sockets
import string                 # string functions
```

```python
import time                    # for sleep(1) function

# define global variables

HOST = ''                # Symbolic name meaning the local host
PORT = 4000                 # Arbitrary non-privileged server
endl = "\r\n"             # standard terminal line ending


userlist = []            # list of connected users
done = 0                 # set to 1 to shut this down


kAskName = 0             # some constants used to flag
kWaitName = 1            #    the state of each user
kOK = 2



# class to store info about connected users

class User:
    def __init__(self):
        self.name = ""
        self.addr = ""
        self.conn = None
        self.step = kAskName


    def Idle(self):
        if self.step == kAskName: self.AskName()


    def AskName(self):
        self.conn.send("Name? ")
        self.step = kWaitName


    def HandleMsg(self, msg):
        print "Handling message: ",msg
        global userlist

        # if waiting for name, record it
        if self.step == kWaitName:
```

```
                    # try to trap garb initiall sent by some telnets:
                    if len(msg) < 2 or msg=="#": return
                    print "Setting name to: ",msg
                    self.name = msg
                    self.step = kOK
                    self.conn.send("Hello, "+self.name+endl)
                    broadcast(self.name+" has connected."+endl)
                    return

               # check for commands
               if msg == "quit":
                    broadcast(self.name+" has quit.\n")
                    self.conn.close()
                    userlist.remove(self)
                    return

               # otherwise, broadcast msg
               broadcast( self.name+": "+msg+endl )


# routine to check for incoming connections

def pollNewConn():
    try:
        conn, addr = s.accept()
    except:
        return None
    print "Connection from", addr
    conn.setblocking(0)
    user = User();
    user.conn = conn
    user.addr = addr
    return user


# routine to broadcast a message to all connected users

def broadcast(msg):
    for u in userlist:
```

```
            u.conn.send(msg)


# MAIN PROGRAM


# set up the server

s = socket(AF_INET, SOCK_STREAM)
s.bind(HOST, PORT)
s.setblocking(0)
s.listen(1)
print "Waiting for connection(s)..."

# loop until done, handling connections and incoming messages

while not done:
    time.sleep(1)          # sleep to reduce processor usage
    u = pollNewConn()      # check for incoming connections
    if u:
        userlist.append(u)
        print len(userlist),"connection(s)"

    for u in userlist:     # check all connected users
        u.Idle()
        try:
            data = u.conn.recv(1024)
            data = filter(lambda x: x>=' ' and x<='z', data)
            data = string.strip(data)
            if data:
                print "From",u.name,': ['+data+']'
                u.HandleMsg(data)
                if data == "shutdown": done=1
        except:
            pass

for u in userlist:
    u.conn.close()
```

How It Works

Using this script you can have others telnet to your machine on port 4000 and hold a chat session. The script even informs users when somebody logs on. To my mind, server.py just cries out for a Tkinter GUI presentation, but that will be left for you to play with.

The main program sets up the server—opening a socket, binding it, and so forth. The script then goes into an indefinite loop waiting for others to log on. Each new participant has their information stored with the class User.

pollNewConn() continually checks for new connections and, when it finds one, instantiates User().

Joe Strout is a scientific software developer at the Salk Institute in La Jolla, CA.

With techniques that have been successfully used to win the All-England Summarize Proust Competition three years running.

Chapter 10: Strings and Other Data Types

A h, strings. Python does a great job with strings. You can slice, rearrange, concatenate, and do lots of other fun things. And it's all remarkably easy.

strplay.py

This script doesn't do much to earn its keep, but it illustrates several of the basic string functions. It could be readily modified to, for example, open a file and search for a word or letter. To run strplay.py, copy it to the right Python directory, set permissions for execution, and type

```
python strplay.py
```

Then press the Enter key. You should see the prompt:

```
Type a few words for me, please:
```

Type a few words and press the Enter key again.

```
#!/usr/bin/python
#
 play
import string

def string_play(instring):
    print "You typed: ", instring
    ecount=string.count(instring, "e")
    print "There are",ecount, "instances of e in this sample."
    upstring=string.upper(instring)
    dnstring=string.lower(instring)
    print "All uppercase:", upstring
    print "All lowercase:", dnstring
    outstring=string.split(instring)
    print "The string breaks into these elements: ",outstring
    lenstring=len(outstring)
    print "Which number: ", lenstring
    if lenstring<3:
        print "I would do a slice, but a I need at least 3 elements."
    else:
```

```
        sliced=outstring[:2]
        print "The first two elements are:", sliced
    outstring.sort()
    print "Sorted, it looks like this:",outstring
    outstring.reverse()
    print "In reverse order:", outstring


if __name__ == "__main__":
    instring=raw_input("Type a few words for me please:  ")
    string_play(instring)
```

How It Works

This script illustrates some of the basic string-handling concepts in Python. The script starts executing with the main, which is simply:

```
if __name__ == "__main__":
    instring=raw_input("Type a few words for me please:  ")
    string_play(instring)
```

The "if" statement is used when the script is expected to be used as a main program, rather than as a module. You could also run this script by starting the interpreter in interactive mode, importing strplay, and executing a line like:

```
>>>strplay.string_play("I'll have your Spam")
```

The next thing that happens in the script is the execution of the raw_input() statement. This statement puts a prompt on the screen, takes the input from the standard input device (here the keyboard), and loads the variable instring with the string value. The value can be any length. After the user types some words and presses the Enter key, string_play() is called, passing instring.

The function string_play() has all of the processing code. The script imports the module string so that string's methods are available. The first few lines are simple string-handling functions.

- The first line prints the string exactly the way you originally typed it.
- The second line checks for the existence of the letter "e" and counts how many instances there are. Then the result is printed in the third line.
- The fourth and fifth lines use two more of the string module's methods: upper() and lower().
- The sixth and seventh lines print the results of the uppercase and lowercase conversions.

```
print "You typed: ", instring
ecount=string.count(instring, "e")
print "There are",ecount, "instances of e in this sample."
upstring=string.upper(instring)
dnstring=string.lower(instring)
print "All uppercase:", upstring
print "All lowercase:", dnstring
```

The ensuing lines are subtly different. The first line

```
outstring=string.split(instring)
```

changes the whole structure of the data, because it converts a string of characters into a list, using yet another of the string module's methods. Now each word you typed becomes a list element.

The significance of this is that you've crossed the line from string functions into list functions. It's easy to forget that the data type has changed and to keep writing code to work with strings when you actually have a list. The next line demonstrates this pretty graphically, by printing the list:

```
print "The string breaks into these elements: ",outstring
```

The script then figures out how long the list is

```
lenstring=len(outstring)
```

and then prints the number of elements:

```
print "Which number: ", lenstring
```

The next few lines do some simple error checking and slicing. *Slicing* means to copy selected elements from a sequence. But you can't slice out two elements if you have only one, for example. Python won't complain if you try, returning just the one element. But if a method is looking for two elements and gets only one, you're going to get an exception. Hence error checking for the number of elements.

So, before slicing, the if statement checks to see if there are at least three elements. If there aren't at least three, the script prints the warning. If there are three or more elements, the else statements are executed.

The slice expression uses an index. In Python, every sequence has an index that can be directly addressed. The number to the left of the colon is the starting point, while the number to the right is the ending point. The count starts with zero. So variable[1:5] would slice out the second through fifth elements, stopping just short of number 5 in the index.

As an example, if the user types, **"It's a fair cop"**, it's converted to ["It's", "a", "fair", "cop"]. The sliced elements are in the variable outstring. By giving the index as [:2], I'm telling Python to start with the first element and take everything up to the third element, for a total of two. In the example, this would be ["It's", "a"].

```
if lenstring<3:
    print "I would do a slice, but a I need at least 3 elements."
else:
    sliced=outstring[:2]
    print "The first two elements are:", sliced
```

The new shortened list is then printed. There are several variations on the indexed slice statement. The statement sequence[:] gets back all of the sequence. Sequence[1:] gets all elements from number 2 to the end. You can even use negatives to move around in the index. Sequence[:-1] gives you all the elements from the first to the one just before the end.

The last few lines are:

```
outstring.sort()
print "Sorted, it looks like this:",outstring
outstring.reverse()
print "In reverse order:", outstring
```

Here, in order, I've sorted the elements of outstring, printed the sorted list, then reversed the sorted list and printed it again. For fun, run this script with the words "It's a fair cop" and see what happens. Look at the sorted list. For some reason, "It's" is ahead of "a". The sort algorithm looks for capital letters first, then lower-case. If you want to sort for real, it's usually best to make sure that all elements are equally capitalized.

Gotcha

Remember that Python's list indexes start with 0, not 1. mylist[1] is the second element in mylist, not the first.

dog.py

Input your age, and this script gives you back your age in dog years.

```
### get the original age
age = input("Enter your age (in human years): ")
print # print a blank line
### do some range checking, then print result
if age < 0:
    print "Negative age?!? I don't think so."
elif age < 3 or age > 110:
```

```
        print "Frankly, I don't believe you"
else:
print "That's", age*7, "in dog years."
### pause for Return key (so window doesn't disappear)
raw_input("press Return")
```

How It Works

You enter your age; the script multiplies by seven and prints the result. However, it also does some error checking to make sure you're not trying to gull the script.

```
if age < 0:
    print "Negative age?!? I don't think so."
elif age < 3 or age > 110:
    print "Frankly, I don't believe you."
else:
print "That's", age*7, "in dog years."
```

The script looks at the age you typed to see if it's a negative number, if it's under three, or over 110. It works in three steps: an if statement, an elif, and an else. Finally, when the script is satisfied with your honesty, it prints the results.

Joe Strout is a scientific software developer at the Salk Institute in La Jolla, California.

banner.py

This script prints a "banner", a larger-than-life rendering of a word or phrase you type in. An easy way to run this script is to fire up Python in interactive mode, import banner, and then use the command

```
banner.Banner("string", "character")
```

which makes the script use the string as the banner lettering and the character as the individual elements in the banner.

```
'''

This module contains the function Banner() which can be used to print
a banner message like the UNIX banner(1) function.
'''


import sys
'''
```

The array letters contains the information on how to print each character
between 32 and 126, inclusive. There are 8 bytes for each character and
each byte represents one line of the font. The high byte of the first
number is the first line of 8 bits, the next byte is the next line, and
so on. I got these numbers by writing a little script that analyzed the
output of somebody's banner program...
'''

```
letters = [
    [ 0x00000000, 0x00000000 ], [ 0x30303030, 0x30003000 ],
    [ 0x6c6c6c00, 0x00000000 ], [ 0x6c6cfe6c, 0xfe6c6c00 ],
    [ 0x187e407e, 0x027e1800 ], [ 0xc2c60c18, 0x3066c600 ],
    [ 0x3828387b, 0xd6cc7700 ], [ 0x60204000, 0x00000000 ],
    [ 0x1c70c0c0, 0xc0701c00 ], [ 0x701c0606, 0x061c7000 ],
    [ 0x006c38fe, 0x386c0000 ], [ 0x303030fc, 0x30303000 ],
    [ 0x00000000, 0x00602040 ], [ 0x0000007c, 0x00000000 ],
    [ 0x00000000, 0x00060600 ], [ 0x02060c18, 0x3060c000 ],
    [ 0x7cc6ced6, 0xe6c67c00 ], [ 0x10703030, 0x30307800 ],
    [ 0x78cc0c18, 0x3062fe00 ], [ 0x78cc0c38, 0x0ccc7800 ],
    [ 0x0c1c6ccc, 0xfe0c1e00 ], [ 0x7e40407c, 0x06c67c00 ],
    [ 0x3c64c0fc, 0xc6c67c00 ], [ 0xfe860c18, 0x18181800 ],
    [ 0x3c66663c, 0x66663c00 ], [ 0x7cc6c67e, 0x064c7800 ],
    [ 0x00006060, 0x00606000 ], [ 0x00006060, 0x00602040 ],
    [ 0x183060c0, 0x60301800 ], [ 0x00007c00, 0x7c000000 ],
    [ 0xc0603018, 0x3060c000 ], [ 0x78cc8c1c, 0x30003000 ],
    [ 0x3c46c2ce, 0xcc407800 ], [ 0x183c6666, 0x7e666600 ],
    [ 0xfc66667c, 0x6666fc00 ], [ 0x3c66c0c0, 0xc2663c00 ],
    [ 0xfc666666, 0x6666fc00 ], [ 0xfe626878, 0x6862fe00 ],
    [ 0xfe626878, 0x6860f000 ], [ 0x3c64c0c0, 0xce663a00 ],
    [ 0xccccccfc, 0xcccccc00 ], [ 0x3c181818, 0x18183c00 ],
    [ 0x3c181818, 0x98d87000 ], [ 0xe6666c78, 0x6c66e600 ],
    [ 0xf0606060, 0x6066fe00 ], [ 0xc6eefed6, 0xc6c6c600 ],
    [ 0xc6e6f6de, 0xcec6c600 ], [ 0x7cc6c6c6, 0xc6c67c00 ],
    [ 0xfc66667c, 0x6060f000 ], [ 0x7cc6c6c6, 0xc6c67c06 ],
    [ 0xfc66667c, 0x6c66e600 ], [ 0x7ec2c07c, 0x0686fc00 ],
    [ 0x7e5a1818, 0x18183c00 ], [ 0x66666666, 0x66663c00 ],
    [ 0xc6c6c66c, 0x6c381000 ], [ 0xc6c6c6d6, 0xfeeec600 ],
    [ 0xee6c3810, 0x386cee00 ], [ 0xc3663c18, 0x18183c00 ],
    [ 0xfe860c18, 0x3062fe00 ], [ 0x7c606060, 0x60607c00 ],
```

```
    [ 0xc0603018, 0x0c060200 ], [ 0x3e060606, 0x06063e00 ],
    [ 0x10386cc6, 0x00000000 ], [ 0x00000000, 0x00007c00 ],
    [ 0x0c080400, 0x00000000 ], [ 0x00007c04, 0xfc8cfa00 ],
    [ 0xe060607c, 0x6666fc00 ], [ 0x00007cc6, 0xc0c67c00 ],
    [ 0x1c0c0c7c, 0xcccc7a00 ], [ 0x00007cc2, 0xfec07c00 ],
    [ 0x386c60f8, 0x6060f000 ], [ 0x00007bc6, 0xc67e047c ],
    [ 0xe060606e, 0x7666e700 ], [ 0x18003818, 0x18183c00 ],
    [ 0x18003c18, 0x1818d870 ], [ 0xe060666c, 0x706ce600 ],
    [ 0x38181818, 0x18183c00 ], [ 0x0000ecd6, 0xd6c6e700 ],
    [ 0x00006e76, 0x66666600 ], [ 0x00003c66, 0x66663c00 ],
    [ 0x0000dc66, 0x667c60f0 ], [ 0x000076cc, 0xcc7c0c1e ],
    [ 0x0000dc76, 0x6060f000 ], [ 0x0000fec0, 0xfe06fe00 ],
    [ 0x10307c30, 0x30361c00 ], [ 0x0000cecc, 0xcccc7600 ],
    [ 0x00006666, 0x663c1800 ], [ 0x0000c6d6, 0xd6fe6c00 ],
    [ 0x0000c66c, 0x386cc600 ], [ 0x0000c6c6, 0xc67e0478 ],
    [ 0x0000fc98, 0x3064fc00 ], [ 0x0c181830, 0x18180c00 ],
    [ 0x10101000, 0x10101000 ], [ 0x60303018, 0x30306000 ],
    [ 0x66980000, 0x00000000 ]
    ]


def Banner(string, char_to_use):
    global letters
    out = [ [], [], [], [], [], [], [], [] ] # 8 lines of data
    for ltr in range(len(string)):
        char = string[ltr]
        if ord(char) < 32 or ord(char) > 126:
            char = " "
        ix = ord(char)-32
        bytes = []
        lines = letters[ix][0]
        #print "Lines = 0x%08x" % lines
        out[0].append((((lines & (0xff << 24)) >> 24) & 0xff)
        out[1].append((((lines & (0xff << 16)) >> 16) & 0xff)
        out[2].append((((lines & (0xff <<  8)) >>  8) & 0xff)
        out[3].append(lines & 0xff)
        lines = letters[ix][1]
        #print "Lines = 0x%08x" % lines
        out[4].append((((lines & (0xff << 24)) >> 24) & 0xff)
        out[5].append((((lines & (0xff << 16)) >> 16) & 0xff)
```

```
            out[6].append(((lines & (0xff << 8)) >> 8) & 0xff)
            out[7].append(lines & 0xff)
    for element in out:
        for byte in element:
            PrintByteLine(byte, char_to_use)
        sys.stdout.write("\n")
    sys.stdout.write("\n")


def PrintByteLine(byte, char_to_use):
    for ix in range(8):
        if byte & (1 << (8 - ix)):
            sys.stdout.write("%s" % char_to_use)
        else:
            sys.stdout.write(" ")


if __name__ == '__main__':
    import sys
    if len(sys.argv) < 2:
        print "Usage:  banner <string>"
        sys.exit(1)
    Banner(sys.argv[1], "X")
```

How It Works

The function Banner (and remember that Python is case sensitive, so don't try to
call it with "banner") is defined with two variables, the string and the character to
use to construct the banner. The next line declares the variable letters to be a global
variable, but this isn't really necessary in today's versions of Python. The variable
out is declared to be a list of eight lists, all of which are empty.

```
def Banner(string, char_to_use):
    global letters
    out = [ [], [], [], [], [], [], [], [] ]  # 8 lines of data
```

Now the script has to process the string and convert it into lines of graphical representation, rather than strings. To do that, the script needs a lookup table that
shows how letters look built from single characters. The list letters is just such a
lookup table. Python doesn't have a matrix or array data type, but a list of list
elements does much the same job. The lines

```
        if ord(char) < 32 or ord(char) > 126:
            char = " "
```

check for unprintable ASCII characters, those lower than 32 or higher than 126. The printable characters are stored in the list letters, so the script is now ready to see which characters to use. The line

```
ix = ord(char)-32
```

resets an index to characters from a bottom of 32 to a bottom of zero. The lines

```
out[0].append(((lines & (0xff << 24)) >> 24) & 0xff)
out[1].append(((lines & (0xff << 16)) >> 16) & 0xff)
out[2].append(((lines & (0xff <<  8)) >>  8) & 0xff)
out[3].append(lines & 0xff)
```

illustrate how the append method works. The variable out, remember, is a list of eight lists. Starting with element zero, you want to write to each of the eight lists in the variable out. This gives you one of the vertical lines for the banner.

These lines are really packed. In the first line, for example, the script is appending (or "replacing" if you like) the first list in the variable out with the result of the bitwise operations within the parentheses. 0xff is the hexadecimal representation for the decimal 255. Notice, though, that four separate bitwise operations are going on in each of the first three lines. Now that's efficiency. The line

```
sys.stdout.write("%s" % char_to_use)
```

in the function PrintByteLine is particularly interesting. First, it uses sys.stdout.write instead of the ordinary print statement. And it uses formatting. The code snippet "%s" % char_to_use makes use of "%s" as a character placeholder that will substitute whatever character is in char_to_use. It will do this over and over, as PrintByteLine is called by Banner.

Contributor anonymous

ebcdic.py

IBM way back when created its own character set, called EBCDIC (*Extended Binary Coded Decimal Interchange Code*). Both ASCII and EBCDIC are eight-bit formats, but EBCDIC actually uses all eight bits, while ASCII uses only seven. EBCDIC is still used on IBM Big Iron (mainframes), and there are times when you might see data out of a Big Blue mainframe that's still in this format. You might want to convert EBCDIC to the more common ASCII, which is where this script comes into the story. ebcdic.py converts both ways, from ASCII to EBCDIC and vice versa.

This script is intended as a module, not as a stand-alone program. If you run it alone, it will test itself.

```
'''
ASCII <=> EBCDIC conversion functions.  The arrays were taken from
the Snippets collection.
'''


a2eG = [
     0,  1,  2,  3, 55, 45, 46, 47, 22,  5, 37, 11, 12, 13, 14, 15,
    16, 17, 18, 19, 60, 61, 50, 38, 24, 25, 63, 39, 28, 29, 30, 31,
    64, 79,127,123, 91,108, 80,125, 77, 93, 92, 78,107, 96, 75, 97,
   240,241,242,243,244,245,246,247,248,249,122, 94, 76,126,110,111,
   124,193,194,195,196,197,198,199,200,201,209,210,211,212,213,214,
   215,216,217,226,227,228,229,230,231,232,233, 74,224, 90, 95,109,
   121,129,130,131,132,133,134,135,136,137,145,146,147,148,149,150,
   151,152,153,162,163,164,165,166,167,168,169,192,106,208,161,  7,
    32, 33, 34, 35, 36, 21,  6, 23, 40, 41, 42, 43, 44,  9, 10, 27,
    48, 49, 26, 51, 52, 53, 54,  8, 56, 57, 58, 59,  4, 20, 62,225,
    65, 66, 67, 68, 69, 70, 71, 72, 73, 81, 82, 83, 84, 85, 86, 87,
    88, 89, 98, 99,100,101,102,103,104,105,112,113,114,115,116,117,
   118,119,120,128,138,139,140,141,142,143,144,154,155,156,157,158,
   159,160,170,171,172,173,174,175,176,177,178,179,180,181,182,183,
   184,185,186,187,188,189,190,191,202,203,204,205,206,207,218,219,
   220,221,222,223,234,235,236,237,238,239,250,251,252,253,254,255
    ]


e2aG = [
     0,  1,  2,  3,156,  9,134,127,151,141,142, 11, 12, 13, 14, 15,
    16, 17, 18, 19,157,133,  8,135, 24, 25,146,143, 28, 29, 30, 31,
   128,129,130,131,132, 10, 23, 27,136,137,138,139,140,  5,  6,  7,
   144,145, 22,147,148,149,150,  4,152,153,154,155, 20, 21,158, 26,
    32,160,161,162,163,164,165,166,167,168, 91, 46, 60, 40, 43, 33,
    38,169,170,171,172,173,174,175,176,177, 93, 36, 42, 41, 59, 94,
    45, 47,178,179,180,181,182,183,184,185,124, 44, 37, 95, 62, 63,
   186,187,188,189,190,191,192,193,194, 96, 58, 35, 64, 39, 61, 34,
   195, 97, 98, 99,100,101,102,103,104,105,196,197,198,199,200,201,
   202,106,107,108,109,110,111,112,113,114,203,204,205,206,207,208,
   209,126,115,116,117,118,119,120,121,122,210,211,212,213,214,215,
```

```
      216,217,218,219,220,221,222,223,224,225,226,227,228,229,230,231,
      123, 65, 66, 67, 68, 69, 70, 71, 72, 73,232,233,234,235,236,237,
      125, 74, 75, 76, 77, 78, 79, 80, 81, 82,238,239,240,241,242,243,
       92,159, 83, 84, 85, 86, 87, 88, 89, 90,244,245,246,247,248,249,
       48, 49, 50, 51, 52, 53, 54, 55, 56, 57,250,251,252,253,254,255
]

def AsciiToEbcdic(str):
    '''Return the ASCII string str in EBCDIC form.
    '''
    global a2eG
    if type(str) != type(""):
        raise "Bad data", "Expected a string argument"
    if len(str) == 0:  return str
    newstr = ""
    for ix in xrange(len(str)):
        newstr = newstr + chr(a2eG[ord(str[ix])])
    return newstr

def EbcdicToAscii(str):
    global e2aG
    if type(str) != type(""):
        raise "Bad data", "Expected a string argument"
    if len(str) == 0:  return str
    newstr = ""
    for ix in xrange(len(str)):
        newstr = newstr + chr(e2aG[ord(str[ix])])
    return newstr

def Test():
    str = "The dog jumped over the lazy brown fox in 1.234567890 seconds"
    str1 = EbcdicToAscii(AsciiToEbcdic(str))
    if str != str1:
        raise "Test failed"

if __name__ == '__main__':
    Test()
```

How It Works

This script can be viewed as two big lookup tables surrounded by a life-support system. When a value str is passed to one of the script's two functions, the script performs error checking to make sure that the data is a string type, using this code:

```
if type(str) != type(""):
    raise "Bad data", "Expected a string argument"
```

The donkey work of conversion is done in a single line in each function of this type:

```
newstr = newstr + chr(e2aG[ord(str[ix])])
```

Notice that this script uses nothing but Python's built-in statements. No modules were abused in the course of making this script.

Contributor anonymous

lc.py

Unlike the previous scripts in this chapter that take their input from the keyboard, this one takes input from a file. lc.py counts the number of lines in an input file and prints the result.

```
lc.py
'''
Counts the number of lines in the input file.  The input file is assumed
to be text, but it doesn't have to be.
'''

import sys, glob

def count_lines(files):
    retval = 0
    for file in sys.argv[1:]:
        if not IsFile(file):  continue
        try:
            fp = open(file, "rb")
            lines = fp.readlines()
            fp.close()
            print "%-8d  %s" % (len(lines), file)
        except:
            sys.stderr.write("Couldn't read \"%s\"\n" % file)
            retval = 1
```

Gotcha

You can get input from a command line in a couple of ways: input() and raw_input(). If you're looking for numbers, the difference between them is important. raw=input("Type a number: ") will produce an integer 10 in the variable raw when the user types "10". If you use raw=raw_input("Type a number: ") you'll get the same prompt, but the variable raw will contain a string "10". In general, it's better to use raw_input(), so if you're retrieving a number, convert it with another statement, such as int().

```
        return retval

def IsFile(file_name):
    '''Return 1 if file_name is a file; otherwise return 0.
    '''
    import os
    try:
        s = os.stat(file_name)
        return ((0100000 & s[0]) == 0100000)
    except:
        return 0


if __name__ == "__main__":
    if len(sys.argv) < 2:
        print "Usage:  lc file1 [file2...]"
        sys.exit(1)
    sys.exit(count_lines(sys.argv[1:]))
```

How It Works

This script is a neat illustration of both file opening and closing and of the use of readline(). The file is opened with the line:

```
        fp = open(file, "rb")
```

This opens the file with read permission ("r") and allows the use of a binary file on some platforms ("b"). The next line

```
        lines = fp.readlines()
```

reads the lines from beginning to end, returning a list of them. The file is then closed with the line

```
        fp.close()
```

and the resulting number of lines is calculated and printed in one line:

```
        print "%-8d  %s" % (len(lines), file)
```

Contributor anonymous

sample.py

This module can pull a random sample number. It's copiously commented, which is perhaps one of the finest things any coder can do for future generations.

```
'''

This module contains functions to do sampling with and without
replacement and random shuffling.  The algorithms are from
Knuth, vol. 2, section 3.4.2.

sample_wr(population_size, sample_size)
    Sample with replacement from a set of integers from 1 to
    population_size.  It returns a list of sample_size integers
    that were selected.  The sampling distribution is binomial.

sample_wor(population_size, sample_size)
    Sample without replacement from a set of integers from 1 to
    population_size.  It returns a list of sample_size integers
    that were selected.  The sampling distribution is
    hypergeometric.

shuffle(sample_size)
    Returns a random permutation of the integers 1 to sample_size.

deal(deck_size, num_hands, num_per_hand)
    Returns a dictionary of hands (list of integers) dealt from
    the integers 1 to deck_size.  The hands are keyed by
    1, 2, ..., num_hands.  Any leftover "cards" go into the list
    keyed by 0.

deal_deck(num_hands, num_per_hand)
    Returns a dictionary of a dealt card hand.  The deal() function
    is used, but the routine also maps the integers to a string that
    contains the card identifications.  For example, 1 -> 2S, 2 -> 3S,
    ..., etc.


'''


import whrandom

# Note:  it's important to make the generator global.  If you put it into
# one of the functions and call that function rapidly, the generator will
# be initialized using the clock.  If the calls are fast enough, you'll
```

```
# see distinctly nonrandom behavior.


def sample_wor(population_size, sample_size):
    assert type(population_size) == type(0) and \
           type(sample_size) == type(0)      and \
           population_size > 0                and \
           sample_size > 0                    and \
           sample_size <= population_size
    global rand_num_generatorG
    m = 0  # number of records selected so far
    t = 1  # Candidate integer to select if frac is right
    list = []
    while m < sample_size:
        unif_rand = rand_num_generatorG.random()
        frac = 1.0 * (sample_size - m) / (population_size - (t-1))
        if unif_rand < frac:
            list.append(t)
            m = m + 1
        t = t + 1
    return list


def sample_wr(population_size, sample_size):
    assert type(population_size) == type(0) and \
           type(sample_size) == type(0)      and \
           population_size > 0                and \
           sample_size > 0
    global rand_num_generatorG
    list = []
    for ix in xrange(sample_size):
        list.append(rand_num_generatorG.randint(1, population_size))
    return list


def shuffle(sample_size):
    '''Moses and Oakford algorithm.  See Knuth, vol 2, section 3.4.2.
    Returns a random permutation of the integers from 1 to
    sample_size.
    '''
    assert type(sample_size) == type(0) and sample_size > 0
```

```
        global rand_num_generatorG
        list = range(1, sample_size + 1)
        for ix in xrange(sample_size - 1, 0, -1):
            rand_int = rand_num_generatorG.randint(0, ix)
            if rand_int == ix:
                continue
            tmp = list[ix]
            list[ix] = list[rand_int]
            list[rand_int] = tmp
        return list


def shuffle_set(set):
    '''Returns a copy of the sequence set that has been randomly
    shuffled.  Works with lists and tuples.
    '''
    if type(set) == type([]):
        shuffled_set = []
    elif type(set) == type(()):
        shuffled_set = ()
    else:
        raise "Bad data", "must be list or tuple"
    numlist = shuffle(len(set))
    for jx in numlist:
        ix = jx - 1
        shuffled_set.append(set[ix])
    return shuffled_set


def deal(deck_size, num_hands, num_per_hand):
    '''Returns a dictionary of dealt hands from the integers 1 to
    deck_size.  Each dictionary element (indexed by 1, 2, ...,
    num_hands) is a list of num_per_hand integers.  The element
    indexed by 0 is the remaining integers that were not selected
    for one of the hands.
    '''
    assert deck_size                             and \
           deck_size >= num_hands * num_per_hand and \
           num_hands > 0                         and \
           type(num_hands) == type(0)            and \
           num_per_hand > 0                      and \
```

```
                type(num_per_hand) == type(0)
    dict = {}
    # Generate the integers that will be in the hands
    sample = shuffle_set(range(1, deck_size + 1))
    for ix in range(num_hands):     # Partition into the dictionary
        start = ix * num_per_hand
        stop  = start + num_per_hand
        dict[ix+1] = sample[start : stop]
    dict[0] = sample[stop:]
    return dict


def deal_deck(num_hands, num_per_hand):
    '''Returns a dictionary of a dealt card hand.  The deal() function
    is used, but the routine also maps the integers to a string that
    contains the card identifications.  For example, 1 -> 2S, 2 -> 3S,
    ..., 13 -> AS, 14 -> 2C, etc.
    '''
    cards = deal(52, num_hands, num_per_hand)
    # Now go through and put identifier on the cards (and change them
    # from type integer to type string).
    suit_name = "SCHD"              # Spades, clubs, hearts, diamonds
    card_name = "A234567890JQK"    # Note 10 will need special handling...
    for hand in cards.keys():
        new_hand = []
        for card_num in cards[hand]:
            # We subtract 1 from card_num because cards are numbered 1 to 52
            suit_index, card_index = divmod(card_num-1, 13)
            #print "suit_index =", suit_index, " card_index =", card_index, "
card_num =", card_num
            suit = suit_name[suit_index]
            card = ("1" * (card_index == 9)) + card_name[card_index]
            new_hand.append(card + suit)
        cards[hand] = new_hand
    return cards
```

How It Works

As with most modules or scripts that deal in probabilities, this one uses a random
number generator, the whrandom module. In particular, the line

```
rand_num_generatorG = whrandom.whrandom()
```

creates a new variable rand_num_generatorG out of whrandom's whrandom class. rand_num_generatorG is then explicitly stated to be global. This isn't generally done with variables, but here it seems to be necessary.

Another unusual feature of this module is the use of the assert statement. This statement is normally used for debugging. The assert statement examines the __debug__ variable to see if it's true, and if it is, whether the expression is false. If __debug__ is true and the expression is false, then assert raises the AssertionError.

To run this script, you may have to insert the line

```
rand_num_generatorG = whrandom
```

at line 43.

Contributor anonymous

xref.py

This module makes a dictionary out of an imported text file. The dictionary is a cross-reference of the file's contents.

```
'''

Implements the Xref function which will generate a dictionary of the
tokens separated by whitespace and punctuation in a text file.  The
contents of the dictionary are the line numbers (1-based) the tokens
appear on.

'''


import re

punctuation_reG=re.compile("/|\"|'|\.|\,|\?|\s|\<|\>|\[|\]|\{|\}|:|;|\||\\\\|~|"\
||@|#|\$|%|\^|&|\*|\(|\)|-|=|\+")


def Xref(filename, preserve_case = 0):
    import string
    global punctuation_reG, whitespaceG
    try:
        fp = open(filename, "r")
        lines = fp.readlines()
```

```
            fp.close()
    except:
        raise "Couldn't read input file \"%s\"" % filename
    # Convert all punctuation to spaces.
    for line_num in xrange(len(lines)):
        line = punctuation_reG.sub(" ", lines[line_num])
        if not preserve_case:
            lines[line_num] = string.lower(line)
        else:
            lines[line_num] = line

    # Now split lines into words and build the list of words
    dict = {}
    for line_num in xrange(len(lines)):
        if lines[line_num] == "":  continue
        words = re.split("  *", lines[line_num])
        for word in words:
            if word == "":  continue
            if not dict.has_key(word):
                dict[word] = []
            line_num_1_based = line_num + 1
            if line_num_1_based not in dict[word]:
                dict[word].append(line_num_1_based)
    return dict

if __name__ == '__main__':
    import sys
    if len(sys.argv) != 2:
        print "Usage:  xref file"
        sys.exit(1)
    words = Xref(sys.argv[1], 1)
    list = []
    # Find longest word
    maxlen = 0
    for key in words.keys():
        if len(key) > maxlen:
            maxlen = len(key)
    # Now print the output
```

```
template = "%%-%ds: " % maxlen
for key in words.keys():
    str = template % key
    for line_num in words[key]:
        s = "%d," % line_num
        str = str + s
    str = str[:len(str)-1]  # Remove last comma
    list.append(str)
list.sort()
for s in list:
    print s
```

How It Works

The function Xref opens a text file, cuts the file into elements separated by white space and punctuation, and compiles a dictionary of the results. The module does its appointed task by using the module re (for "regular expression"). re hands you a bundle of commands for manipulating regular expressions.

Operation starts with some setup, importing re, importing string, and declaring some global variables. Then you have these lines of code:

```
try:
    fp = open(filename, "r")
    lines = fp.readlines()
    fp.close()
except:
    raise "Couldn't read input file \"%s\"" % filename
```

This sequence uses Python's ability to run lines of code within a monitored error-trapping environment. The lines under the try statement may or may not work right, but if an exception arises during operation (as it just might if the file can't be opened), then execution falls through to the except statement and the raise statement executes. The raise statement implicitly causes an exception.

After the file is opened and read, all punctuation is stripped out and replaced with spaces. This is done rather cleverly with the re module. This lengthy statement

```
punctuation_reG=re.compile("/|\"|'|\.|\,|\?|\s|\<|\>|\[|\]|\{|\}|:|;|\||\\\\|~|"|\
|@|#|\$|%|\^|&|\*|\(|\)|-|=|\+")
```

both creates a new object of re.compile() and loads the new object with every conceivable form of punctuation. This object will be used later for pattern matching.

Last, the lines are split into words, and the words are assembled into a dictionary.

Contributor anonymous

It's easy to examine strings in Python. For example, to search a list of strings, you could do it this way:

```
target="sheep"
list_of_stuff=["Victoria", "sheep", "Scotsmen"]
if target in list_of_stuff:
    print "Got it"
```

piglatin.py

Remember pig Latin, that odd twist on English that most of us practiced at some time in our lives? If we'd had this script, we could have just commanded Python to do the translation for us. This script goes both ways, from English to pig Latin and back again.

```
# piglatin.py  8/16/96 JJS
# # piglatin(s) -- returns piglatin of plaintext string s
# depiglatin(s) -- returns plaintext of piglatin string s
# # WARNING: Export of this code to foreign countries may
# constitute a violation of national security.
#-------------------------------------------------------------
from string import splitfields, uppercase, lowercase, upper, lower

def append(w,suffix):
    if not w: return suffix
    elif w[-1] in uppercase: return w + upper(suffix)
    else: return w + lower(suffix)

def piglatin(s):
    out = "
    for word in splitfields(s,' '):
        if word:
```

```
            # check for punctuation
            p = 0
            while word[p-1] not in uppercase+lowercase:
                p = p-1
            if p:
                punc = word[p:]
                word = word[:p]
            else: punc = "
            # and pre-punc (e.g., parentheses)
            p = 0
            while word[p] not in uppercase+lowercase:
                p = p+1
            prepunc = word[:p]
            word = word[p:]
            # note capitalization
            if word[0] in uppercase: caps = 1
            else: caps = 0
            # remove up to the first vowel to make suffix
            p = 0
            while p < len(word) and word[p] not in "aoeuiyAOEUIY": p=p+1
            if not p:
                word=append(word, "yay")
            else:
                word=append(word[p:], word[:p]+"ay")
            #recapitalize, as appropriate
            if caps: word=upper(word[0])+word[1:]

            #restore any punctuation
            word=prepunc+word+punc
        out=out+"+word
    return out[1:]

def depiglatin(s):
    out="
    for word in splitfields(s,' '):
        if word:
            #check for punctuation
            p=0
            while word[p-1] not in uppercase+lowercase:
```

```
                    p=p-1
            if p:
                punc=word[p:0]
                word=word[:p]
            else: punc="

            #and pre-punc (e.g. parentheses)
            p=0
            while word[p] not in uppercase+lowercase:
                p=p+1
            prepunc=word[:p]
            word=word[p:]
            #note capitalization
            if word[0] in uppercase: caps=1
            else: caps=0

            #find the suffix
            if lower(word[-3:]) =="yay":
                word=word[:-3]
            else:
                if lower(word[-4:1]) in ['tray', 'stay', 'shay', 'play', 'quay',\
'thay', 'whay']:
                    suflen=4
                else: suflen=3
                if word[1] in lowercase:
                    word=lower(word[0])+word[1:]
                word=word[-suflen:-2]+word[word[:-suflen]
                if caps:
                    word=upper(word[0])+word[1:]
            #restore any punctuation
            word=prepunc+word+punc
        out=out+' '+word
    return out[1:]

if __name__ == "__main__":
    print "PigLatin demo (enter 'quit" to quit)."
    s="
    while lower(s) != 'quit':
        s=raw_input(">")
```

```
        print "-->", piglatin(s)
        print "<--", depiglatin(piglatin(s))
    print piglatin("Thank you, have a nice day!")
```

How It Works

Okay, so it may not be quite the high-tech product that it seems to be from the warning at the top, but it's fun. Believe it or not, dozens of Web sites out there are devoted to pig Latin. One of them is **www.achiever.com/freehmpg/cryptology/ pig.html.** It has the rules for conversion. Pig Latin even has its own dialects. For instance, there's a hyphenated dialect: foo-yay, as opposed to fooyay.

piglatin.py has two functions. One converts from English to pig Latin; the other goes from pig Latin to English. Both functions begin similarly, and the first job up is to detect punctuation. The script does this rather simply with these lines:

```
# check for punctuation
p = 0
while word[p-1] not in uppercase+lowercase:
    p = p-1
if p:
    punc = word[p:]
    word = word[:p]
else: punc = "
```

The code checks the variable word, which has part of the input sequence in it, to see if there's anything that isn't in the string module's list of uppercase and lowercase letters. Anything else, presumably, is punctuation. This is in contrast to the opposite approach, which scans for known punctuation marks. The variable p is used as a counter. If p is still nonzero after the scanning operation is done, then there's a punctuation mark and it's written into the variable punc. The variable word is given everything else. If there's no punctuation, punc is empty.

It's important to note that the variable word doesn't have a string inside; it has a list of strings. This sleight was done with the line:

```
for word in splitfields(s,' '):
```

This code walks through the input file s, plucking out words one at a time and putting them into the variable word. Each word in the input string is therefore handled separately.

The code also has a routine for checking on "precapitalization," like parentheses.

Here the two functions diverge. They're both searching their respective inputs, but for different things. piglatin(s) looks for consonants by listing vowels and looking for non-vowels.

```
while p < len(word) and word[p] not in "aoeuiyAOEUIY": p=p+1
if not p:
    word=append(word, "yay")
else:
    word=append(word[p:], word[:p]+"ay")
```

After that, any capitals are restored and punctuation is replaced. depiglatin(s)'s job is different. It has to detect a specific set of endings. Then it has to carve away the pig Latin endings, restructure the words, and restore the English endings.

```
#find the suffix
if lower(word[-3:]) =="yay":
    word=word[:-3]
else:
    if lower(word[-4:1]) in ['tray', 'stay', 'shay', \
'play', 'quay', 'thay', 'whay']:
        suflen=4
    else: suflen=3
```

The code has to make sure that it's not being tripped by a mixture of upper- and lowercase letters, so it explicitly uses the lower() method of the string module. These lines result in the variable suflen being either three or four.

The rest of the code shears off the suffixes, using slice expressions, and puts back capitalization and punctuation. Then it fetches another word from the input string, if there's another word to get, and starts over.

Joe Strout is a scientific software developer at the Salk Institute in La Jolla, California.

Gotcha

The multiplication operator (*) works differently on strings and numbers, but it works on both. For numbers, it multiplies the numbers. For strings, it duplicates the string the number of times called for. The one thing the multiplication operator won't do is multiply two strings. Sorry.

For example:

```
>>> 24.0 * 2
48.0
>>> "spam " * 2
'spam spam '
>>> "spam " * "eggs"
Traceback (innermost last):
  File "<stdin>", line 1, in ?
TypeError: can't multiply \
sequence with non-int
```

Where the proper incantations can
prevent the penguin from exploding.

Chapter 11: System Operations and Programming

P ython can do interesting things that relate to the system and programming, such as walking a directory tree or translating Python code into C.

This chapter has a wide variety of scripts that bear on the system itself or on programming.

spinner.py

```
'''
Implements a text spinner.  Prints to stdout.
'''

import sys

class Spinner:
    def __init__(self, type=0):
        if type == 0:
            self.char = ['.', 'o', 'O', 'o']
        else:
            self.char = ['|', '/', '-', '\\', '-']
        self.len  = len(self.char)
        self.curr = 0

    def Print(self):
        self.curr = (self.curr + 1) % self.len
        str = self.char[self.curr]
        sys.stdout.write("\b \b%s" % str)

    def Done(self):
        sys.stdout.write("\b \b")

if __name__ == "__main__":
    s = Spinner()
    # This works OK on my old & slow computer; you'll have to adjust
    # it for yours.
```

```
for jx in xrange(100):
    for ix in xrange(40000):
        pass
    s.Print()
s.Done()
print
```

How It Works

This script can be used as a main or as a module. It puts a spinner on the screen to let the user know that the system isn't suffering from catatonia but is just working hard in the back room.

spinner.py is actually two spinners in one. In the definition __init__ you'll find two lists with text. One is for a "zero based" spinner, and the other for a "slash based" one. If the variable type is zero, then you see the zero-based one. If the variable is anything else, you get the slash spinner.

Check out the following lines:

```
sys.stdout.write("\b \b%s" % str)


    def Done(self):
        sys.stdout.write("\b \b")
```

Gotcha

Remember that Python's variables are case sensitive.

What's with the "\b"? It's an escape character, the backspace. A spinner doesn't look too good skittering each of its animation frames across the screen: ".oOo.oOo." You need to back up the cursor each time. \b does this job. The %s is a placeholder for the contents of str.

tabfix.py

The contributor says that he wrote this script to solve a cross-platform problem. UNIX systems often have text editors that can handle only eight-space tabs because of limitations in the VT100 terminal that we all loved many years ago. Modern text editors on other platforms often have four-space tab widths. This discrepancy makes sharing Python scripts a little difficult because Python is, of course, indentation based. This script accepts a file name, changes the tabs, and closes the file.

```
# tabfix.py by Joe Strout
#
```

```
# converts a file built with 4-space tabs into a
# similar file made with 8-space tabs and strings of 4 spaces.

import sys
import string
import regex


TAB = '\t'
endspace = regex.compile(' * $')


def fixTabs(str):
    # first, replace all tabs with spaces
    str = string.expandtabs(str,4) # assuming 4-space tabs
    # now collapse spaces to tabs, where possible
    tabsize = 8
    col = (len(str)/tabsize)*tabsize
    while col >= 0:
        # check for at least spaces ending before the next tab stop;
        # if found, replace with tabs
        pos = col + endspace.search( str[col:col+tabsize] )
        if pos >= col:
            str = str[:pos] + TAB + str[col+tabsize:]
        col = col - tabsize
    return str


def processFile(filename):
    try:
        file = open( filename, 'r' ) # open the file
    except:
        print "Error opening",filename
        return
    lines = file.readlines() # read it
    for i in range(0,len(lines)): # process it...
        lines[i] = fixTabs(lines[i])
    file = open( filename, 'w' ) # open it again
    file.writelines(lines) # write it
```

```
        print len(lines), "lines processed in",filename

# end of processFile() function

def run(filename=''):
    if filename=='':
        filename = raw_input('Enter name of a textfile to read: ')
processFile(filename)

# end of run() function
# immediate-mode commands, for drag-and-drop or execfile() execution

if __name__ == '__main__':
    if len(sys.argv) == 2:
        processFile(sys.argv[1]) # accept a command-line filename
    else:
        run()
    print raw_input("press Return")
else:
    print "Module tabfix imported."
    print "To run, type: tabfix.run()"
    print "To reload after changes to the source, type: reload(tabfix)"

# end of tabfix.py
```

How It Works

See the readme file on the companion CD for hints about making this script run.

tabfix.py has two modes. If you run it as a main program, sending it arguments from the command line, it starts processing with processFile(). You can also start tabfix.py as a real-time interaction by importing it and firing it with tabfix.run().

If the script is run from the command line with arguments, it starts processing with processFile(), which opens a file, reads its lines, processes each line in turn, writes it back, then closes the file.

fixTabs() is where the conversion takes place. It uses the string module's expandtabs() function to replace the four-space tabs spaces. The next lines replace eight spaces with a tab.

Joe Strout is a scientific software developer at the Salk Institute in La Jolla, CA.

python2c.py

This script illustrates some basics about file conversions and filtering. It actually changes a limited amount of Python code to an equally limited amount of C++.

If you want to run this script as is, you need a module named wmod, which is a specially written debugging module. This module isn't included with this script, but its calling line is commented out anyway, so don't worry about using the script as it stands.

```
#--------------------------------------------------------------------------
# python2c.py joe@strout.net
#
# This is a cheezy little program that converts some Python code
# into C++ code. It has a very limited range, but it does a good
# job on the example code it was built around! =)
#
# first release: 3/21/97 JJS
#
# Changes by Dirk Heise 01-12-98 (Thanks, Dirk!)
# - created a very simple file interface
# - some more rules for C++ support
# - added another "action" that may contain a python statement to
# be executed on match, so a match can trigger something
# - create a class header
# - temporarily buffer output in several lists of strings
# - added DEVELOPING option to help in examining operation of rules #--------------
------------------------------------------------------------


import regex
import string
import wmod

# dirk heise, for debug output - not a standard module
# supplies a function DEBUGWRITE(str), that's all

DEVELOPING = 1

# set this to 0 for simple translation
# set this to 1 if you want to have supplementary comments in the
```

```
# generated C++ code that help finding out what PYTHON2C did
# dirk heise:


# --------------------------- RULES ----------------------------


# All these rules work on single lines of input text !
# Every rule consists of three strings (the third may be None)
# - regex
# If you wanna create new rules: # the regex must contain one or more "\(.*\)"
patterns,
# - replacement rule
# the replacement rule can refer to the patterns mentioned above
# with "^1","^2", "^3" etc. to insert the substring swallowed by that subexpr.
# - None or a Python statement to be executed on match.
# When this statement is executed, it can refer to the subexpressions
# eaten by the regex as "sub[1]", "sub[2]" etc.
# you can use this to store info from the parsed text into string
# variables.
# IMPORTANT : the line you're defining works in a local namespace;
# it can NOT setup global variables in this program directly
# (i suspect it might be a bug in Python1.4)
# My workaround suggestion:
# When you define such a line, simply call a function you define yourself!
# That function (see SetClassName() below) can access every global object.
# The rules are applied from top to bottom of list!
# You can exploit this by first catching special cases and later
# catch more generalized cases! (In other words, the sequence order
# might be important)

trans = [
    # COMMENTS
    # 0
    ["\(.*\)#\(.*\)", "^1//^2", None],

    # STRING LITERALS
    # 1
    ["\(.*\)'\(.*\)'\(.*\)", '^1"^2"^3', None],

    # WHILE LOOPS
```

```
# 2
["while \(.*\):\(.*\)", "while (^1)^2", None],

# FOR LOOPS
# loops that iterate integers can easily be converted:
# 3
["for \(.*\) in range(\(.*\),\(.*\)):\(.*\)",
   "for (int ^1=^2; ^1<^3; ^1++) {^4", None],
  # an attempt to make sense of loops that iterate over some sequence/list:
  # (rule sequence is important here as the following rule is a superset
  # of the last one!):
# 4
["for \(.*\) in \(.*\):\(.*\)",
   "for (int ^1i=0; ^1i<^2.Length(); ^1i++) { int ^1 = ^2[^1i]; ^3", None],
  # Here, i assume that a Python sequence is represented by some
  # C++ container, and this container offers a method Length()
  # to find out its number of elements.
  # While a Python loop does not need an int counter variable for
  # this, iterating a C++ dynamic array-like container requires
  # a counter int. And it requires accessing the container content
  # explicitly. This rule constructs some code for that.
  # Even if it doesn't compile, it'll notify you of the necessity of
  # explicit indirection, it's a thing easily overlooked.
  # TODO : replace Length() with something more flexible
  #   or define a complete container interface somewhere...

# IF LINES
# 5
["if \(.*\):\(.*\)", "if (^1)^2", None],

# ELSE LINES
# 6
["else:\(.*\)", "else^1", None],

# PRINT LINES
# 7
["print \(.*\),$", "cout << ^1 << ' ';", None],
# 8
```

```
["print \(.*\)", "cout << ^1 << endl;", None],

# INPUT STATEMENTS
# 9
['\(.*\)=\(.*\)raw_input("\(.*\)")\(.*\)',
   'cout << "^3"; cin >> ^1;^4', None],
# 10
["\(.*\)=\(.*\)raw_input(\(.*\))\(.*\)",
   "cin >> ^1;^4", None],
# 11
['\(.*\)=\(.*\)input("\(.*\)")\(.*\)',
   'cout << "^3"; cin >> ^1;^4', None],
# 12
["\(.*\)=\(.*\)input(\(.*\))\(.*\)",
   "cin >> ^1;^4", None],


# C++ RULES
# some more rules by dirk heise
# MEMBER VARIABLE PREFIXES (TREATING "SELF.")
   # this is done by two rules, the sequence is important!
# 13
#["\(.*\)self\.\(\(\(\|[a-z]\|[A-Z]\)+\)\)(\(.*\)" , "^1^2(^4" , None],
   # this catches "self.id("
   # first catch function calls to the object itself, and simply kill
   # ".self"
   # TODO this regex fails... why? and find an easier way to catch
   #    id char set
["\(.*\)self\.\(.*\)" , "^1m_^2" , None],
   # catch the rest: member variable accesses
   # this rule assumes the C++ programmer has the habit of calling member variables
   # "m_something" (which is a habit of mine)
   # Change this rule to fit your personal C++ naming conventions!


# CLASS DECLARATIONS
["class \(.*\):" , "", "SetClassName(sub[1])"],
   # assign the detected class name to a global string


# FUNCTION & METHOD DECLARATIONS
```

```
    # first catch method declarations:
  ["def \(.*\)(self):\(.*\)" , "void ^c::^1()^2", None],
  ["def \(.*\)(self,\(.*\)" , "void ^c::^1(^2", None],
    # put classname in front of function name, eat parameter "self"
    # the "void" is just a guess, of course.
    # TODO : ^c for classname is quite arbitrary.
    #        Setting up "classname" is okay cause its a clean way of
    #        extending but ^c is built into the translate function and
    #        it shouldn't
    #
    # now catch normal function declarations (they have no "self" argument):
  ["def \(.*\)" , "void ^1", None],
    # again, the void is a guess.
]


# -------------------- EXTENSIONS --------------------------
# These variables and functions are used by user-defined python statements
# (see descriptions of rules)

header = [] # will store list of strings for class header
            # only used when a class definition is found
def hprint(s):
  # append string to class header text
  header.append(s)

classname = ""
  # dirk heise
  # global variable to keep a detected class name

def SetClassName(s):
  # dirk heise
  # set up class name , to be used in user executable statements
  # i suppose here that this function is called when a Python class
  # is defined.
  # So create some code that will work as a template for a header file
  global classname
  classname = s
  hprint ("VERY ROUGH HEADER FILE TEMPLATE FOR CLASS "+classname)
  hprint ("copy this into its own file and refine it by hand."  )
```

```
hprint ("// "+classname+".H"                                    )
hprint ("//"                                                    )
hprint ("//"                                                    )
hprint ("#ifndef _"+classname+"_H_"                             )
hprint ("#define _"+classname+"_H_"                             )
hprint ('#include "globs.h"'                                    )
hprint ("class "+classname                                      )
hprint (" {"                                                    )
hprint ("  public:"                                             )
hprint ("    "+classname+"();"                                  )
hprint ("   virtual ~"+classname+"();"                          )
hprint ("  protected:"                                          )
hprint ("  private:"                                            )
hprint (" };"                                                   )
hprint ("#endif // _"+classname+"_H_"                           )
hprint ("END OF HEADER FILE TEMPLATE FOR CLASS "+classname      )
    # TODO why all the mess with hprint? Well, the idea is to extend this
    #      one: First write only until destructor prototype, later
    #      when fetching a "def NAME(" "print" translation and "hprint"
    #      line as prototype (so this header file will contain
    #      more accurate info)
    #      In the end, "hprint" the rest of the header file.
# dirk heise: added parameter exe
def translate(s,keys,values,exe):
  # translate line s
  # find a match among keys
  # returns transformed "s" and a history string telling numbers of
  # transformations applied, in the form of a C++ comment
  global classname # dirk heise
  changed = 1
  history = ""
    # history builds up a string of transformation numbers so later we can
    # see what trafos have been applied
  while changed:
    changed = 0
    for i in range(0,len(keys)):
      if keys[i].match(s) >= 0:
        # found a match ... apply translation
        history = history + str(i) + " "
```

```python
      # make sure history string entries are separated by spaces
      # to facilitate parsing these comments later (if someone wants
      # to)
s = values[i]
# we've got a response... stuff in adjusted text where indicated
pos = string.find(s,'^')
while pos > -1:
    # dirk heise : special : ^c means "classname"
    # TODO: this is a nonsystematic hasty improvement hack
    #     (see the annotation in the rules section, seek TODO)
    if s[pos+1] == 'c' :
      # insert "classname" into our string
      left = s[:pos]
      right = s[pos+2:]
      k = classname
    else:
      num = string.atoi(s[pos+1:pos+2])
      # s = s[:pos] + keys[i].group(num) + s[pos+2:]
      # dirk heise : i splitted that to make it more understandable
      # for me
      left = s[:pos]
      right = s[pos+2:]
      k = keys[i].group(num)
      if k==None :
        # give advice:
        raise "Error in rule: missing a \\(.*\\) pattern in regex!"
    s = left + k + right

    # find another caret:
    pos = string.find(s,'^')
# dirk heise : execute user statement if one is given:
if exe[i] <> None :
  # before execution, setup "environment" strings:
  sub  = []
  sub.append("")
  k = " "
  num = 1
  while num <> 0:
    k = keys[i].group(num)
```

```
                if k==None :
                  num = 0 # to quit the loop
                else:
                  num = num + 1
                  sub.append(k)
            # sub is now a list of strings containing parsed subexpressions
            exec(exe[i])
          changed = 1    # check for more matches!


    # special case: add semicolon after most statements
    pos = string.find(s+"//", "//")
    endpos = len(string.rstrip(s[:pos])) - 1
    if s <> "":
      # dirk heise: to allow rules that return an empty string
      endchar = s[endpos]
      if endpos >= 3 and s[endpos-3:endpos+1] == 'else' and \
            (endpos == 3 or s[endpos-4] in " \t"):
        # found dangling keyword -- no semicolon needed
        return (s," //$$$ trafos applied: "+history)
      if endpos > 0 and endchar not in "{});:":
        s = s[:endpos+1] + ';' + s[endpos+1:]


    return (s," //$$$ trafos applied: "+history)
      # I use "//$$$" as a marker for the history string to facilitate later
      # automatic wipeaway of these comments


# dirk heise: added parameter exe :
def processLine(s,keys,values,exe):
    # find the indentation
    global gIndents
    qtywhitechars = regex.match("[\t ]*", s)
    if qtywhitechars > -1: whitechars = s[:qtywhitechars]
    else: whitechars = ''

    if len(whitechars) > len(gIndents[-1]):
        print gIndents[-1] + "{"
        gIndents.append(whitechars)
    else:
        while gIndents and gIndents[-1] != whitechars:
```

```
              del gIndents[-1]
              if gIndents: print gIndents[-1] + "}"
     # if not gIndents: raise "Inconsistent indentation"
     # dirk heise: Come on... Never give up!
     if not gIndents:
       print "WARNING! Inconsistent indentation."
       gIndents.append(whitechars)


  # dirk heise: added exe , take care for history return value:
  s,history = translate(s[qtywhitechars:], keys, values, exe)
  return gIndents[-1] + s , gIndents[-1] + "  " + history


# set up gKeys and gValues
# dirk heise: and gExe
gKeys = map(lambda x:regex.compile(x[0]), trans)
gValues = map(lambda x:x[1], trans)
gExe = map(lambda x:x[2], trans)
gEndWhite = regex.compile("\(.*\)\([ \t]*\)$")


gIndents = ['']


s = ""
# Dirk Heise 12.01.97 : commented this away
# print "Enter python code below, 'quit' when done."
# while s != 'quit':
#     s = raw_input()
#     print processLine(s, gKeys, gValues,gExe)


# Dirk Heise 12.01.97 : a very simple file interface.
# Modified by JJS to be platform-independent.
s = raw_input("Enter pathname of .py file:")
try:
  f = open(s)
  lines = f.readlines()
  for s in lines:
    # wmod.DEBUGWRITE("PROCESSING <"+s+">")
    cs,history = processLine(s, gKeys, gValues,gExe)
    print cs
    if DEVELOPING :
```

```
      # print numbers of transformations applied
      print history


  # now output class header if there is one:
  for s in header:
    print s


except IOError:
  result.SetFailure("File not found!")
```

How It Works

See the readme file on the companion CD for hints about making this script run.

This is one of the longest scripts in this book. A lot of the script is lookups and conversion code. Here's an example of code fed to this script by its contributor:

```
# this is a test
x = -1
while x:     # loop until 0 spam
    x = input('\nHow much spam?')
    if x:
        print "We have:"
        for i in range(0,x):
            print 'spam',
            if i == x-2:    # (don't forget the beans!)
                print "baked beans and",
    else:
        print "Enjoy!"

# all done!
```

which spewed out the following C++ code in response:

```
// this is a test
x = -1;
while (x)    // loop until 0 spam
{
    cout << "\nHow much spam?"; cin >> x ;
    if (x)
    {
        cout << "We have:" << endl;
        for (i=0; i<x; i++) {
```

```
        {
            cout << "spam" << " ";
            if (i == x-2)   // (don't forget the beans!)
            {
                cout << "baked beans and" << " ";
            }
        }
    }
    else
    {
        cout << "Enjoy!" << endl;
    }
}
// all done!
```

The script starts out with a bunch of rules for doing the conversions. Then there are slews of lists that are essentially lookup tables. A closer look at all those lists reveals that they all fit within one humongous list called trans. This is followed by the functions.

The code looks hard to follow in spots, sometimes, paradoxically, because it's so heavily commented. To see the entry code, you need to drop nearly to the end of the script, to the statement:

```
s=raw_input("Enter pathname of .py file:")
```

Then there's a try statement to test the ensuing few lines and handle any exceptions. When you input a file name, it's opened and read. This is where the module wmod would come in handy. The original script has the debug line commented out, so you can just leave it alone.

The original script expected a line of Python code, which it then translated. The script was then modified to read a whole Python file. The file's lines are passed to the function processLine(), along with four parameters. Three of these parameters have been set up with regex lines earlier in the script.

Regex is a module that can compile strings into efficient little packages for searching and matching. For details, look up the specifics in the documentation that comes with your distribution. But for now, look at the following lines:

```
gKeys = map(lambda x:regex.compile(x[0]), trans)
gValues = map(lambda x:x[1], trans)
```

```
gExe = map(lambda x:x[2], trans)
gEndWhite = regex.compile("\(.*\)\([ \t]*\)$")
```

These lines do a lot of setup. Remember the list of lists named trans? Here's where it's used. Consider one such list from trans:

```
["\(.*\)'\(.*\)'\(.*\)", '^1"^2"^3", None]
```

There are three items in this list. The first item is a search string with search parameters you can look up in the documentation. The line

```
gKeys = map(lambda x:regex.compile(x[0]), trans)
```

reads each of trans' lists in turn. It then copies the first list element (the x[0] part of the statement) in each list to gKeys. gKeys is therefore a tuple of compiled search patterns.

The other two list elements in each of trans' lists (which are, in reality, rules) are copied to their respective tuples, to gValues, and to gExe. These, however, aren't compiled. They stay as ordinary strings. gEndWhite is initialized as a simple regex compiled search pattern.

Now the search and match operation is ready to march onward in earnest. All of these values are passed to the function processLine(), which finds indentation. Indentation, of course, is the key to understanding Python code, so processLine() is an indispensable place to start.

After the line is processed, both the keys and the values tuples are passed to the function translate(). There the matching is performed between Python statements and C++ statements. The keys and values could have been put into a dictionary just as easily, rather than having them exist separately as tuples. However, this works out well.

It would be interesting to reduce all of the translation functions to a class and feed it the variable trans as a separate data file, thus permitting the script to translate Python into other languages, too.

Contributor anonymous

Private attributes are used only within the class they're declared in. In Python, private attributes are given leading double underlines: __attribute. You can also tack on a trailing single underline if you want, but nobody ever does. Attributes with both leading and trailing doubles are used by Python for internal purposes. Keep in mind that Python won't actually forbid accessing private attributes.

TIP

otp.py

Need some one-time pad (OTP) sequences? These are handy for any application that requires lengthy alphanumeric sequences that are 128-bit numbers. The chances of getting two identical OTPs within one lifetime are extremely low.

. . .

This module provides an otp object that can be used to get one time
pad strings. It should be adequate for situations that don't require
high security.

You can call the module directly as a script; it will want the
number of otp strings to print out and an optional seed number.
For example, 'python otp.py 20' will print out 20 otp strings.

You may pass in a function to the constructor. This function takes
an integer parameter (defaults to 0) and must return a string.
This string is hashed with the MD5 algorithm and the hex
representation of the hash is returned. If you do not pass in a
string generating function, an internal function is used that is
based on the whrandom module.

Once you have constructed an otp object, call the Get() method to
return an otp string. The Get() method can have an integer
parameter that is passed to the str_function() function. For the
default function (GenerateString()), if the seed is nonzero, the
Wichmann-Hill generator is started over and initialized from the
seed.

Each call to Get generates a new random string, sends it to
md5.update(), (which appends it to its own internal copy of all the
strings it's been sent), and then a new md5 hash is gotten, which is
converted to the hex representation with 32 hex characters.

This module could be made to provide cryptographically secure
one time pads by substituting a cryptographic quality random
number generator for the whrandom object. You can go out on

the web and search for "random number" and find some hardware
devices to do this.

```
'''
import md5, whrandom

whG = whrandom.whrandom()

def GenerateString(seed = 0):
    '''Generate a string from a four byte integer.  The string is the
    4 bytes of the integer, each converted to a character.
    '''
    global whG
    if seed:        # seed != 0 means to restart; whrandom seeds from time.
        whG.seed(seed & 0xff,
                (seed & 0xff00) >> 8,
                (seed & 0xff0000) >> 16)
    n = whG.randint(0, 2**30-1)
    str = ""
    str = str + chr((n & 0xFF000000) >> 24)
    str = str + chr((n & 0x00FF0000) >> 16)
    str = str + chr((n & 0x0000FF00) >>  8)
    str = str + chr((n & 0x000000FF) >>  0)
    return str

class Otp:
    def __init__(self, str_function = GenerateString, seed = 0):
        str_function(seed) # Initialize random number generator
        self.m = md5.new()

    def Get(self, seed=0):
        '''Return an OTP.
        '''
        self.m.update(GenerateString(seed))
        string = self.m.digest()
        str = ""
        for ix in xrange(len(string)):
            str = str + "%02X" % ord(string[ix])
```

```
        return str

if __name__ == "__main__":
    import sys
    num = 1
    seed = 0
    if len(sys.argv) < 2:
        print "Usage:  otp num_times [seed]"
        sys.exit(1)
    num = int(sys.argv[1])
    if len(sys.argv) == 3:
        seed = int(sys.argv[2])
    o = Otp(seed=seed)
    for ix in xrange(num):
        print o.Get()
```

How It Works

The action of this script is actually rather straightforward. It needs a string to submit to an MD5 function, which is conveniently available from the MD5 module. The string can be passed in by the user, or it can be internally generated with the random number generator module whrandom. If it's internally generated, it's a four-byte integer that's converted into characters.

This script uses bitwise operators, which is a rare occurrence in Python scripts. The lines

```
str = ""
    str = str + chr((n & 0xFF000000) >> 24)
    str = str + chr((n & 0x00FF0000) >> 16)
    str = str + chr((n & 0x0000FF00) >>  8)
    str = str + chr((n & 0x000000FF) >>  0)
    return str
```

take the random number, perform an AND with the hex masks, and side-shift the result to the right the stated number of bit positions. The syntax is almost exactly the same as C's. The result is cumulative as the interpreter moves through the lines of code.

Contributor anonymous

Gotcha

There is a difference between class variables and instance variables in classes. In the first class Horsie, num_hooves is a class variable. It'll be shared by all instances of Horsie:

```
class Horsie:
    num_hooves = 4
    def figure_hooves(self):
        print Horsie.num_hooves
```

In the second class Horsie, num_hooves is an instance variable, and will be used only by the class:

```
class Horsie:
    def __init__(self, hooves=4):
        self.num_hooves = hooves
    def hoof_report(self):
        print self.num_hooves
```

space.py

Want to know how much space you've used in any number of directories? This
script tells you.

```
'''
This module provides a function that constructs a list containing
the sizes of directories under a specified directory.

It is about an order of magnitude slower than a C implementation
would be, but it only took a short time to develop...  :)
'''


import os

listG = []

def GetTotalFileSize(dummy_param, directory, list_of_files):
    '''Given a list of files and the directory they're in, add the
    total size and directory name to the global list listG.
    '''
    global listG
    currdir = os.getcwd()
    os.chdir(directory)
    total_size = 0
    if len(list_of_files) != 0:
        for file in list_of_files:
            if file == ".." or file == ".":  continue
            size = os.stat(file)[6]
            total_size = total_size + size
    listG.append([total_size, directory])
    os.chdir(currdir)

def GetSize(directory):
    '''Returns a list of the form [ [a, b], [c, d], ... ] where
    a, c, ... are the number of total bytes in the directory and
    b, d, ... are the directory names.  The indicated directory
    is recursively descended and the results are sorted by directory
    size with the largest directory at the beginning of the list.
```

```
    '''
    import os
    global listG
    listG = []
    os.path.walk(directory, GetTotalFileSize, "")
    listG.sort()
    listG.reverse()


def ShowBiggestDirectories(directory):
    import regsub
    GetSize(directory)
    # Get total number of bytes
    total_size = 0
    for dir in listG:
        total_size = total_size + dir[0]
    if total_size != 0:
        print "For directory '%s':    " % directory,
        print "[total bytes = %.1f MB]" % (total_size / (1024.0*1024))
        print "Percent"
        print "of total    Directory"
        print "--------    " + "-" * 50
        not_shown_count = 0
        for dir in listG:
            dir[0] = 100.0 * dir[0] / total_size
            dir[1] = regsub.gsub("\\\\", "/", dir[1])
            if dir[0] >= 0.1:
                print "%6.1f     %s" % (dir[0], dir[1])
            else:
                not_shown_count = not_shown_count + 1
        print "              [%d directories not shown]" % not_shown_count


if __name__ == '__main__':
    import sys
    name = sys.argv[0]
    sys.argv = sys.argv[1:]
    if len(sys.argv) != 1:
        print "Usage:  %s directory_to_summarize" % name
        sys.exit(1)
    ShowBiggestDirectories(sys.argv[0])
```

How It Works

This script illustrates several of the methods of the os module. Many Python scripts need to delve into a directory structure, and the os module makes the job relatively painless. As of this writing, the os module is available for Windows, Mac, and UNIX machines, including Linux.

In space.py, for example, the current directory is discovered with the os method os.getcwd. Changing the current directory to another is done with os.chdir(directory). There are dozens of other methods in the os and os.path modules for everything from process parameters to file and directory information.

The os/os.path modules aren't available for every platform, though, so be cautious if you're away from the Windows/Mac/UNIX axis.

Note that the os/os.path modules aren't the same as the sys module. The sys module is basically for working with the interpreter's environment and interfacing with common system functions like standard input and output. Note, too, that in space.py, the module os is input both at the top of the script and in the function GetSize(). This duplication isn't necessary.

Contributor anonymous

tree.py

Sometimes you need to have a peek into a particular directory structure. Explore the tree with this script. To use it as a module, import tree and call the function tree.Tree(directory, indent, leading character).

```
'''

$Id: tree.py 1.2 1998/08/30 21:24:14 donp Exp $

This module defines the Tree() function.  This function will return
a list of strings that represent the directory tree for the directory
passed into the function.  The calling syntax is:

    Tree(dir, indent, leading_char)

The variable indent controls how much each subdirectory is indented
on each line.  The variable leading_char sets the leading character
```

```
in the list; '|' might not be a bad choice.

If you call the module as a script, it will print the tree to stdout
for the directory you pass in on the command line (defaults to '.').

'''

def visit(list, dirname, names):
    list.append(dirname)

def Tree(dir, indent=4, leading_char=" "):
    import os, string, re
    list = []
    dir_list = []
    os.path.walk(dir, visit, list)
    list.sort()
    head = re.compile("^" + dir)
    indent_str = leading_char +  " " * (indent - 1)
    for directory in list:
        if directory == ".":
            continue
        y = string.replace(directory, "\\", "/")
        y = head.sub("", y)
        fields = string.split(y, "/")
        count = len(fields) - 1
        if dir == "/":
            count = count + 1
        if fields[-1]:
            str = indent_str * count + fields[-1]
            dir_list.append(str)
    return [dir] + dir_list

if __name__ == "__main__":
    import sys
    dir_to_process = "."
    if len(sys.argv) == 2:
        dir_to_process = sys.argv[1]
    leading_char = "|"
    if sys.platform == "win32":
```

```
        leading_char = "3"
    for dir in Tree(dir_to_process, leading_char=leading_char):
        print dir
```

How It Works

tree.py essentially divides its operations into two parts. First it checks on the directory structure using the module os. Then it manipulates the directory names as text strings. The module re contributes by performing a substitution function.

The script runs through the directories using the line

```
os.path.walk(dir, visit, list)
```

which starts at a root point defined by variable dir. The script then puts all of the directories it finds under the root into the variable list. The rest is string manipulation. Before the list is redone, it looks like this:

```
['/home/ftp', '/home/ftp/bin', '/home/ftp/etc'
```

and so forth. The preliminary (and redundant) /home/ftp is stripped out for each occurrence, and the resulting list is given its indents and its leading character.

The output isn't a nicely formatted tree. Rather, with a call like

```
import tree
tree.Tree("/home", indent=1, leading_char="|")
```

it looks something like

```
['home', '|ftp', '||bin', '||etc', '||lib', '||pub'
```

and so on until the end. If you call for a walk through a particularly deep set of nested directories, the CPU takes quite some time to chew on it before erupting with a vast number of directories. A nifty way to turn the returned value into a nicely formatted tree is:

```
import string, tree
string.join(tree.Tree("/home", indent=1, leading_char="|"), "\n")
```

Contributor anonymous

Can you find Mr. Neutron?

Chapter 12: Games and Artificial Intelligence

Python can build some interesting games. And although it isn't really an AI (*Artificial Intelligence*) language, Python can make nice little AI-style programs. therapist.py, in particular, can fool some of the more gullible among us for quite some time.

logic.py

This script is a guessing game. The script comes up with a letter, and you get to ask questions about that letter in the hopes of guessing what it is. There's a built-in bug, as the comment lines attest. See if you can catch it as you read the code. You ask questions of this script by typing succinct characters. From the code itself, this is a sample session:

```
Sample transcript:
    Next? curves?
    1.
    Good question.
    Next? c
    You don't have enough information yet.
    How do you know it isn't c, for example?
    Next? horizontals?
    0.
    Next? s
    You don't have enough information yet.
    How do you know it isn't c, for example?
```

This script is a classic case of several separated developers contributing to a work. This is common in the Open Source community.

```
import whrandom, string
# Logic game
# From a program by Judith Haris, John Swets, and Wallace Feurzeig
# Reference: The Secret Guide to Computers, by Russ Walter, 18th ed 1993. # \
Written in Python by A.M. Kuchling (amk@magnet.com)
# For each letter, we need the various characteristics:
# (curves, loose ends, obliques, horizontals, verticals).
# There should really be a sample character set for the user to look
```

```
# at; otherwise, there are ambiguities. For example, does B have
# horizontals? Does D? How about P and R?
# There's a bug lurking in this data! Can you catch it?
# (See the bottom of the program for the answer.)
letter_stats={'a': (0, 2, 2, 1, 0), 'b':(2, 0, 0, 3, 1),
'c': (1, 2, 0, 0, 0), 'd':(1, 0, 0, 0, 1),
'e': (0, 3, 0, 3, 1), 'f':(0, 3, 0, 2, 1),
'g': (1, 2, 0, 1, 1), 'h':(0, 4, 0, 1, 2),
'i': (0, 2, 0, 0, 1), 'j':(1, 2, 0, 0, 1),
'k': (0, 4, 2, 0, 1), 'l':(0, 2, 0, 1, 1),
'm': (0, 2, 2, 0, 2), 'n':(0, 2, 1, 0, 2),
'o': (1, 0, 0, 0, 0), 'p':(1, 1, 0, 2, 1),
'q': (1, 2, 1, 0, 0), 'r':(1, 2, 1, 0, 1),
's': (1, 2, 0, 0, 0), 't':(0, 3, 0, 1, 1),
'u': (1, 2, 0, 0, 2), 'v':(0, 2, 2, 0, 0),
'w': (0, 2, 4, 0, 0), 'x':(0, 4, 2, 0, 0),
'y': (0, 3, 2, 0, 1), 'z':(0, 2, 1, 2, 0)}


# We'll define constants for the various statistics; each constant is
# equal to the position of the statistic in the tuples in
#letter_stats. CURVES=0 ; LOOSE_ENDS=1 ; OBLIQUES=2 ; HORIZONTALS=3 ; VERTICALS=4
# This dictionary is used to map questions to corresponding
# statistics. Note that different keys can map to the same value;
# for example, 'obliques' and 'diagonals' both map to the OBLIQUES constant.\
questions={'curves':CURVES, 'looseends':LOOSE_ENDS, 'obliques':OBLIQUES, \
'diagonals':OBLIQUES, 'horizontals':HORIZONTALS, 'verticals':VERTICALS}


# Play a single game

def play_once():
    # Choose a random number between 0 and 26, inclusive.    choice=\
26*whrandom.random()
    # Convert the numeric choice to a letter: 0-a, 1-b, etc.    choice=\
chr(ord('a')+choice)
    #choice=raw_input("What should I choose?") # (for debugging)
    # We'll track how many possibilities the user still has available.
    # Start with all of the letters.    possibilities=\
string.lower("ABCDEFGHIJKLMNOPQRSTUVWXYZ")
    # We'll also track which questions have been asked, and chide the
```

```
        # user when he repeats a question.
    asked=[]

    # Loop forever; the play_once() function will exit by hitting a
    # 'return' statement inside the loop.
    while (1):
        try:
            #print possibilities
            # (for debugging)
            # Get input from the user
            query=raw_input('Next? ')
            # Convert the input to lowercase           query=string.lower(query)
            # Remove all non-letter characters              query=filter(lambda x: x
in string.lowercase, query)
            # Remove whitespace
            query=string.strip(query)
        except (EOFError, KeyboardInterrupt):
            # End-Of-File : the user
            print '\nOK; give up if you like.'
            return
    if len(query)==1:
        # The query is one character long, so it's a guess
        if query not in possibilities:
            print ("Wrong! That guess is inconsistent " "with the information \
you've been given.\n" "I think you made that guess just to see " "what I would \
say.")
        elif len(possibilities)1:
            print "You don't have enough information yet."
            # Temporarily remove the user's guess from
            # possibilities, and pick a random letter.
temp=filter(lambda x, query=query: x!=query, possibilities)
            r=int(whrandom.random()*len(temp))
            print "How do you know it isn't",temp[r]+',',
            print "for example?"
        else:
            # query is in possibilities, and
            # len(possibilities)==1, so the user is right.              print \
"Yes, you've done it. Good work!" ; return
    elif questions.has_key(query):
```

```
        # Get the field of the letter_stats tuple to compare.        field=\
questions[query]
        # Determine the answer for the computer's letter        result=\
letter_stats[choice][field]        original_length=len(possibilities)
        # Exclude possibilities that don't match those of the
        # mystery letter.
        # filter(func, sequence) calls func() on each element in
        # the sequence, and returns a new sequence object
        # containing only elements for which func() returned true.
        # For strings, each character is an element. Instead of
        # defining a formal function, a lambda is used to create        # an \
anonymous function (one without a name).
        # Various other things required by the function are set
        # as default arguments, so they're accessible inside the
        # scope of the anonymous function.        possibilities=filter(lambda \
letter, letter_stats=letter_stats, field=field, result=result: \
letter_stats[letter][field]==result, possibilities)
        new_length=len(possibilities)
        if field in asked:
            print "You asked me that already."
            print "The answer is the same as before:",
        else: asked.append(field)
        # Note that this question was asked.
        print str(result)+'.'
        if (original_length==new_length):
            print 'That was a wasted question; it did not exclude any \
possibilities.'
        elif (new_length < original_length/2 or new_length==1):
            print "Good question."
    else:
        print "I don't understand the question."

#Print the instructions
print """This is a guessing game about capital letters. You can ask various \
questions about the features of the letter: curves, loose ends, obliques \
(or diagonals), horizontals, verticals. To make a guess, just enter the letter \
of your choice.

Sample transcript:
```

```
    Next? curves?
    1.
    Good question.
    Next? c
    You don't have enough information yet.
    How do you know it isn't c, for example?
    Next? horizontals?
    0.
    Next? s
    You don't have enough information yet.
    How do you know it isn't c, for example?
"""

#Play a single game
play_once()
raw_input("Press Return>")


# The solution to the bug-hunt is below...
# It's not a bug that the Python interpreter can catch; instead, it's
# a specification bug:
# # 'C' and 'S' both have the same stats: 1 curve, 2 loose ends,
# and no obliques, horizontals, or verticals. If either C or S is
# chosen as the computer's letter, the user can never get the right
# answer, because he/she can't narrow down the possibilities to just
# one! To fix this, you'd have to add another statistic, like
# number of intersections or number of closed loops. However, the
# statistic would have to be *different* for 'C' and 'S', and neither
# of those two suggestions qualify. Can you think of a property to
# distinguish between the two letters?
```

How It Works

The script relies on the fact that letters can have five attributes: curves, loose ends, obliques, horizontals, and verticals. The letter Z, for example, has no curves, two loose ends, one oblique, two horizontals, and no verticals. Therefore you can define Z as (0, 2, 1, 2, 0), and that's the way it's defined in the lookup table letter_state.

The game begins with the user pressing the return key. The script then generates a random number and converts it into a letter. Here's the conversion code:

```
     # Choose a random number between 0 and 26, inclusive.     choice=\
26*whrandom.random()
     # Convert the numeric choice to a letter: 0-a, 1-b, etc.     choice=\
chr(ord('a')+choice)
```

Take a moment and look at how these lines work. The variable choice is loaded with a value that's a decimal float less than one, multiplied by 26. At a stroke, you now have a random number between 1 and 26.

Then the script needs to convert this number to a letter. The line

```
     choice=chr(ord('a')+choice)
```

now makes the variable *choice* equal to a character that's the ASCII equivalent of lowercase *a* plus whatever *choice* is. That makes *a* the baseline, resulting in a pretty random choice of a letter.

Okay, so much for the selection process. Now the script has to interact with the user. The line

```
query=raw_input('Next? ')
```

prompts the user for input. The input is held in the variable query, which is then filtered with these lines:

```
          # Convert the input to lowercase
query=string.lower(query)
          # Remove all non-letter characters
     query=filter(lambda x: x in string.lowercase, query)
          # Remove whitespace
          query=string.strip(query)
```

If the user input causes an EOF (*End of File*) error or if there's a keyboard interrupt, the except statement after these lines catches it.

The user can type two different valid responses. The first would be a word like *curves* to see if the letter has any curves. Or the user could type a guess.

The script checks to see if the input is a guess with the line

```
if len(query)==1:
```

which checks the length of the variable query's contents. If the length is one, the input was a guess. There's an interesting twist to the subsequent logic. Further along, the script keeps track of the total number of remaining possibilities. If there is more than one, the game wants to tease the user a little bit if the user guesses wrong. The game removes the user's guess from the variable possibilities, which holds all valid remaining possibilities, retrieves a random letter from the variable possibilities, and presents it to the user saying, "How do you know it wasn't...?"

The twist in this case is how the variable possibilities is examined for the presence of the guessed letter. It's done with this code:

```
temp=filter(lambda x, query=query: x!=query, possibilities)
```

This is a Python lambda function, which is given precious little space in most Python books and documentation. Primarily, that's because it has only limited usefulness. The lambda function is a one-shot, unnamed function. But if all you need is a one-shot, it's perfect.

The lambda here is used with the filter function. In the previous code line, the variable temp is loaded with the results of a filter operation on the variable possibilities. In the filter function, there are declarations to the left of the colon and an expression to the right. Notice the odd practice of making query equal to query. This is necessary as a workaround because Python has only two scopes: local and global. Lambda operations aren't really either one, so to pass a value in or out you have to declare a variable so that the lambda function can operate on it. In this case, the parameter for the lambda function is given the same name as the variable. These two names don't have to be identical. In practice, though, they often are.

If the user inputs a word, it's assumed to be a request for information and it's passed to the elif part of the if tree. This part also has a lambda filter function. As to the bug, the game can't distinguish between a lowercase c and a lowercase s because they have the same characteristics: 1,2,0,0. But doesn't an s have two curves and one oblique? In that case, you can define s as having 2,3,1,0,0, which distinguishes it from c.

Joe Strout is a scientific software developer at the Salk Institute in La Jolla, CA.

If you have trouble running this script, try this version, courtesy of Mitch Chapman:

```
#letters logic game
import whrandom, string
# Logic game
# From a program by Judith Haris, John Swets, and Wallace Feurzeig
# Reference: The Secret Guide to Computers, by Russ Walter, 18th ed 1993. # Written
in Python by A.M. Kuchling (amk@magnet.com)
# For each letter, we need the various characteristics:
# (curves, loose ends, obliques, horizontals, verticals).
```

```
# There should really be a sample character set for the user to look
# at; otherwise, there are ambiguities. For example, does B have
# horizontals? Does D? How about P and R?
# There's a bug lurking in this data! Can you catch it?
# (See the bottom of the program for the answer.)
letter_stats={'a': (0, 2, 2, 1, 0), 'b':(2, 0, 0, 3, 1),
'c': (1, 2, 0, 0, 0), 'd':(1, 0, 0, 0, 1),
'e': (0, 3, 0, 3, 1), 'f':(0, 3, 0, 2, 1),
'g': (1, 2, 0, 1, 1), 'h':(0, 4, 0, 1, 2),
'i': (0, 2, 0, 0, 1), 'j':(1, 2, 0, 0, 1),
'k': (0, 4, 2, 0, 1), 'l':(0, 2, 0, 1, 1),
'm': (0, 2, 2, 0, 2), 'n':(0, 2, 1, 0, 2),
'o': (1, 0, 0, 0, 0), 'p':(1, 1, 0, 2, 1),
'q': (1, 2, 1, 0, 0), 'r':(1, 2, 1, 0, 1),
's': (1, 2, 0, 0, 0), 't':(0, 3, 0, 1, 1),
'u': (1, 2, 0, 0, 2), 'v':(0, 2, 2, 0, 0),
'w': (0, 2, 4, 0, 0), 'x':(0, 4, 2, 0, 0),
'y': (0, 3, 2, 0, 1), 'z':(0, 2, 1, 2, 0)}


# We'll define constants for the various statistics; each constant is
# equal to the position of the statistic in the tuples in
#letter_stats.
CURVES=0 ; LOOSE_ENDS=1 ; OBLIQUES=2 ; HORIZONTALS=3 ; VERTICALS=4
# This dictionary is used to map questions to corresponding
# statistics. Note that different keys can map to the same value;
# for example, 'obliques' and 'diagonals' both map to the OBLIQUES constant.
questions={'curves':CURVES, 'looseends':LOOSE_ENDS, 'obliques':OBLIQUES,
           'diagonals':OBLIQUES, 'horizontals':HORIZONTALS,
           'verticals':VERTICALS}


# Play a single game

def play_once():
    # Choose a random number between 0 and 26, inclusive.
     choice=26*whrandom.random()
    # Convert the numeric choice to a letter: 0-a, 1-b, etc.
     choice=chr(ord('a')+choice)
    #choice=raw_input("What should I choose?") # (for debugging)
    # We'll track how many possibilities the user still has available.
    # Start with all of the letters.
```

```
        possibilities=string.lower("ABCDEFGHIJKLMNOPQRSTUVWXYZ")
        # We'll also track which questions have been asked, and chide the
        # user when he repeats a question.
        asked=[]

        # Loop forever; the play_once() function will exit by hitting a
        # 'return' statement inside the loop.
        while (1):
            try:
                #print possibilities
                # (for debugging)
                # Get input from the user
                query=raw_input('Next? ')
                # Convert the input to lowercase
                 query=string.lower(query)
                # Remove all non-letter characters
                 query=filter(lambda x: x in string.lowercase, query)
                # Remove whitespace
                query=string.strip(query)
            except (EOFError, KeyboardInterrupt):
                # End-Of-File : the user
                print '\nOK; give up if you like.'
                return
                    if len(query)==1:
                            # The query is one character long, so it's a guess
                            if query not in possibilities:
                                    print ("Wrong! That guess is inconsistent "
                                           "with the information you've been given.\n"
                                           "I think you made that guess just to see "
                                           "what I would say.")
                            elif len(possibilities) > 1:
                                    print "You don't have enough information yet."
                                    # Temporarily remove the user's guess from
                                    # possibilities, and pick a random letter.
                                    temp=filter(lambda x, query=query: x!=query, \
possibilities)
                                    r=int(whrandom.random()*len(temp))
                                    print "How do you know it isn't",temp[r]+',',
                                    print "for example?"
```

```
                       else:
                                # query is in possibilities, and
                                # len(possibilities)==1, so the user is right.
                                print "Yes, you've done it. Good work!"
                                return
                elif questions.has_key(query):
                        # Get the field of the letter_stats tuple to compare.
                        field=questions[query]
                        # Determine the answer for the computer's letter
                        result=letter_stats[choice][field]
                        original_length=len(possibilities)
                        # Exclude possibilities that don't match those of the
                        # mystery letter.
                        # filter(func, sequence) calls func() on each element in
                        # the sequence, and returns a new sequence object
                        # containing only elements for which func() returned true.
                        # For strings, each character is an element. Instead of
                        # defining a formal function, a lambda is used to create
                        # an anonymous function (one without a name).
                        # Various other things required by the function are set
                        # as default arguments, so they're accessible inside the
                        # scope of the anonymous function.
                        possibilities=filter(lambda letter, \
letter_stats=letter_stats,
                                        field=field, result=result:
                                        letter_stats[letter][field]==result,\
possibilities)
                        new_length=len(possibilities)
                        if field in asked:
                                print "You asked me that already."
                                print "The answer is the same as before:",
                        else: asked.append(field)
                        # Note that this question was asked.
                        print str(result)+'.'
                        if (original_length==new_length):
                                print 'That was a wasted question; it did not \
exclude any possibilities.'
                        elif (new_length < original_length/2 or new_length==1):
                                print "Good question."
```

```
                    else:
                        print "I don't understand the question."

#Print the instructions
print """This is a guessing game about capital letters. You can ask various \
questions about the features of the letter: curves, loose ends, obliques (or \
diagonals), horizontals, verticals. To make a guess, just enter the letter of \
your choice.

Sample transcript:
    Next? curves?
    1.
    Good question.
    Next? c
    You don't have enough information yet.
    How do you know it isn't c, for example?
    Next? horizontals?
    0.
    Next? s
    You don't have enough information yet.
    How do you know it isn't c, for example?
"""
#Play a single game
play_once()
raw_input("Press Return>")
```

shaney.py

According to the lore, Mark Shaney was a participant in a group called net.singles several years ago. His replies were, according to list members, either poetically penetrating or merely nuts. As the story goes, "Mark V. Shaney" was actually a program running on a server at Bell Labs. Here's an attempt to re-create some of the Shaney magic.

The following code is Joe Strout's original script. I modified it, and my modification appears immediately after Joe's version.

```
# shaney.py by Greg McFarlane
# some editing by Joe Strout
```

```
#
# search for "Mark V. Shaney" on the WWW for more info!

import sys
import rand
import string


def run(filename=''):
    if filename=='':
        file = open( raw_input('Enter name of a textfile to read:'), 'r')
    else:
        file = open( filename, 'r')
    text = file.read()
    file.close()
    words = string.split(text)
    end_sentence = []
    dict = {}
    prev1 = ''
    prev2 = ''
    for word in words:
        if prev1 != '' and prev2 != '':
            key = (prev2, prev1)
            if dict.has_key(key):
                dict[key].append(word)
            else:
                dict[key] = [word]
                if prev1[-1:] == '.':
end_sentence.append(key)
        prev2 = prev1
        prev1 = word
    if end_sentence == []:
        print 'Sorry, there are no sentences in the text.'
        return
    key = ()
    count = 10
    while 1:
        if dict.has_key(key):
            word = rand.choice(dict[key])
```

```
                print word,
                key = (key[1], word)
                if key in end_sentence:
                    print
                    count = count - 1
                    if count <= 0:
                        break
        else:
                key = rand.choice(end_sentence)
# end of run() function
# immediate-mode commands, for drag-and-drop or execfile() execution

if __name__ == '__main__':
    if len(sys.argv) == 2:
        run(sys.argv[1]) # accept a command-line filename
    else:
        run()
    print
    raw_input("press Return")
else:
    print "Module shaney imported."
    print "To run, type: shaney.run()"
    print "To reload after changes to the source,type:reload(shaney)"
# end of shaney.py
```

My version begins here. I changed the module name from rand to random. There is no longer a rand module in the Python distribution.

```
# shaney.py by Greg McFarlane
# some editing by Joe Strout
# some more editing by Tim Altom
# search for "Mark V. Shaney" on the WWW for more info!

import sys
import random
import string

def run(filename=''):
    if filename=='':
        file = open( raw_input('Enter name of a textfile to read:'), 'r')
```

```
        else:
            file = open( filename, 'r')
        text = file.read()
        file.close()
        words = string.split(text)
        end_sentence = []
        dict = {}
        prev1 = ''
        prev2 = ''
        for word in words:
            if prev1 != '' and prev2 != '':
                key = (prev2, prev1)
                if dict.has_key(key):
                    dict[key].append(word)
                else:
                    dict[key] = [word]
                    if prev1[-1:] == '.':
end_sentence.append(key)
            prev2 = prev1
            prev1 = word
        if end_sentence == []:
            print 'Sorry, there are no sentences in the text.'
            return
        key = ()
        count = 10
        while 1:
            if dict.has_key(key):
                word = random.choice(dict[key])
                print word,
                key = (key[1], word)
                if key in end_sentence:
                    print
                    count = count - 1
                    if count <= 0:
                        break
            else:
                key = random.choice(end_sentence)
# end of run() function
```

```
# immediate-mode commands, for drag-and-drop or execfile() execution

if __name__ == '__main__':
    if len(sys.argv) == 2:
        run(sys.argv[1]) # accept a command-line filename
    else:
        run()
    print
    raw_input("press Return")
else:
    print "Module shaney imported."
    print "To run, type: shaney.run()"
    print "To reload after changes to the source,type:reload(shaney)"


# end of shaney.py
```

How It Works

The operation of shaney.py is pretty straightforward. Only the output is odd. This script uses a random number generator modulerandom to determine the order in which to print the text from the open file. Older scripts may have used the module random, but many scripts today use the module whrandom.

The effect is much more interesting with longer files. One- or two-line files aren't nearly as much fun. And it makes me wonder if you couldn't hook a similar Shaney script to a dictionary module (not supplied with Python, by the way) to produce truly bizarre and unexpected results. The script would look through the dictionary for a randomly generated word to drop in here or there, or to replace whole phrases. You'd get delightful pseudophilosophy starting with conventional text like

```
This has nothing to do with the subject at hand, you know.
```

And evolve it into something like

```
Something is a bean with the subject at hand.
```

Take your pick: brilliance or nonsense? And before you answer, check out any number of song lyrics from Bob Dylan to John Lennon. "I am the walrus…?" If the sender of the message is acknowledged to be eccentric, would anybody know that it was just a Python script?

Joe Strout is a scientific software developer at the Salk Institute in La Jolla, CA.

> Unpacking can be a real time-saver. If you have a list or a tuple and you want to unpack its values into a number of variables, you can do it quickly like this:
>
> ```
> a,b,c=[1,2,3]
> ```
>
> The variables a, b, and c become loaded with, respectively, 1, 2, and 3. This may not seem all that helpful until you start unpacking lists of names you've culled from a database, for example.

TIP

therapist.py

The Holy Grail of AI programmers is a program that can't be told from a real human when questions are put to it. This is the famous "Turing test," named after Alan Turing, the unfortunate but brilliant mathematician and computing visionary of the early twentieth century. therapist.py isn't going to pass the Turing test, but it's fun.

therapist.py is a kind of Eliza program. Eliza was written in the mid-1960s by Joseph Weizenbaum as a study in AI. It starts by asking, "How are you feeling today?" You type in an answer, and the script churns out a stock answer from one of its stored responses. The script's responses sound much like a bored therapist's reactions to a patient's maunderings.

As its author notes, therapist.py is easily fooled, but it's fun while it lasts.

```
#--------------------------------------------------------------------
# therapist.py # # a cheezy little Eliza knock-off by Joe Strout
# with some updates by Jeff Epler # last revised: 3/17/97
#--------------------------------------------------------------------

import string
import regex
import whrandom

#--------------------------------------------------------------------
# translate: take a string, replace any words found in dict.keys()
# with the corresponding dict.values()
#--------------------------------------------------------------------
def translate(str,dict):
    words = string.split(string.lower(str))
```

```
        keys = dict.keys();
        for i in range(0,len(words)):
            if words[i] in keys:
                words[i] = dict[words[i]]
                    # fix munged punctuation at the end
                    if resp[-2:] == '?.': resp = resp[:-2] + '.'
        return string.join(words)


#----------------------------------------------------------------------
# respond: take a string, a set of regexps, and a corresponding
# set of response lists; find a match, and return a randomly
# chosen response from the corresponding list. #------------------------------------
------------------------------------

def respond(str,keys,values):
    # find a match among keys
    for i in range(0,len(keys)):
        if keys[i].match(str) > 0:
            # found a match ... stuff with corresponding value
            # chosen randomly from among the available options
            respnum = whrandom.randint(0,len(values[i])-1)
            resp = values[i][respnum]
            # we've got a response... stuff in reflected text where indicated
pos = string.find(resp,'%')
            while pos > -1:
                num = string.atoi(resp[pos+1:pos+2])
                resp = resp[:pos]+\
                translate(keys[i].group(num),gReflections) + \
                resp[pos+2:]
                pos = string.find(resp,'%')
                if resp[-2:] == '??': resp = resp[:-2] + '?'
                return resp


#----------------------------------------------------------------------
# gReflections, a translation table used to convert things you say
# into things the computer says back, e.g. "I am" -- "you are" #--------------------
----------------------------------------------------

gReflections = {
```

```
"am" : "are",
"was" : "were",
"i" : "you",
"i'd" : "you would",
"i've" : "you have",
"i'll" : "you will",
"my" : "your",
"are" : "am",
"you've": "I have",
"you'll": "I will",
"your" : "my",
"yours" : "mine",
"you" : "me",
"me" : "you" }


#---------------------------------------------------------------------
# gPats, the main response table. Each element of the list is a
# two-element list; the first is a regexp, and the second is a
# list of possible responses, with group-macros labelled as # %1, %2, etc. #-------
----------------------------------------------------------------


gPats = [
["I need \(.*\)",
["Why do you need %1?",
"Would it really help you to get %1?",
"Are you sure you need %1?"]],


["Why don't you \(.*\)",
["Do you really think I don't %1?",
"Perhaps eventually I will %1.",
"Do you really want me to %1?"]],


["Why can't I \(.*\)",
["Do you think you should be able to %1?",
"If you could %1, what would you do?",
"I don't know -- why can't you %1?",
"Have you really tried?"]],


["I can't \(.*\)",
```

```
[ "How do you know you can't %1?",
"Perhaps you could %1 if you tried.",
"What would it take for you to %1?"]],

["I am \(.*\)",
[ "Did you come to me because you are %1?",
"How long have you been %1?",
"How do you feel about being %1?"]],

["I'm \(.*\)",
[ "How does being %1 make you feel?",
"Do you enjoy being %1?",
"Why do you tell me you're %1?",
"Why do you think you're %1?"]],

["Are you \(.*\)",
[ "Why does it matter whether I am %1?",
"Would you prefer it if I were not %1?",
"Perhaps you believe I am %1.",
"I may be %1 -- what do you think?"]],

["What \(.*\)",
[ "Why do you ask?",
"How would an answer to that help you?",
"What do you think?"]],

["How \(.*\)",
[ "How do you suppose?",
"Perhaps you can answer your own question.",
"What is it you're really asking?"]],

["Because \(.*\)",
[ "Is that the real reason?",
"What other reasons come to mind?",
"Does that reason apply to anything else?",
"If %1, what else must be true?"]],

["\(.*\) sorry \(.*\)",
```

```
[ "There are many times when no apology is needed.",
"What feelings do you have when you apologize?"]],


["Hello\(.*\)",
[ "Hello... I'm glad you could drop by today.",
"Hi there... how are you today?",
"Hello, how are you feeling today?"]],


["I think \(.*\)",
[ "Do you doubt %1?",
"Do you really think so?",
"But you're not sure %1?"]],


["\(.*\) friend\(.*\)",
[ "Tell me more about your friends.",
"When you think of a friend, what comes to mind?",
"Why don't you tell me about a childhood friend?"]],


["Yes",
[ "You seem quite sure.",
"OK, but can you elaborate a bit?"]],


["\(.*\) computer\(.*\)",
[ "Are you really talking about me?",
"Does it seem strange to talk to a computer?",
"How do computers make you feel?",
"Do you feel threatened by computers?"]],


["Is it \(.*\)",
[ "Do you think it is %1?",
"Perhaps it's %1 -- what do you think?",
"If it were %1, what would you do?",
"It could well be that %1."]],


["It is \(.*\)",
[ "You seem very certain.",
"If I told you that it probably isn't %1, what would you feel?"]],


["Can you \(.*\)",
```

```
[ "What makes you think I can't %1?",
"If I could %1, then what?",
"Why do you ask if I can %1?"]],

["Can I \(.*\)",
[ "Perhaps you don't want to %1.",
"Do you want to be able to %1?",
"If you could %1, would you?"]],

["You are \(.*\)",
[ "Why do you think I am %1?",
"Does it please you to think that I'm %1?",
"Perhaps you would like me to be %1.",
"Perhaps you're really talking about yourself?"]],

["You're \(.*\)",
[ "Why do you say I am %1?",
"Why do you think I am %1?",
"Are we talking about you, or me?"]],

["I don't \(.*\)",
[ "Don't you really %1?",
"Why don't you %1?",
"Do you want to %1?"]],

["I feel \(.*\)",
[ "Good, tell me more about these feelings.",
"Do you often feel %1?",
"When do you usually feel %1?",
"When you feel %1, what do you do?"]],

["I have \(.*\)",
[ "Why do you tell me that you've %1?",
"Have you really %1?",
"Now that you have %1, what will you do next?"]],

["I would \(.*\)",
[ "Could you explain why you would %1?",
"Why would you %1?",
```

```
"Who else knows that you would %1?"]],

["Is there \(.*\)",
[ "Do you think there is %1?",
"It's likely that there is %1.",
"Would you like there to be %1?"]],

["My \(.*\)",
[ "I see, your %1.",
"Why do you say that your %1?",
"When your %1, how do you feel?"]],

["You \(.*\)",
[ "We should be discussing you, not me.",
"Why do you say that about me?",
"Why do you care whether I %1?"]],

["Why \(.*\)",
[ "Why don't you tell me the reason why %1?",
"Why do you think %1?" ]],

["I want \(.*\)",
[ "What would it mean to you if you got %1?",
"Why do you want %1?",
"What would you do if you got %1?",
"If you got %1, then what would you do?"]],

["\(.*\) mother\(.*\)",
[ "Tell me more about your mother.",
"What was your relationship with your mother like?",
"How do you feel about your mother?",
"How does this relate to your feelings today?",
"Good family relations are important."]],

["\(.*\) father\(.*\)",
[ "Tell me more about your father.",
"How did your father make you feel?",
"How do you feel about your father?",
"Does your relationship with your father relate to your feelings today?",
```

```
"Do you have trouble showing affection with your family?"]],

["\(.*\) child\(.*\)",
[ "Did you have close friends as a child?",
"What is your favorite childhood memory?",
"Do you remember any dreams or nightmares from childhood?",
"Did the other children sometimes tease you?",
"How do you think your childhood experiences relate to your feelings today?"]],

["\(.*\)\?",
[ "Why do you ask that?",
"Please consider whether you can answer your own question.",
"Perhaps the answer lies within yourself?",
"Why don't you tell me?"]],

["quit",
[ "Thank you for talking with me.",
"Good-bye.",
"Thank you, that will be $150. Have a good day!"]],

["\(.*\)",
[ "Please tell me more.",
"Let's change focus a bit... Tell me about your family.",
"Can you elaborate on that?",
"Why do you say that %1?",
"I see.",
"Very interesting.",
"%1.",
"I see. And what does that tell you?",
"How does that make you feel?",
"How do you feel when you say that?"]] ]


#-------------------------------------------------------------------
# Main program
#-------------------------------------------------------------------

gKeys = map(lambda x:regex.compile(x[0]),gPats)
gValues = map(lambda x:x[1],gPats)

print "Therapist\n--------"
```

```
print "Talk to the program by typing in plain English, using normal upper-"
print 'and lower-case letters and punctuation. Enter "quit" when done.'
print '='*72
print "Hello. How are you feeling today?"
s = ""
while s != "quit":
    try: s = raw_input(">")
    except EOFError:
        s = "quit"
        print s
    while s[-1] in "!.": s = s[:-1]
    print respond(s,gKeys,gValues)
```

How It Works

Most of this script is lookups. The code compares the user's input statement and keys on certain words in the input to give back a randomly chosen response from two to four possible answers stored in the lookup tables.

The program works on the basis that much of conversational English is rather formalized. When we construct sentences, we tend to rely on certain opening words and phrases: *I am, I'm, My,* and so on. Those answering us back have only a narrow range of possible responses, and we expect them to react with appropriately predictable phrasing: "Yes, I can see that you are not happy today," "I'm sorry. Can I help?" and so forth. We tend to be surprised by unpredictable responses, such as "Shoes. You need to buy shoes." But we're not surprised by responses that are boring, vapid, and even unhelpful. Those we can deal with.

This program picks out particular words or phrases as a clue to what sort of statement has been typed. *What* at the beginning, for example, suggests that someone is asking a question. *I think* is the preface for a belief statement. The lookup table gPats holds the key to this exchange. The first element is an important word or phrase from the sentence the user typed in, used as a key. When there's a match with any key, the program picks from the possible two to four responses, possibly adding a variable or two.

The script starts by putting together a regex compiled pattern of first elements in the gPats lists. These are the key words and phrases that the script uses to locate a match. As for the rest of the gPats elements, they're mapped to another variable. Effectively, the script has now split each of the lists in gPats into two forks: keys and possible responses. Here's the code:

```
gKeys = map(lambda x:regex.compile(x[0]),gPats)
gValues = map(lambda x:x[1],gPats)
```

For fun, add a couple of print lines to the main program, like this:

```
gKeys = map(lambda x:regex.compile(x[0]),gPats)
gValues = map(lambda x:x[1],gPats)
print "gKeys:", gKeys
print "gValues:", gValues
```

These lines won't stay. They're only for educational purposes. When you run the script, you'll see that although gValues is a typical list (albeit a really long one!), gKeys is a list of regex objects. See the Python documentation for lots more about regex. For now just remember that regex speeds up processing a lot.

As valuable as regex is, however, you should know that regex is deprecated nowadays in favor of the module re. The key to both is the use of regular expressions. The main program now bundles up the user's input string, gKeys, and gValues and sends them to the respond() function. When they arrive, they become str, keys, and values, respectively. respond() checks for a match. When it finds one, the function generates a random number and uses it to choose the script's response. The response is then assembled and printed.

One little thing to note is the line

```
print '='*72
```

which to all appearances is multiplying a character by an integer. And that's what's happening. This line prints the equal sign 72 times across the screen. Finally, you might consider updating the script by redoing the main code a bit. You can let the script determine if it's been called as a module or as a main:

```
if __name__ == "__main__":
gKeys = map(lambda x:regex.compile(x[0]),gPats)
gValues = map(lambda x:x[1],gPats)

print "Therapist\n--------" .
print "Talk to the program by typing in plain English, using normal upper-"
print 'and lower-case letters and punctuation. Enter "quit" when done.'
print '='*72
print "Hello. How are you feeling today?"
s = ""
while s != "quit":
        try: s = raw_input(">")
```

```
        except EOFError:
            s = "quit"
            print s
        while s[-1] in "!.": s = s[:-1]
        print respond(s,gKeys,gValues)
```

Joe Strout is a scientific software developer at the Salk Institute in La Jolla, CA.

lotto.py

Let this script pick your lottery numbers, in groups of six. It illustrates a number of string functions, as well as actually being useful for picking numbers.

```
# lotto picker by manny juan (juanm@wellsfargo.com or manny@bdt.com)
from whrandom import randint
def pick_lotto():
maxm=53
maxj=6
m=maxm
# create all numbers from 0 to m
r=range(m+1)
# start with an empty result
v=[]
for j in range(maxj):
# get ith number from r...
i=randint(1,m)
n=r[i]
# remove it from r...
r[i:i+1]=[]
m=m-1
# and append to the result
v.append(n)
return v
def run():
done=0
while not done:
try: x=raw_input('\npress Enter for Lotto picks (Q to quit). ')
except EOFError:
x = 'q'
if x and (x[0] == 'q' or x[0] == 'Q'):
```

```
done=1
print 'done'
else:
print pick_lotto()
# immediate-mode commands, for drag-and-drop or execfile() execution
if __name__ == '__main__':
run()
else:
print "Module lotto imported."
print "To run, type: lotto.run()"
print "To reload after changes to the source, type: reload(lotto)"
# end of lotto.py
```

How It Works

The actual selection of numbers is done in pick_lotto(). Here the script creates a list of the numbers from 1 through 53, puts them into a list, generates a random integer, and uses the random integer as an index to pick one of the numbers from the range list. The script does this six times and then returns the result.

 This same general concept could be extended to, for example, generate both alpha and numeric character strings for randomly created passwords. With every keypress, you'd get another random password. If you were issuing passwords to thousands of employees, you could finish the job within seconds.

Joe Strout is a scientific software developer at the Salk Institute in La Jolla, CA.

warmer.py

warmer.py is a Python implementation of the old warmer/colder game. See how many tries it takes to guess the randomly generated number.

```
# warmer.py 3/11/96 by Joe Strout
import rand # handy random-number functions
def run():
# pick a number in the range 1-100
mynum = rand.choice( range(100) ) + 1
yourguess = 200     # what user guessed
lastdist = 0     # last distance to mynum
tries = 0     # number of tries so far
print "I'm thinking of a number from 1 to 100."
```

```
# main loop: repeat until user gets it right
while yourguess != mynum:
tries = tries + 1
yourguess = input("Your guess? ")
if (yourguess != mynum):
# find how far off you are
newdist = abs(yourguess - mynum)
# print warmer/colder than last time
if (lastdist == 0):
print "Guess again..."
elif (newdist > lastdist):
print "You're getting colder."
else:
print "You're getting warmer."
lastdist = newdist
# end of the if statement
# repeat until user gets it right
print "Good job! That took", tries, "tries."
# immediate-mode commands, for drag-and-drop or execfile() execution
if __name__ == '__main__':
run()
print
raw_input("press Return")
else:
print "Module warmer imported."
print "To run, type: warmer.run()"
print "To reload after changes to the source, type: reload(warmer)"
# end of warmer.py
```

How It Works

Once again you see the use of a random number generator. This time the user has to guess the number the script chooses. The action starts with the script creating a list of numbers from 1 to 100. When the user types a guess the first time, there's no difference between this guess and the last guess, so the game calls for another guess. It takes the absolute value of the difference between them and tells you if you're getting hotter or colder. If you hit the number, the game informs and congratulates you.

Joe Strout is a scientific software developer at the Salk Institute in La Jolla, CA.

questor.py

This script actually gets smarter as it plays a guessing game with you.

```
# questor.py 3/11/96 Joe Strout
# define some constants for future use
kQuestion = 'question'
kGuess = 'guess'
# define a function for asking yes/no questions
def yesno(prompt):
ans = raw_input(prompt)
return (ans[0]=='y' or ans[0]=='Y')
# define a node in the question tree (either question or guess)
class Qnode:
# initialization method
def __init__(self,guess):
self.nodetype = kGuess
self.desc = guess
# get the question to ask
def query(self):
if (self.nodetype == kQuestion):
return self.desc + " "
elif (self.nodetype == kGuess):
return "Is it a " + self.desc + "? "
else: return "Error: invalid node type!"
# return new node, given a boolean response
def nextnode(self,answer):
return self.nodes[answer]
# turn a guess node into a question node and add new item
# give a question, the new item, and the answer for that item def makeQuest\
( self, question, newitem, newanswer ):
# create new nodes for the new answer and old answer
newAnsNode = Qnode(newitem)
oldAnsNode = Qnode(self.desc)
# turn this node into a question node
self.nodetype = kQuestion
self.desc = question
# assign the yes and no nodes appropriately
self.nodes = {newanswer:newAnsNode, not newanswer:oldAnsNode}
```

```
def traverse(fromNode):
# ask the question
yes = yesno( fromNode.query() )
# if this is a guess node, then did we get it right?
if (fromNode.nodetype == kGuess):
if (yes):
print "I'm a genius!!!"
return
# if we didn't get it right, return the node
return fromNode
# if it's a question node, then ask another question
return traverse( fromNode.nextnode(yes) )
def run():
# start with a single guess node
topNode = Qnode('python')
done = 0
while not done:
# ask questions till we get to the end
result = traverse( topNode )
# if result is a node, we need to add a question
if (result):
item = raw_input("OK, what were you thinking of? ")
print "Enter a question that distinguishes a",
print item, "from a", result.desc + ":"
q = raw_input()
ans = yesno("What is the answer for " + item + "? ")
result.makeQuest( q, item, ans )
print "Got it."
# repeat until done
print
done = not yesno("Do another? ")
print
# immediate-mode commands, for drag-and-drop or execfile() execution
if __name__ == '__main__':
run()
print
raw_input("press Return")
else:
print "Module questor imported."
```

```
print "To run, type: questor.run()"
print "To reload after changes to the source, type: reload(questor)"
# end of questor.py
```

How It Works

This script formulates questions in response to your answers and stores old responses. To do these things, it needs a question tree, whose nodes are built by the class Qnode. The script stores each addition to the tree in a dictionary self.nodes.

The class Qnode is used several times. For example, in the line

```
topNode = Qnode('python')
```

Qnode is instantiated as topNode and given the default string of 'python' so that there is something for the script to present to the user when the game is started. newAnsNode and oldAnsNode are also examples of using Qnode.

As the author points out, all of the program's legerdemain is temporary because, as written, there's no way to store a copy of the data for the next day's game. Questor must therefore be rebuilt each time you play it. It would be intriguing to write a file routine to open, append, and close a file for the data at the end of the game, which would be read in when the player starts the game again.

Appendix A: Python Programming and Known Bugs FAQ

Building Python and Other Known Bugs

Programming in Python

O ne of the best resources for learning tricks and inside stuff is in FAQs. This FAQ is from python.org. You can pick up a fresh and complete copy at **http://www.python.org**.

Building Python and Other Known Bugs

1.1   Is there a test set?

1.2   When running the test set, I get complaints about floating point operations, but when playing with floating point operations I cannot find anything wrong with them.

1.3   Link errors after rerunning the configure script.

1.4   The Python interpreter complains about options passed to a script (after the script name).

1.5   When building on the SGI, make tries to run Python to create glmodule.c, but Python hasn't been built or installed yet.

1.6   I use VPATH but some targets are built in the source directory.

1.7   Trouble building or linking with the GNU readline library.

1.8   Trouble with socket I/O on older Linux 1.x versions.

1.9   Trouble with prototypes on Ultrix.

1.10   Other trouble building Python on platform X.

1.11   How to configure dynamic loading on Linux.

1.12   I can't get shared modules to work on Linux 2.0 (Slackware96)?

1.13   Trouble when making modules shared on Linux.

1.14   How to use threads on Linux.

1.15   Errors when linking with a shared library containing C++ code.

1.16   I built with tkintermodule.c enabled but get "Tkinter not found."

1.17   I built with Tk 4.0 but Tkinter complains about the Tk version.

1.18   Compilation or link errors for the _tkinter module.

1.19 I configured and built Python for Tcl/Tk but "import Tkinter" fails.

1.20 Tk doesn't work right on DEC Alpha.

1.21 Several common system calls are missing from the posix module.

1.22 ImportError: No module named string, on MS Windows.

1.23 Core dump on SGI when using the gl module.

1.24 "Initializer not a constant" while building DLL on MS-Windows.

1.25 Output directed to a pipe or file disappears on Linux.

1.26 Syntax Errors all over the place in Linux with libc 5.4.

1.27 Crash in XIO on Linux when using Tkinter.

1.28 How can I test if Tkinter is working?

1.29 Is there a way to get the interactive mode of the Python interpreter to perform function/variable name completion?

1.30 Why is the Python interpreter not built as a shared library?

1.31 Build with GCC on Solaris 2.6 (SunOS 5.6) fails.

1.32 Running "make clean" seems to leave problematic files that cause subsequent builds to fail.

Programming in Python

2.1 Is there a source code level debugger with breakpoints, step, etc.?

2.2 Can I create an object class with some methods implemented in C and others in Python (for example through inheritance)? (Also phrased as: Can I use a built-in type as base class?)

2.3 Is there a curses/termcap package for Python?

2.4 Is there an equivalent to C's onexit() in Python?

2.5 When I define a function nested inside another function, the nested function seemingly can't access the local variables of the outer function. What is going on? How do I pass local data to a nested function?

2.6 How do I iterate over a sequence in reverse order?

2.7 My program is too slow. How do I speed it up?

2.8   When I have imported a module, then edit it, and import it again (into the same Python process), the changes don't seem to take place. What is going on?

2.9   How do I find the current module name?

2.10   I have a module in which I want to execute some extra code when it is run as a script. How do I find out whether I am running as a script?

2.11   I try to run a program from the Demo directory but it fails with ImportError: No module named ...; what gives?

2.12   I have successfully built Python with STDWIN but it can't find some modules (for example stdwinevents).

2.13   What GUI toolkits exist for Python?

2.14   Are there any interfaces to database packages in Python?

2.15   Is it possible to write obfuscated one-liners in Python?

2.16   Is there an equivalent of C's "?:" ternary operator?

2.17   My class defines __del__ but it is not called when I delete the object.

2.18   How do I change the shell environment for programs called using os.popen() or os.system()? Changing os.environ doesn't work.

2.19   What is a class?

2.20   What is a method?

2.21   What is self?

2.22   What is an unbound method?

2.23   How do I call a method defined in a base class from a derived class that overrides it?

2.24   How do I call a method from a base class without using the name of the base class?

2.25   How can I organize my code to make it easier to change the base class?

2.26   How can I find the methods or attributes of an object?

2.27   I can't seem to use os.read() on a pipe created with os.popen().

2.28   How can I create a stand-alone binary from a Python script?

2.29   What WWW tools are there for Python?

2.30 How do I run a subprocess with pipes connected to both input and output?

2.31 How do I call a function if I have the arguments in a tuple?

2.32 How do I enable font-lock-mode for Python in Emacs?

2.33 Is there a scanf() or sscanf() equivalent?

2.34 Can I have Tk events handled while waiting for I/O?

2.35 How do I write a function with output parameters (call by reference)?

2.36 Please explain the rules for local and global variables in Python.

2.37 How can I have modules that mutually import each other?

2.38 How do I copy an object in Python?

2.39 How to implement persistent objects in Python? (Persistent == automatically saved to and restored from disk.)

2.40 I try to use __spam and I get an error about _SomeClassName__spam.

2.41 How do I delete a file? And other file questions.

2.42 How to modify urllib or httplib to support HTTP/1.1?

2.43 Unexplicable syntax errors in compile() or exec.

2.44 How do I convert a string to a number?

2.45 How do I convert a number to a string?

2.46 How do I copy a file?

2.47 How do I check if an object is an instance of a given class or of a subclass of it?

2.48 What is delegation?

2.49 How do I test a Python program or component.

2.50 My multidimensional list (array) is broken! What gives?

2.51 I want to do a complicated sort: can you do a Schwartzian Transform in Python?

2.52 How to convert between tuples and lists?

2.53 Files retrieved with urllib contain leading garbage that looks like e-mail headers.

2.54 How do I get a list of all instances of a given class?

2.55 A regular expression fails with regex.error: match failure.

Building Python and Other Known Bugs

1.1   Is there a test set?

Sure. You can run it after building with "make test", or you can run it manually with the command:

```
import test.autotest
```

In 1.4 or earlier, use:

```
import autotest
```

The test set doesn't test all features of Python, but it goes a long way to confirm that Python is actually working.

If "make test" fails, don't just mail the output to the newsgroup — this doesn't give enough information to debug the problem. Instead, find out which test fails, and run that test manually from an interactive interpreter. For example, if "make test" reports that test_spam fails, try this interactively:

```
import test.test_spam
```

This generally produces more verbose output, which can be diagnosed to debug the problem.

TIP

1.2   When running the test set, I get complaints about floating point operations, but when playing with floating point operations I cannot find anything wrong with them

The test set makes occasional unwarranted assumptions about the semantics of C floating point operations. Until someone donates a better floating point test set, you will have to comment out the offending floating point tests and execute similar tests manually.

1.3   Link errors after rerunning the configure script

It is generally necessary to run "make clean" after a configuration change.

1.4   The Python interpreter complains about options passed to a script (after the script name)

You are probably linking with GNU getopt, e.g. through —liberty. Don't. The reason for the complaint is that GNU getopt, unlike System V getopt and other getopt implementations, doesn't consider a non-option to be the end of the option list. A quick (and compatible) fix for scripts is to add "--" to the interpreter, like this:

```
#! /usr/local/bin/python --
```

You can also use this interactively:

```
python -- script.py [options]
```

Note that a working getopt implementation is provided in the Python distribution (in Python/getopt.c) but not automatically used.

1.5   When building on the SGI, make tries to run Python to create glmodule.c, but Python hasn't been built or installed yet

Comment out the line mentioning glmodule.c in Setup and build a Python without gl first; install it or make sure it is in your $PATH, then edit the Setup file again to turn on the gl module, and make again. You don't need to do "make clean"; you do need to run "make Makefile" in the Modules subdirectory (or just run "make" at the toplevel).

1.6   I use VPATH but some targets are built in the source directory

On some systems (e.g. Sun), if the target already exists in the source directory, it is created there instead of in the build directory. This is usually because you have previously built without VPATH. Try running "make clobber" in the source directory.

1.7   Trouble building or linking with the GNU readline library

Consider using readline 2.0. Some hints:

You can use the GNU readline library to improve the interactive user interface: this gives you line editing and command history when calling Python interactively. You need to configure and build the GNU readline library before running the configure script. Its sources are no longer distributed with Python; you can ftp them from any GNU mirror site, or from its home site **ftp://slc2.ins.cwru.edu/ pub/dist/readline-2.0.tar.gz** (or a higher version number — using version 1.x is not recommended). Pass the Python configure script the option —with-readline=DIRECTORY where DIRECTORY is the absolute pathname of the directory where you've built the readline library. Some hints on building and using the readline library: On SGI IRIX 5, you may have to add the following to rldefs.h:

```
#ifndef sigmask
#define sigmask(sig) (1L << ((sig)-1))
#endif
```

On most systems, you will have to add #include "rldefs.h" to the top of several source files, and if you use the VPATH feature, you will have to add dependencies of the form foo.o: foo.c to the Makefile for several values of foo. The readline library requires use of the termcap library. A known problem with this is that it contains entry points which cause conflicts with the STDWIN and SGI GL libraries. The STDWIN conflict can be solved by adding a line saying '#define werase w_erase' to the stdwin.h file (in the STDWIN distribution, subdirectory H). The GL conflict has been solved in the Python configure script by a hack that forces use of the static version of the termcap library. Check the newsgroup **gnu.bash.bug news:gnu.bash.bug** for specific problems with the readline library (I don't read this group but I've been told that it is the place for readline bugs).

1.8   Trouble with socket I/O on older Linux 1.x versions

Once you've built Python, use it to run the regen.py script in the Lib/linux1 directory. Apparently the files as distributed don't match the system headers on some Linux versions.

1.9   Trouble with prototypes on Ultrix

Ultrix cc seems broken — use gcc, or edit config.h to #undef HAVE_PROTOTYPES.

1.10   Other trouble building Python on platform X

Please e-mail the details to **guido@cnri.reston.va.us**. Please provide as many details as possible. In particular, if you don't say what type of computer and what operating system (and version) you are using, it will be difficult to figure out what the problem is. If you get a specific error message, please e-mail it also.

1.11   How to configure dynamic loading on Linux

This is now automatic as long as your Linux version uses the ELF object format (all recent Linuxes do).

1.12   I can't get shared modules to work on Linux 2.0 (Slackware96)

This is a bug in the Slackware96 release. The fix is simple: Make sure that there is a link from /lib/libdl.so to /lib/libdl.so.1 so that the following links are setup: /lib/libdl.so -> /lib/libdl.so.1 /lib/libdl.so.1 -> /lib/libdl.so.1.7.14 You may have to re-run the configure script after rm'ing the config.cache file before you attempt to rebuild Python after this fix.

1.13   Trouble when making modules shared on Linux

This happens when you have built Python for static linking and then enable

```
*shared*
```

in the Setup file. Shared library code must be compiled with "-fpic". If a .o file for the module already exists that was compiled for static linking, you must remove it or do "make clean" in the Modules directory.

1.14   How to use threads on Linux

[Greg Stein] You need to have a very recent libc, or even better, get the LinuxThreads-0.5 distribution. Note that if you install LinuxThreads normally, you shouldn't need to specify the directory to the -with-thread configuration switch. The configure script ought to find it without a problem. To make sure everything builds properly, do a "make clean", remove config.cache, rerun configure with that switch, and then build.

[Andy Dustman] On glibc systems (like RedHat 5.0+), LinuxThreads is obsoleted by POSIX threads (-lpthread). If you upgraded from an earlier Red Hat, remove LinuxThreads with "rpm -e linuxthreads linuxthreads-devel". Then run configure using —with-thread as above.

1.15   Errors when linking with a shared library containing C++ code

Link the main Python binary with C++. Change the definition of LINKCC in Modules/Makefile to be your C++ compiler. You may have to edit config.c slightly to make it compilable with C++.

1.16   I built with tkintermodule.c enabled but get 'Tkinter not found'

Tkinter.py (note uppercase T) lives in a subdirectory of Lib, Lib/tkinter. If you are using the default module search path, you probably didn't enable the line in the Modules/Setup file defining TKPATH; if you use the environment variable PYTHONPATH, you'll have to add the proper tkinter subdirectory.

1.17   I built with Tk 4.0 but Tkinter complains about the Tk version

Several things could cause this. You most likely have a Tk 3.6 installation that wasn't completely eradicated by the Tk 4.0 installation (which tends to add "4.0" to its installed files). You may have the Tk 3.6 support library installed in the place where the Tk 4.0 support files should be (default /usr/local/lib/tk/); you may have compiled Python with the old tk.h header file (yes, this actually compiles!); you may actually have linked with Tk 3.6 even though Tk 4.0 is also around. Similar for Tcl 7.4 vs. Tcl 7.3.

1.18   Compilation or link errors for the _tkinter module

Most likely, there's a version mismatch between the Tcl/Tk header files (tcl.h and tk.h) and the Tcl/Tk libraries you are using (e.g. "-ltk8.0" and "-ltcl8.0" arguments for _tkinter in the Setup file). It is possible to install several versions of the Tcl/Tk libraries, but there can only be one version of the tcl.h and tk.h header files. If the library doesn't match the header, you'll get problems, either when linking the module, or when importing it. Fortunately, the version number is clearly stated in each file, so this is easy to find. Reinstalling and using the latest version usually fixes the problem.

(Also note that when compiling unpatched Python 1.5.1 against Tcl/Tk 7.6/ 4.2 or older, you get an error on Tcl_Finalize. See the 1.5.1 patch page at **http://www.python.org/1.5/patches-1.5.1/**.)

1.19   I configured and built Python for Tcl/Tk but "import Tkinter" fails

Most likely, you forgot to enable the line in Setup that says "TKPATH=:$(DESTLIB)/ tkinter".

1.20   Tk doesn't work right on DEC Alpha

You probably compiled either Tcl, Tk, or Python with gcc. Don't. For this platform, which has 64-bit integers, gcc is known to generate broken code. The standard cc (which comes bundled with the OS!) works. If you still prefer gcc, at least try recompiling with cc before reporting problems to the newsgroup or the author; if this fixes the problem, report the bug to the gcc developers instead. (As far as we know, there are no problems with gcc on other platforms — the instabilities seem to be restricted to the DEC Alpha.)

There's also a 64-bit bugfix for Tcl/Tk; see **http://grail.cnri.reston.va.us/grail/ info/patches/tk64bit.txt**

1.21 Several common system calls are missing from the posix module

Most likely, *all* test compilations run by the configure script are failing for some reason or another. Have a look in config.log to see what could be the reason. A common reason is specifying a directory to the —with-readline option that doesn't contain the libreadline.a file.

1.22 ImportError: No module named string, on MS Windows

Most likely, your PYTHONPATH environment variable should be set to something like:

```
set PYTHONPATH=c:\python;c:\python\lib;c:\python\scripts
```

(assuming Python was installed in c:\python).

1.23 Core dump on SGI when using the gl module

There are conflicts between entry points in the termcap and curses libraries and an entry point in the GL library. There's a hack of a fix for the termcap library if it's needed for the GNU readline library, but it doesn't work when you're using curses. Concluding, you can't build a Python binary containing both the curses and gl modules.

1.24 "Initializer not a constant" while building DLL on MS-Windows

Static type object initializers in extension modules may cause compiles to fail with an error message like "initializer not a constant". Fredrik Lundh, **Fredrik.Lundh@image.combitech.se** explains:

This shows up when building DLL under MSVC. There are two ways to address this: either compile the module as C++, or change your code to something like:

```
statichere PyTypeObject bstreamtype = {
    PyObject_HEAD_INIT(NULL) /* must be set by init function */
    0,
    "bstream",
    sizeof(bstreamobject),
...
void
initbstream()
{
    /* Patch object type */
    bstreamtype.ob_type = &PyType_Type;
    Py_InitModule("bstream", functions);
```

```
    ...
}
```

1.25 Output directed to a pipe or file disappears on Linux

Some people have reported that when they run their script interactively, it runs great, but that when they redirect it to a pipe or file, no output appears.

```
% python script.py
...some output...
% python script.py >file
% cat file
% # no output
% python script.py | cat
% # no output
%
```

Nobody knows what causes this, but it is apparently a Linux bug. Most Linux users are *not* affected by this.

There's at least one report of someone who reinstalled Linux (presumably a newer version) and Python and got rid of the problem; so this may be the solution.

1.26 Syntax Errors all over the place in Linux with libc 5.4

"I have installed python1.4 on my Linux system. When I try run the import statement I get the following error message:"

```
File "<stdin>", line 1
    import sys
        ^
Syntax Error: "invalid syntax"
```

Did you compile it yourself? This usually is caused by an incompatibility between libc 5.4.x and earlier libc's. In particular, programs compiled with libc 5.4 give incorrect results on systems that had libc 5.2 installed because the ctype.h file is broken. In this case, Python can't recognize which characters are letters and so on. The fix is to install the C library that was used when building the binary that you installed, or to compile Python yourself. When you do this, make sure the C library header files that get used by the compiler match the installed C library. (Adapted from an answer by Martin V. Loewis).

Also, (adapted from Andreas Jung) if you have upgraded to libc 5.4.x, and the problem persists, check your library path for an older version of libc. Try to clean update libc with the libs and the header files and then try to recompile all.

1.27   Crash in XIO on Linux when using Tkinter

When Python is built with threads under Linux, use of Tkinter can cause crashes like the following:

```
>>> from Tkinter import *
>>> root = Tk()
XIO:  fatal IO error 0 (Unknown error) on X server ":0.0"
      after 45 requests (40 known processed) with 1 events remaining.
```

The reason is that the default Xlib is not built with support for threads. If you rebuild Xlib with threads enabled the problems go away. Alternatively, you can rebuild Python without threads ("make clean" first!).

1.28   How can I test if Tkinter is working?

Try the following:

```
python
>>> import _tkinter
>>> import Tkinter
>>> Tkinter._test()
```

This should pop up a window with two buttons, one "Click me" and one "Quit".

If the first statement (import _tkinter) fails, your Python installation probably has not been configured to support Tcl/Tk. On UNIX, if you have installed Tcl/Tk, you have to rebuild Python after editing the Modules/Setup file to enable the _tkinter module and the TKPATH environment variable.

It is also possible to get complaints about Tcl/Tk version number mismatches or missing TCL_LIBRARY or TK_LIBRARY environment variables. These have to do with Tcl/Tk installation problems.

A common problem is to have installed versions of tcl.h and tk.h that don't match the installed version of the Tcl/Tk libraries; this usually results in linker errors or (when using dynamic loading) complaints about missing symbols during loading the shared library.

1.29   Is there a way to get the interactive mode of the Python interpreter to perform function/variable name completion?

(From a posting by Guido van Rossum.) On UNIX, if you have enabled the readline module (for example if Emacs-style command line editing and bash-style history works for you), you can add this by importing the undocumented standard library module "rlcompleter". When completing a simple identifier, it completes keywords, built-ins and globals in __main__; when completing NAME.NAME..., it evaluates (!) the expression up to the last dot and completes its attributes.

This way, you can do "import string", type "string.", hit the completion key twice, and see the list of names defined by the string module.

To use the tab key as the completion key, call:

```
readline.parse_and_bind("tab: complete")
```

You can put this in a ~/.pythonrc file, and set the PYTHONSTARTUP environment variable to ~/.pythonrc. This will cause the completion to be enabled whenever you run Python interactively.

TIP

Notes (see the docstring for rlcompleter.py for more information):

- The evaluation of the NAME.NAME... form may cause arbitrary application defined code to be executed if an object with a __getattr__ hook is found. Since it is the responsibility of the application (or the user) to enable this feature, I consider this an acceptable risk. More complicated expressions (e.g. function calls or indexing operations) are *not* evaluated.

- GNU readline is also used by the built-in functions input() and raw_input(), and thus these also benefit/suffer from the complete features. Clearly an interactive application can benefit by specifying its own completer function and using raw_input() for all its input.

- When stdin is not a tty device, GNU readline is never used, and this module (and the readline module) are silently inactive.

1.30 Why is the Python interpreter not built as a shared library?

(This is a UNIX question; on Mac and Windows, it *is* a shared library.) It's just a nightmare to get this to work on all different platforms. Shared library portability is a pain. And yes, I know about GNU libtool — but it requires me to use its conventions for file names, etc., and it would require a complete and utter rewrite of all the makefile and config tools I'm currently using.

In practice, few applications embed Python — it's much more common to have Python extensions, which already are shared libraries. Also, serious embedders often want total control over which Python version and configuration they use, so they wouldn't want to use a standard shared library anyway. So while the motivation of saving space when lots of apps embed Python is nice in theory, I doubt that it will save much in practice. (Hence the low priority I give to making a shared library.)

1.31   Build with GCC on Solaris 2.6 (SunOS 5.6) fails

If you have upgraded Solaris 2.5 or 2.5.1 to Solaris 2.6, but you have not upgraded your GCC installation, the compile may fail, like this:

```
In file included from /usr/include/sys/stream.h:26,
                 from /usr/include/netinet/in.h:38,
                 from /usr/include/netdb.h:96,
                 from ./socketmodule.c:121:
/usr/include/sys/model.h:32: #error "No DATAMODEL_NATIVE specified"
```

Solution: rebuild GCC for Solaris 2.6. You might be able to simply rerun fixincludes, but people have had mixed success with doing that.

1.32   Running "make clean" seems to leave problematic files that cause subsequent builds to fail

Use "make clobber" instead. Use "make clean" to reduce the size of the source/build directory after you're happy with your build and installation. If you have already tried to build Python and you'd like to start over, you should use "make clobber". It does a "make clean" and also removes files such as the partially built Python library from a previous build.

Programming in Python

2.1   Is there a source code level debugger with breakpoints, step, etc.?

Yes. Check out module pdb. It is documented in the Library Reference Manual; pdb.help() also prints the documentation. You can write your own debugger by using the code for pdb as an example.

Pythonwin also has a GUI debugger available, based on bdb, which colors breakpoints and has quite a few cool features (including debugging non-Pythonwin programs). The interface needs some work, but is interesting none the less. A reference can be found in **http://www.python.org/ftp/python/pythonwin/pwindex.html**

Richard Wolff has created a modified version of pdb, called Pydb, for use with the popular Data Display Debugger (DDD). Pydb can be found at **http://daikon.tuc.noao.edu/python/**, and DDD can be found at **http://www.cs.tu-bs.de/softech/ddd/**

2.2 Can I create an object class with some methods implemented in C and others in Python (for example through inheritance)? (Also phrased as: Can I use a built-in type as base class?)

No, but you can easily create a Python class which serves as a wrapper around a built-in object, for example (for dictionaries):

```
# A user-defined class behaving almost identical
# to a built-in dictionary.
class UserDict:
        def __init__(self): self.data = {}
        def __repr__(self): return repr(self.data)
        def __cmp__(self, dict):
             if type(dict) == type(self.data):
                     return cmp(self.data, dict)
             else:
                     return cmp(self.data, dict.data)
        def __len__(self): return len(self.data)
        def __getitem__(self, key): return self.data[key]
        def __setitem__(self, key, item): self.data[key] = item
        def __delitem__(self, key): del self.data[key]
        def keys(self): return self.data.keys()
        def items(self): return self.data.items()
        def values(self): return self.data.values()
        def has_key(self, key): return self.data.has_key(key)
```

See Jim Fulton's ExtensionClass for an example of a mechanism which allows you to have superclasses which you can inherit from in Python — that way you can have some methods from a C superclass (call it a mixin) and some methods from either a Python superclass or your subclass. See **http://www.digicool.com/releases/ExtensionClass/** .

2.3 Is there a curses/termcap package for Python?

[Andrew Kuchling] The standard Python distribution comes with a curses module in the Modules/ subdirectory, though it's not compiled by default. However, that module only supports plain curses; you can't use ncurses features like colors with it (though it will link with ncurses).

Oliver Andrich has an enhanced module that does support such features; there's a version available at **http://andrich.net/python/selfmade.html#ncursesmodule.**

2.4   Is there an equivalent to C's onexit() in Python?

Yes, if you import sys and assign a function to sys.exitfunc, it will be called when your program exits, is killed by an unhandled exception, or (on UNIX) receives a SIGHUP or SIGTERM signal.

2.5   When I define a function nested inside another function, the nested function seemingly can't access the local variables of the outer function. What is going on? How do I pass local data to a nested function?

Python does not have arbitrarily nested scopes. When you need to create a function that needs to access some data which you have available locally, create a new class to hold the data and return a method of an instance of that class, for example:

```
class MultiplierClass:
    def __init__(self, factor):
        self.factor = factor
    def multiplier(self, argument):
        return argument * self.factor
def generate_multiplier(factor):
    return MultiplierClass(factor).multiplier
twice = generate_multiplier(2)
print twice(10)
# Output: 20
```

An alternative solution uses default arguments, for example:

```
def generate_multiplier(factor):
    def multiplier(arg, fact = factor):
        return arg*fact
    return multiplier
twice = generate_multiplier(2)
print twice(10)
# Output: 20
```

2.6   How do I iterate over a sequence in reverse order?

If it is a list, the fastest solution is:

```
list.reverse()
try:
        for x in list:
                "do something with x"
```

```
        finally:
                list.reverse()
```

This has the disadvantage that while you are in the loop, the list is temporarily reversed. If you don't like this, you can make a copy. This appears expensive but is actually faster than other solutions:

```
rev = list[:]
rev.reverse()
for x in rev:
        <do something with x>
```

If it's not a list, a more general but slower solution is:

```
for i in range(len(sequence)-1, -1, -1):
        x = sequence[i]
        <do something with x>
```

A more elegant solution is to define a class that acts as a sequence and yields the elements in reverse order (solution due to Steve Majewski):

```
class Rev:
        def __init__(self, seq):
                self.forw = seq
        def __len__(self):
                return len(self.forw)
        def __getitem__(self, i):
                return self.forw[-(i + 1)]
```

You can now simply write:

```
for x in Rev(list):
        <do something with x>
```

Unfortunately, this solution is slowest of all, due to the method call overhead.

2.7 My program is too slow. How do I speed it up?

That's a tough one, in general. There are many tricks to speed up Python code; I would consider rewriting parts in C only as a last resort. One thing to notice is that function and (especially) method calls are rather expensive; if you have designed a purely OO interface with lots of tiny functions that don't do much more than get or set an instance variable or call another method, you may consider using a more direct way, such as directly accessing instance variables. Also see the standard module "profile" (described in the Library Reference manual), which makes it possible to find out where your program is spending most of its time (if you have some patience — the profiling itself can slow your program down by an order of magnitude).

Remember that many standard optimization heuristics you may know from other programming experience may well apply to Python. For example, it may be faster to send output to output devices using larger writes rather than smaller ones in order to avoid the overhead of kernel system calls. Thus CGI scripts that write all output in "one shot" may be notably faster than those that write lots of small pieces of output.

Also, be sure to use "aggregate" operations where appropriate. For example, the "slicing" feature allows programs to chop up lists and other sequence objects in a single tick of the interpreter mainloop using highly optimized C implementations. Thus to get the same effect as:

```
L2 = []
for i in range[3]:
    L2.append(L1[i])
```
it is much shorter and far faster to use
```
L2 = list(L1[:3]) # "list" is redundant if L1 is a list.
```

Note that the map() function, particularly used with builtin methods or builtin functions can be a convenient accelerator. For example, to pair the elements of two lists together:

```
>>> map(None, [1,2,3], [4,5,6])
[(1, 4), (2, 5), (3, 6)]
```

or to compute a number of sines:

```
>>> map( math.sin, (1,2,3,4))
[0.841470984808, 0.909297426826, 0.14112000806,  -0.756802495308]
```

The map operation completes very quickly in such cases.

Other examples of aggregate operations include the join, joinfields, split, and splitfields methods of the standard string builtin module. For example, if s1..s7 are large (10K+) strings, then string.joinfields([s1,s2,s3,s4,s5,s6,s7], "") may be far faster than the more obvious s1+s2+s3+s4+s5+s6+s7, since the "summation" will compute many subexpressions, whereas joinfields does all copying in one pass. For manipulating strings also consider the regular expression libraries and the "substitution" operations String % tuple and String % dictionary. Also be sure to use the list.sort builtin method to do sorting, and see FAQ's 2.51 and 2.59 for examples of moderately advanced usage — list.sort beats other techniques for sorting in all but the most extreme circumstances.

There are many other aggregate operations available in the standard libraries and in contributed libraries and extensions. Another common trick is to "push loops into functions or methods." For example, suppose you have a program that runs slowly and you use the profiler (profile.run) to determine that a Python function ff is being called lots of times. If you notice that ff

```
def ff(x):
    ...do something with x computing result...
    return result
```

tends to be called in loops like (A)

```
list = map(ff, oldlist)
```

or (B)

```
for x in sequence:
    value = ff(x)
    ...do something with value...
```

then you can often eliminate function call overhead by rewriting ff to

```
def ffseq(seq):
    resultseq = []
    for x in seq:
        ...do something with x computing result...
        resultseq.append(result)
    return resultseq
```

and rewrite (A) to

```
list = ffseq(oldlist)
```

and (B) to

```
for value in ffseq(sequence):
    ...do something with value...
```

Other single calls ff(x) translate to ffseq([x])[0] with little penalty. Of course, this technique is not always appropriate and there are other variants, which you can figure out.

You can gain some performance by explicitly storing the results of a function or method lookup into a local variable. A loop like

```
for key in token:
    dict[key] = dict.get(key, 0) + 1
```

resolves dict.get every iteration. If the method isn't going to change, a faster implementation is

```
dict_get = dict.get   # look up the method once
for key in token:
    dict[key] = dict_get(key, 0) + 1
```

Default arguments can be used to determine values once at compile time instead of at run time. This can only be done for functions or objects that will not be changed during program execution, such as replacing

```
def degree_sin(deg):
    return math.sin(deg * math.pi / 180.0)
```

with

```
def degree_sin(deg, factor = math.pi/180.0, sin = math.sin):
    return sin(deg * factor)
```

Because this trick uses default arguments for terms that should not be changed, it should only be used when you are not concerned with presenting a possibly confusing API to your users. For an anecdote related to optimization, see **http://www.python.org/doc/essays/list2str.html**.

2.8 When I import a module, then edit it, and import it again (into the same Python process), the changes don't seem to take place. What is going on?

For reasons of efficiency as well as consistency, Python only reads the module file on the first time a module is imported. (Otherwise a program consisting of many modules, each of which imports the same basic module, would read the basic module over and over again.) To force rereading of a changed module, do this:

```
import modname
reload(modname)
```

Be warned — this technique is not 100 percent fool-proof. In particular, modules containing statements like

```
from modname import some_objects
```

will continue to work with the old version of the imported objects.

2.9 How do I find the current module name?

A module can find out its own module name by looking at the (predefined) global variable __name__. If this has the value '__main__' you are running as a script.

2.10 I have a module in which I want to execute some extra code when it is run as a script. How do I find out whether I am running as a script?

See the previous question. For example, if you put the following on the last line of your module, main() is called only when your module is running as a script:

```
if __name__ == '__main__': main()
```

2.11 I try to run a program from the Demo directory but it fails with ImportError: No module named ...; what gives?

This is probably an optional module (written in C!) which hasn't been configured on your system. This especially happens with modules like "Tkinter", "stdwin", "gl", "Xt" or "Xm". For Tkinter, STDWIN and many other modules, see Modules/ Setup.in for info on how to add these modules to your Python, if it is possible at all. Sometimes you will have to ftp and build another package first (such as Tcl and Tk for Tkinter). Sometimes the module only works on specific platforms (for example gl only works on SGI machines).

Note that if the complaint is about "Tkinter" (uppercase T) and you have already configured module "tkinter" (lowercase t), the solution is *not* to rename tkinter to Tkinter or vice versa. There is probably something wrong with your module search path. Check out the value of sys.path.

For X-related modules (Xt and Xm) you will have to do more work: they are currently not part of the standard Python distribution. You will have to ftp the Extensions tar file, i.e. **ftp://ftp.python.org/pub/python/src/X-extension.tar.gz** and follow the instructions there. See also the next question.

2.12 I have successfully built Python with STDWIN but it can't find some modules (for example stdwinevents)

There's a subdirectory of the library directory named 'stdwin', which should be in the default module search path. There's a line in Modules/Sctup(.in) that you have to enable for this purpose — unfortunately in the latest release it's not near the other STDWIN-related lines, so it's easy to miss it.

2.13 What GUI toolkits exist for Python?

Depending on what platform(s) you are aiming at, there are several. There's a neat object-oriented interface to the Tcl/Tk widget set, called Tkinter. It is part of the standard Python distribution and well-supported — all you need to do is build and install Tcl/Tk and enable the _tkinter module and the TKPATH definition in Modules/Setup when building Python. This is probably the easiest to install and use, and the most complete widget set. It is also very likely that in the future the standard Python GUI API will be based on or at least look very much like the Tkinter interface. For more info about Tk, including pointers to the source, see the Tcl/Tk home page at **http://www.scriptics.com**. Tcl/Tk is now fully portable to the Mac and Windows platforms (NT and 95 only); you need Python 1.4beta3 or later and Tk 4.1patch1 or later.

There's an interface to X11, including the Athena and Motif widget sets (and a few individual widgets, like Mosaic's HTML widget and SGI's GL widget) available from **ftp://ftp.python.org/pub/python/src/X-extension.tar.gz**. Support by Sjoerd Mullender **sjoerd@cwi.nl**.

On top of the X11 interface there's the (recently revived) vpApp toolkit by Per Spilling, now also maintained by Sjoerd Mullender **sjoerd@cwi.nl**. See **ftp://ftp.cwi.nl/pub/sjoerd/vpApp.tar.gz**.

The Mac port has a rich and ever-growing set of modules that support the native Mac toolbox calls. See the documentation that comes with the Mac port. See **ftp://ftp.python.org/pub/python/mac**. Support by Jack Jansen **jack@cwi.nl**.

The NT port supported by Mark Hammond **MHammond@skippinet.com.au** includes an interface to the Microsoft Foundation Classes and a Python programming environment using it that's written mostly in Python. See **ftp://ftp.python.org/pub/python/pythonwin/**.

There's an object-oriented GUI based on the Microsoft Foundation Classes model called WPY, supported by Jim Ahlstrom jim@interet.com. Programs written in WPY run unchanged and with native look and feel on Windows NT/95, Windows 3.1 (using win32s), and on UNIX (using Tk). Source and binaries for Windows and Linux are available in **ftp://ftp.python.org/pub/python/wpy/**.

Obsolete or minority solutions:

There's an interface to wxWindows. wxWindows is a portable GUI class library written in C++. It supports XView, Motif, and Windows as targets. There is some support for Macs and CURSES as well. wxWindows preserves the look and feel of the underlying graphics toolkit. Support for wxPython (by Harri Pasanen **pa@tekla.fi**) appears to have a low priority.

For SGI IRIX only, there are unsupported interfaces to the complete GL (Graphics Library — low level but very good 3-D capabilities) as well as to FORMS (a buttons-and-sliders-etc. package built on top of GL by Mark Overmars — ftp'able from **ftp://ftp.cs.ruu.nl/pub/SGI/FORMS/**). This is probably also becoming obsolete, as OpenGL takes over.

There's an interface to STDWIN, a platform-independent low-level windowing interface for Mac and X11. This is totally unsupported and rapidly becoming obsolete. The STDWIN sources are at **ftp://ftp.cwi.nl/pub/stdwin/**. (For info about STDWIN 2.0, please refer to Steven Pemberton **steven@cwi.nl** — I believe it is also dead.)

There is an interface to WAFE, a Tcl interface to the X11 Motif and Athena widget sets. WAFE is at **http://www.wu-wien.ac.at/wafe/wafe.html**. (The Fresco port that was mentioned in earlier versions of this FAQ no longer seems to exist. Inquire with Mark Linton.)

2.14 Are there any interfaces to database packages in Python?

There's a whole collection of them in the contrib area of the ftp server. See **http://www.python.org/ftp/python/contrib/Database/**.

2.15 Is it possible to write obfuscated one-liners in Python?

Yes. See the following three examples, courtesy of Ulf Bartelt:

```
# Primes < 1000
print filter(None,map(lambda y:y*reduce(lambda x,y:x*y!=0,
map(lambda x,y=y:y%x,range(2,int(pow(y,0.5)+1))),1),range(2,1000)))
# First 10 Fibonacci numbers
print map(lambda x,f=lambda x,f:(x<=1) or (f(x-1,f)+f(x-2,f)): f(x,f),
range(10))
# Mandelbrot set
print (lambda Ru,Ro,Iu,Io,IM,Sx,Sy:reduce(lambda x,y:x+y,map(lambda y,
Iu=Iu,Io=Io,Ru=Ru,Ro=Ro,Sy=Sy,L=lambda yc,Iu=Iu,Io=Io,Ru=Ru,Ro=Ro,i=IM,
Sx=Sx,Sy=Sy:reduce(lambda x,y:x+y,map(lambda x,xc=Ru,yc=yc,Ru=Ru,Ro=Ro,
i=i,Sx=Sx,F=lambda xc,yc,x,y,k,f=lambda xc,yc,x,y,k,f:(k<=0)or (x*x+y*y
>=4.0) or 1+f(xc,yc,x*x-y*y+xc,2.0*x*y+yc,k-1,f):f(xc,yc,x,y,k,f):chr(
64+F(Ru+x*(Ro-Ru)/Sx,yc,0,0,i)),range(Sx))):L(Iu+y*(Io-Iu)/Sy),range(Sy
))))(-2.1, 0.7, -1.2, 1.2, 30, 80, 24)
#    \___ ___/ \___ ___/ |   |   |__ lines on screen
#        V         V     |   |_____ columns on screen
#        |         |     |_____ maximum of "iterations"
#        |         |_____ range on y axis
#        |_____ range on x axis
```

Don't try this at home, kids!

2.16   Is there an equivalent of C's "?:" ternary operator?

Not directly. In many cases you can mimic a?b:c with "a and b or c", but there's a flaw: if b is zero (or empty, or None — anything that tests false) then c will be selected instead. In many cases you can prove by looking at the code that this can't happen (e.g. because b is a constant or has a type that can never be false), but in general this can be a problem.

Tim Peters (who wishes it was Steve Majewski) suggested the following solution: (a and [b] or [c])[0]. Because [b] is a singleton list it is never false, so the wrong path is never taken; then, applying [0] to the whole thing gets the b or c that you really wanted. Ugly, but it gets you there in the rare cases where it is really inconvenient to rewrite your code using 'if'.

2.17   My class defines __del__ but it is not called when I delete the object

There are several possible reasons for this. The del statement does not necessarily call __del__ — it simply decrements the object's reference count, and if this reaches zero __del__ is called.

If your data structures contain circular links (e.g. a tree where each child has a parent pointer and each parent has a list of children) the reference counts will never go back to zero. You'll have to define an explicit close() method which removes those pointers. Please don't ever call __del__ directly — __del__ should call close() and close() should make sure that it can be called more than once for the same object.

If the object has ever been a local variable (or argument, which is really the same thing) to a function that caught an expression in an except clause, chances are that a reference to the object still exists in that function's stack frame as contained in the stack trace. Normally, deleting (or better, assigning None to) sys.exc_traceback will take care of this. If a stack was printed for an unhandled exception in an interactive interpreter, delete sys.last_traceback instead.

There is code that deletes all objects when the interpreter exits, but it is not called if your Python has been configured to support threads (because other threads may still be active). You can define your own cleanup function using sys.exitfunc (see question 2.4).

Finally, if your __del__ method raises an exception, this will be ignored. Starting with Python 1.4beta3, a warning message is printed to sys.stderr when this happens.

2.18   How do I change the shell environment for programs called using os.popen() or os.system()? Changing os.environ doesn't work.

You must be using either a version of Python before 1.4, or on a (rare) system that doesn't have the putenv() library function.

Before Python 1.4, modifying the environment passed to subshells was left out of the interpreter because there seemed to be no well-established portable way to do it (in particular, some systems, have putenv(), others have setenv(), and some have none at all). As of Python 1.4, almost all UNIX systems *do* have putenv(), and so does the Win32 API, and thus the os module was modified so that changes to os.environ are trapped and the corresponding putenv() call is made.

2.19 What is a class?

A class is the particular object type that is created by executing a class statement. Class objects are used as templates, to create class instance objects, which embody both the data structure and program routines specific to a datatype.

2.20 What is a method?

A method is a function that you normally call as x.name(arguments...) for some object x. The term is used for methods of classes and class instances as well as for methods of built-in objects. (The latter have a completely different implementation and only share the way their calls look in Python code.) Methods of classes (and class instances) are defined as functions inside the class definition.

2.21 What is self?

Self is merely a conventional name for the first argument of a method — i.e. a function defined inside a class definition. A method defined as meth(self, a, b, c) should be called as x.meth(a, b, c) for some instance x of the class in which the definition occurs; the called method will think it is called as meth(x, a, b, c).

2.22 What is an unbound method?

An unbound method is a method defined in a class that is not yet bound to an instance. You get an unbound method if you ask for a class attribute that happens to be a function. You get a bound method if you ask for an instance attribute. A bound method knows which instance it belongs to and calling it supplies the instance automatically; an unbound method only knows which class it wants for its first argument (a derived class is also OK). Calling an unbound method doesn't "magically" derive the first argument from the context — you have to provide it explicitly.

2.23 How do I call a method defined in a base class from a derived class that overrides it?

If your class definition starts with "class Derived(Base): ..." then you can call method meth defined in Base (or one of Base's base classes) as Base.meth(self, arguments...). Here, Base.meth is an unbound method (see previous question).

2.24 How do I call a method from a base class without using the name of the base class?

DON'T DO THIS. REALLY. I MEAN IT. It appears that you could call self.__class__.__bases__[0].meth(self, arguments...) but this fails when a doubly-derived method is derived from your class: for its instances, self.__class__.__bases__[0] is your class, not its base class — so (assuming you are doing this from within Derived.meth) you would start a recursive call.

Often when you want to do this you are forgetting that classes are first class in Python. You can "point to" the class you want to delegate an operation to either at the instance or at the subclass level. For example if you want to use a "glorp" operation of a superclass you can point to the right superclass to use.

```
class subclass(superclass1, superclass2, superclass3):
    delegate_glorp = superclass2
    ...
    def glorp(self, arg1, arg2):
        ... subclass specific stuff ...
        self.delegate_glorp.glorp(self, arg1, arg2)
    ...
class subsubclass(subclass):
    delegate_glorp = superclass3
    ...
```

Note, however, that setting delegate_glorp to subclass in subsubclass would cause an infinite recursion on subclass.delegate_glorp. Careful! Maybe you are getting too fancy for your own good. Consider simplifying the design (?).

2.25 How can I organize my code to make it easier to change the base class?

You could define an alias for the base class, assign the real base class to it before your class definition, and use the alias throughout your class. Then all you have to change is the value assigned to the alias. Incidentally, this trick is also handy if you want to decide dynamically (depending on availability of resources) which base class to use. Example:

```
BaseAlias = <real base class>
class Derived(BaseAlias):
    def meth(self):
        BaseAlias.meth(self)
        ...
```

2.26 How can I find the methods or attributes of an object?

This depends on the object type. For an instance x of a user-defined class, instance attributes are found in the dictionary x.__dict__, and methods and attributes defined by its class are found in x.__class__.__bases__[i].__dict__ (for i in range(len(x.__class__.__bases__))). You'll have to walk the tree of base classes to find *all* class methods and attributes.

Many, but not all, built-in types define a list of their method names in x.__methods__, and if they have data attributes, their names may be found in x.__members__. However, this is only a convention. For more information, read the source of the standard (but undocumented) module newdir.

2.27 I can't seem to use os.read() on a pipe created with os.popen()

os.read() is a low-level function that takes a file descriptor (a small integer). os.popen() creates a high-level file object — the same type used for sys.std{in,out,err} and returned by the builtin open() function. Thus, to read n bytes from a pipe p created with os.popen(), you need to use p.read(n).

2.28 How can I create a stand-alone binary from a Python script?

The "freeze" tool in "Tools/freeze/" does what you want. See the README. This works by scanning your source recursively for import statements (both forms) and looking for the modules on the standard Python path as well as in the source directory (for built-in modules). It then "compiles" the modules written in Python to C code (array initializers that can be turned into code objects using the marshal module) and creates a custom-made config file that only contains those built-in modules which are actually used in the program. It then compiles the generated C code and links it with the rest of the Python interpreter to form a self-contained binary which acts exactly like your script.

> The freeze program only works if your script's file name ends in ".py".

TIP

2.29 What WWW tools are there for Python?

See the chapter titled "Internet and WWW" in the Library Reference Manual. There's also a Web browser written in Python, called Grail (included on this book's CD-ROM) — see **http://grail.cnri.reston.va.us/grail/**.

2.30 How do I run a subprocess with pipes connected to both input and output?

Use the standard popen2 module. For example:

```
import popen2
fromchild, tochild = popen2.popen2("command")
tochild.write("input\n")
tochild.flush()
output = fromchild.readline()
```

Note on a bug in popen2: unless your program calls wait() or waitpid(), finished child processes are never removed, and eventually calls to popen2 will fail because of a limit on the number of child processes. Calling os.waitpid with the os.WNOHANG option can prevent this; a good place to insert such a call would be before calling popen2 again.

In many cases, all you really need is to run some data through a command and get the result back. Unless the data is infinite in size, the easiest (and often the most efficient!) way to do this is to write it to a temporary file and run the command with that temporary file as input. The standard module tempfile exports a function mktemp(), which generates unique temporary file names.

Note that many interactive programs (such as vi) don't work well with pipes substituted for standard input and output. You will have to use pseudo ttys ("ptys") instead of pipes. There is some undocumented code to use these in the library module pty.py — I'm afraid you're on your own here.

A different answer is a Python interface to Don Libes' "expect" library. A Python extension that interfaces to expect is called "expy" and available from **ftp://ftp.python.org/pub/python/contrib/System/**.

A pure Python solution that works like expect is PIPE by John Croix. A prerelease of PIPE is available from **ftp://ftp.python.org/pub/python/contrib/System/**.

2.31 How do I call a function if I have the arguments in a tuple?

Use the built-in function apply(). For instance,

```
func(1, 2, 3)
```

is equivalent to

```
args = (1, 2, 3)
apply(func, args)
```

Note that func(args) is not the same — it calls func() with exactly one argument, the tuple args, instead of three arguments, the integers 1, 2 and 3.

2.32 How do I enable font-lock-mode for Python in Emacs?

If you are using XEmacs 19.14 or later, any XEmacs 20, FSF Emacs 19.34 or any Emacs 20, font-lock should work automatically for you if you are using the latest python-mode.el.

If you are using an older version of XEmacs or Emacs you will need to put this in your .emacs file:

```
(defun my-python-mode-hook ()
  (setq font-lock-keywords python-font-lock-keywords)
  (font-lock-mode 1))
(add-hook 'python-mode-hook 'my-python-mode-hook)
```

2.33 Is there a scanf() or sscanf() equivalent?

Not as such. For simple input parsing, the easiest approach is usually to split the line into whitespace-delimited words using string.split(), and to convert decimal strings to numeric values using string.atoi(), string.atol() or string.atof(). (Python's atoi() is 32-bit and its atol() is arbitrary precision.) If you want to use another delimiter than whitespace, use string.splitfield() (possibly combining it with string.strip(), which removes surrounding whitespace from a string).

For more complicated input parsing, regular expressions (see module regex) are better suited and more powerful than C's sscanf(). There's a contributed module that emulates sscanf(), by Steve Clift; see contrib/Misc/sscanfmodule.c of the site:
http://www.python.org/ftp/python/contrib/Misc/sscanfmodule.c

2.34 Can I have Tk events handled while waiting for I/O?

Yes, and you don't even need threads! But you'll have to restructure your I/O code a bit. Tk has the equivalent of Xt's XtAddInput() call, which allows you to register a callback function which will be called from the Tk mainloop when I/O is possible on a file descriptor. Here's what you need:

```
from Tkinter import tkinter
tkinter.createfilehandler(file, mask, callback)
```

The file may be a Python file or socket object (actually, anything with a fileno() method), or an integer file descriptor. The mask is one of the constants tkinter.READABLE or tkinter.WRITABLE. The callback is called as follows:

```
callback(file, mask)
```

You must unregister the callback when you're done, using

```
tkinter.deletefilehandler(file)
```

Note that since you don't know how many bytes are available for reading, you can't use the Python file object's read or readline methods, since these will insist on reading a predefined number of bytes. For sockets, the recv() or recvfrom() methods will work fine; for other files, use os.read(file.fileno(), maxbytecount).

2.35 How do I write a function with output parameters (call by reference)?

[Mark Lutz] The thing to remember is that arguments are passed by assignment in Python. Since assignment just creates references to objects, there's no alias between an argument name in the caller and callee, and so no call-by-reference per se. But you can simulate it in a number of ways:

1. By using global variables; but you probably shouldn't

2. By passing a mutable (changeable in-place) object:

```
def func1(a):
    a[0] = 'new-value'      # 'a' references a mutable list
    a[1] = a[1] + 1         # changes a shared object
args = ['old-value', 99]
func1(args)
print args[0], args[1]      # output: new-value 100
```

3. By returning a tuple, holding the final values of arguments:

```
def func2(a, b):
    a = 'new-value'         # a and b are local names
    b = b + 1               # assigned to new objects
    return a, b             # return new values
x, y = 'old-value', 99
x, y = func2(x, y)
print x, y                  # output: new-value 100
```

4. And other ideas that fall out from Python's object model. For instance, it might be clearer to pass in a mutable dictionary:

```
def func3(args):
    args['a'] = 'new-value'     # args is a mutable dictionary
    args['b'] = args['b'] + 1   # change it in-place
args = {'a':' old-value', 'b': 99}
func3(args)
print args['a'], args['b']
```

5. Or bundle up values in a class instance:

```
class callByRef:
    def __init__(self, **args):
        for (key, value) in args.items():
            setattr(self, key, value)
def func4(args):
    args.a = 'new-value'          # args is a mutable callByRef
    args.b = args.b + 1           # change object in-place
args = callByRef(a='old-value', b=99)
func4(args)
print args.a, args.b
```

But there's probably no good reason to get this complicated.

2.36 Please explain the rules for local and global variables in Python

[Ken Manheimer] In Python, procedure variables are implicitly global, unless they are assigned anywhere within the block. In that case they are implicitly local, and you need to explicitly declare them as global.

Though a bit surprising at first, a moment's consideration explains this. On one hand, requirement of global for assigned vars provides a bar against unintended side-effects. On the other hand, if global were required for all global references, you'd be using global all the time. Therefore, you'd have to declare as global every reference to a built-in function, or to a component of an imported module. This clutter would defeat the usefulness of the global declaration for identifying side-effects.

2.37 How can I have modules that mutually import each other?

Jim Roskind recommends the following order in each module:

First: all exports (like globals, functions, and classes that don't need imported base classes).

Second: all import statements.

Finally: all active code (including globals that are initialized from imported values).

2.38 How do I copy an object in Python?

There is no generic copying operation built into Python; however, most object types have some way to create a clone. Here's how for the most common objects:

For immutable objects (numbers, strings, tuples), cloning is unnecessary since their value can't change. For lists (and generally for mutable sequence types), a clone is created by the expression l[:]. For dictionaries, the following function returns a clone:

```
def dictclone(o):
    n = {}
    for k in o.keys(): n[k] = o[k]
    return n
```

Finally, for generic objects, the "copy" module defines two functions for copying objects. copy.copy(x) returns a copy as shown by the above rules. copy.deepcopy(x) also copies the elements of composite objects. See the section on this module in the Library Reference Manual.

2.39 How to implement persistent objects in Python (Persistent == automatically saved to and restored from disk)

The library module "pickle" now solves this in a very general way (though you still can't store things like open files, sockets or windows), and the library module "shelve" uses pickle and (g)dbm to create persistent mappings containing arbitrary Python objects. For possibly better performance also look for the latest version of the relatively recent cPickle module.

A more awkward way of doing things is to use pickle's little sister, marshal. The marshal module provides very fast ways to store noncircular basic Python types to files and strings, and back again. Although marshal does not do fancy things like store instances or handle shared references properly, it does run extremely fast. For example, loading a half-megabyte of data may take less than a third of a second (on some machines). This often beats doing something more complex and general such as using gdbm with pickle/shelve.

2.40 I try to use __spam and I get an error about _SomeClassName__spam

Variables with double-leading underscore are "mangled" to provide a simple but effective way to define class private variables. See "New in Release 1.4" in the Python Tutorial.

2.41 How do I delete a file? And other file questions?

Use os.remove(filename) or os.unlink(filename); for documentation, see the posix section of the library manual. They are the same — unlink() is simply the UNIX name for this function. In earlier versions of Python, only os.unlink() was available.

To remove a directory, use os.rmdir(); use os.mkdir() to create one. To rename a file, use os.rename(). To truncate a file, open it using f = open(filename, "r+"), and use f.truncate(offset); offset defaults to the current seek position. (The "r+" mode opens the file for reading and writing.) There's also os.ftruncate(fd, offset) for files opened with os.open() — for advanced UNIX hacks only.

2.42 How to modify urllib or httplib to support HTTP/1.1

Apply the following patch to the vanilla Python 1.4 httplib.py:

```
41c41
< replypat = regsub.gsub('\\.', '\\\\.', HTTP_VERSION) + \

--

> replypat = regsub.gsub('\\.', '\\\\.', 'HTTP/1.[0-9]+') + \
```

2.43 Unexplicable syntax errors in compile() or exec

When a statement suite (as opposed to an expression) is compiled by compile(), exec, or execfile(), it *must* end in a newline. In some cases, when the source ends in an indented block it appears that at least two newlines are required.

2.44 How do I convert a string to a number?

For integers, use the built-in int() function, such as int('144') == 144. Similarly, long() converts from string to long integer, such as long('144') == 144L; and float() to floating-point, such as float('144') == 144.0.

Note that these are restricted to decimal interpretation, so that int('0144') == 144 and int('0x144') raises ValueError.

For greater flexibility, or before Python 1.5, import the module string and use the string.atoi() function for integers, string.atol() for long integers, or string.atof() for floating-point. For example, string.atoi('100', 16) == string.atoi('0x100', 0) == 256. See the library reference manual section for the string module for more details.

While you could use the built-in function eval() instead of any of those, this is not recommended, because someone could pass you a Python expression that might have unwanted side effects (like reformatting your disk).

2.45 How do I convert a number to a string?

To convert, for example, the number 144 to the string '144', use the built-in function repr() or the backquote notation (these are equivalent). If you want a hexadecimal or octal representation, use the built-in functions hex() or oct(), respectively. For fancy formatting, use the % operator on strings, just like C printf formats, for example "%04d" % 144 yields '0144' and "%.3f" % (1/3.0) yields '0.333'. See the library reference manual for details.

2.46 How do I copy a file?

Most of the time this will do:

```
infile = open("file.in", "rb")
outfile = open("file.out", "wb")
outfile.write(infile.read())
```

However, for huge files you may want to do the reads/writes in pieces (or you may have to), and if you dig deeper you may find other technical problems.

Unfortunately, there's no totally platform independent answer. On UNIX, you can use os.system() to invoke the "cp" command (see your UNIX manual for how it's invoked). On DOS or Windows, use os.system() to invoke the "COPY" command. On the Mac, use macostools.copy(srcpath, dstpath). It will also copy the resource fork and Finder info.

There's also the shutil module, which contains a copyfile() function that implements the copy loop; but in Python 1.4 and earlier it opens files in text mode, and even in Python 1.5 it still isn't good enough for the Macintosh: it doesn't copy the resource fork and Finder info.

2.47 How do I check if an object is an instance of a given class or a subclass of it?

If you are developing the classes from scratch, it might be better to program in a more proper object-oriented style — instead of doing a different thing based on class membership, why not use a method and define the method differently in different classes?

However, there are some legitimate situations where you need to test for class membership. In Python 1.5, you can use the built-in function isinstance(obj, cls).

The following approaches can be used with earlier Python versions:

An unobvious method is to raise the object as an exception and to try to catch the exception with the class you're testing for:

```
def is_instance_of(the_instance, the_class):
    try:
      raise the_instance
    except the_class:
```

```
        return 1
    except:
        return 0
```

This technique can be used to distinguish "subclassness" from a collection of classes as well:

```
try:
                raise the_instance
except Audible:
                the_instance.play(largo)
except Visual:
                the_instance.display(gaudy)
except Olfactory:
                sniff(the_instance)
except:
                raise ValueError, "dunno what to do with this!"
```

This uses the fact that exception catching tests for class or subclass membership.

A different approach is to test for the presence of a class attribute that is presumably unique for the given class. For instance:

```
class MyClass:
    ThisIsMyClass = 1

    ...
def is_a_MyClass(the_instance):
    return hasattr(the_instance, 'ThisIsMyClass')
```

This version is easier to inline, and probably faster (inlined it is definitely faster). The disadvantage is that someone else could cheat:

```
class IntruderClass:
    ThisIsMyClass = 1    # Masquerade as MyClass

    ...
```

but this may be seen as a feature (anyway, there are plenty of other ways to cheat in Python). Another disadvantage is that the class must be prepared for the membership test. If you do not "control the source code" for the class it may not be advisable to modify the class to support testability.

2.48 What is delegation?

Delegation refers to an object-oriented technique Python programmers may implement with particular ease. Consider the following:

```
from string import upper
class UpperOut:
      def __init__(self, outfile):
            self.__outfile = outfile
      def write(self, str):
            self.__outfile.write( upper(str) )
      def __getattr__(self, name):
            return getattr(self.__outfile, name)
```

Here the UpperOut class redefines the write method to convert the argument string to uppercase before calling the underlying self.__outfile.write method, but all other methods are delegated to the underlying self.__outfile object. The delegation is accomplished via the "magic" __getattr__ method. Please see the language reference for more information on the use of this method.

Note that for more general cases delegation can get trickier. Particularly when attributes must be set as well as gotten the class must define a __settattr__ method too, and it must do so carefully.

The basic implementation of __setattr__ is roughly equivalent to the following:

```
class X:
    ...
    def __setattr__(self, name, value):
        self.__dict__[name] = value
    ...
```

Most __setattr__ implementations must modify self.__dict__ to store local state for self without causing an infinite recursion.

2.49 How do I test a Python program or component?

First, it helps to write the program so that it may be easily tested by using good modular design. In particular your program should have almost all functionality encapsulated in either functions or class methods — and this sometimes has the surprising and delightful effect of making the program run faster (because local variable accesses are faster than global accesses). Furthermore, the program should avoid depending on mutating global variables, since this makes testing much more difficult to do. The "global main logic" of your program may be as simple as

```
if __name__=="__main__":
    main_logic()
```

at the bottom of the main module of your program.

Once your program is organized as a tractible collection of functions and class behaviors, you should write test functions that exercise the behaviors. A test suite can be associated with each module which automates a sequence of tests. This sounds like a lot of work, but since Python is so terse and flexible it's surprisingly easy. You can make coding much more pleasant and fun by writing your test functions in parallel with the "production code," since this makes it easy to find bugs and even design flaws earlier.

"Support modules" that are not intended to be the main module of a program may include a "test script interpretation" which invokes a self test of the module.

```
if __name__ == "__main__":
    self_test()
```

Even programs that interact with complex external interfaces may be tested when the external interfaces are unavailable by using "fake" interfaces implemented in Python. For an example of a "fake" interface, the following class defines (part of) a "fake" file interface:

```
import string
testdata = "just a random sequence of characters"
class FakeInputFile:
  data = testdata
  position = 0
  closed = 0
  def read(self, n=None):
      self.testclosed()
      p = self.position
      if n is None:
         result= self.data[p:]
      else:
          result= self.data[p: p+n]
      self.position = p + len(result)
      return result
  def seek(self, n, m=0):
      self.testclosed()
      last = len(self.data)
      p = self.position
      if m==0:
         final=n
      elif m==1:
         final=n+p
```

```
        elif m==2:
            final=len(self.data)+n
        else:
            raise ValueError, "bad m"
        if final<0:
            raise IOError, "negative seek"
        self.position = final
    def isatty(self):
        return 0
    def tell(self):
        return self.position
    def close(self):
        self.closed = 1
    def testclosed(self):
        if self.closed:
            raise IOError, "file closed"
Try f=FakeInputFile() and test out its operations.
```

2.50 My multidimensional list (array) is broken! What gives?

You probably tried to make a multidimensional array like this.

```
A = [[None] * 2] * 3
```

This makes a list containing three references to the same list of length two. Changes to one row will show in all rows, which is probably not what you want. The following works much better:

```
A = [None]*3
for i in range(3):
    A[i] = [None] * 2
```

This generates a list containing three different lists of length two.

If you feel weird, you can also do it in the following way:

```
w, h = 2, 3
A = map(lambda i,w=w: [None] * w, range(h))
```

2.51 I want to do a complicated sort: can you do a Schwartzian Transform in Python?

Yes, and in Python you only have to write it once:

```
def st(List, Metric):
    def pairing(element, M = Metric):
```

```
        return (M(element), element)
    paired = map(pairing, List)
    paired.sort()
    return map(stripit, paired)
def stripit(pair):
    return pair[1]
```

This technique, attributed to Randal Schwartz, sorts the elements of a list by a metric which maps each element to its "sort value." For example, if L is a list of string then

```
import string
Usorted = st(L, string.upper)
def intfield(s):
        return string.atoi( string.strip(s[10:15] ) )
Isorted = st(L, intfield)
```

Usorted gives the elements of L sorted as if they were uppercase, and Isorted gives the elements of L sorted by the integer values that appear in the string slices starting at position 10 and ending at position 15. Note that Isorted may also be computed by

```
def Icmp(s1, s2):
        return cmp( intfield(s1), intfield(s2) )
Isorted = L[:]
Isorted.sort(Icmp)
```

but since this method computes intfield many times for each element of L, it is slower than the Schwartzian Transform.

2.52 How to convert between tuples and lists

The function tuple(seq) converts any sequence into a tuple with the same items in the same order. For example, tuple([1, 2, 3]) yields (1, 2, 3) and tuple('abc') yields ('a', 'b', 'c'). If the argument is a tuple, it docs not make a copy but returns the same object, so it is cheap to call tuple() when you aren't sure that an object is already a tuple.

The function list(seq) converts any sequence into a list with the same items in the same order. For example, list((1, 2, 3)) yields [1, 2, 3] and list('abc') yields ['a', 'b', 'c']. If the argument is a list, it makes a copy just like seq[:] would.

2.53 Files retrieved with urllib contain leading garbage that looks like e-mail headers

The server is using HTTP/1.1; the vanilla httplib in Python 1.4 only recognizes HTTP/1.0. See question 2.42 for a patch.

2.54 How do I get a list of all instances of a given class?

Python does not keep track of all instances of a class (or of a built-in type). You can program the class's constructor to keep track of all instances, but unless you're very clever, this has the disadvantage that the instances never get deleted, because your list of all instances keeps a reference to them.

(The trick is to regularly inspect the reference counts of the instances you've retained, and if the reference count is below a certain level, remove it from the list. Determining that level is tricky — it's definitely larger than 1.)

2.55 A regular expression fails with regex.error: match failure

This is usually caused by too much backtracking; the regular expression engine has a fixed size stack which holds at most 4000 backtrack points. Every character matched by ".*" accounts for a backtrack point, so even a simple search like

```
regex.match('.*x',"x"*5000)
```

will fail.

This is fixed in the re module introduced with Python 1.5; consult the Library Reference section on re for more information.

2.56 I can't get signal handlers to work

The most common problem is that the signal handler is declared with the wrong argument list. It is called as

```
handler(signum, frame)
```

so it should be declared with two arguments:

```
def handler(signum, frame):
    ...
```

2.57 I can't use a global variable in a function? Help!

Did you do something like this?

```
x = 1 # make a global
def f():
    print x # try to print the global
    ...
    for j in range(100):
        if q>3:
            x=4
```

If you did, all references to x in f are local, not global, by virtue of the "x=4" assignment. Any variable assigned in a function is local to that function unless it is declared global. Consequently, the "print x" attempts to print an uninitialized local variable and will trigger a NameError.

2.58 What's a negative index? Why doesn't list.insert() use them?

Python sequences are indexed with positive numbers and negative numbers. For positive numbers 0 is the first index, 1 is the second index, and so forth. For negative indices -1 is the last index, -2 is the pentultimate (next to last) index, and so forth. Think of seq[-n] as the same as scq[len(seq)-n].

Using negative indices can be very convenient. For example, if the string Line ends in a newline, then Line[:-1] is all of Line except the newline.

Sadly, the list builtin method L.insert does not observe negative indices. This feature could be considered a mistake, but since existing programs depend on this feature it may stay around forever. L.insert for negative indices inserts at the start of the list. To get "proper" negative index behavior use L[n:n] = [x] in place of the insert method.

2.59 How can I sort one list by values from another list?

You can sort lists of tuples.

```
>>> list1 = ["what", "I'm", "sorting", "by"]
>>> list2 = ["something", "else", "to", "sort"]
>>> pairs = map(None, list1, list2)
>>> pairs
[('what', 'something'), ("I'm", 'else'), ('sorting', 'to'), ('by', 'sort')]
>>> pairs.sort()
>>> pairs
[("I'm", 'else'), ('by', 'sort'), ('sorting', 'to'), ('what', 'something')]
>>> result = pairs[:]
>>> for i in xrange(len(result)): result[i] = result[i][1]
...
>>> result
['else', 'sort', 'to', 'something']
```

Note that "I'm" sorts before "by" because uppercase "I" comes before lowercase "b" in the ascii order. Also see 2.51.

2.60 Why doesn't dir() work on builtin types like files and lists?

It should have — and it does starting with Python 1.5 (currently in development). Using 1.4, you can find out which methods a given object supports by looking at its __methods__ attribute:

```
>>> List = []
>>> List.__methods__
['append', 'count', 'index', 'insert', 'remove', 'reverse', 'sort']
```

2.61 How can I mimic CGI form submission (METHOD=POST)?

I would like to retrieve Web pages that are the result of POSTing a form. Is there existing code that would let me do this easily? Yes. Here's a simple example that uses httplib.

```
#!/usr/local/bin/python
import httplib, sys, time
### build the query string
qs = "First=Josephine&MI=Q&Last=Public"
### connect and send the server a path
httpobj = httplib.HTTP('www.some-server.out-there', 80)
httpobj.putrequest('POST', '/cgi-bin/some-cgi-script')
### now generate the rest of the HTTP headers...
httpobj.putheader('Accept', '*/*')
httpobj.putheader('Connection', 'Keep-Alive')
httpobj.putheader('Content-type', 'application/x-www-form-urlencoded')
httpobj.putheader('Content-length', '%d' % len(qs))
httpobj.endheaders()
httpobj.send(qs)
### find out what the server said in response...
reply, msg, hdrs = httpobj.getreply()
if reply != 200:
    sys.stdout.write(httpobj.getfile().read())
```

Note that in general for "url encoded posts" (the default) query strings must be "quoted" to; for example, change equals signs and spaces to an encoded form when they occur in name or value. Use urllib.quote to perform this quoting. For example, to send name="Guy Steele, Jr.":

```
>>> from urllib import quote
>>> x = quote("Guy Steele, Jr.")
>>> x
```

```
'Guy%20Steele,%20Jr.'
>>> query_string = "name="+x
>>> query_string
'name=Guy%20Steele,%20Jr.'
```

2.62 If my program crashes with a bsddb (or anydbm) database open, it gets corrupted. How come?

Databases opened for write access with the bsddb module (and often by the anydbm module, since it will preferentially use bsddb) must explicitly be closed using the close method of the database. The underlying libdb package caches database contents which need to be converted to on-disk form and written, unlike regular open files which already have the on-disk bits in the kernel's write buffer, where they can just be dumped by the kernel with the program exits.

If you have initialized a new bsddb database but have not written anything to it before the program crashes, you will often wind up with a zero-length file and encounter an exception the next time the file is opened.

2.63 How do I make a Python script executable on UNIX?

You need to do two things: the script file's mode must be executable (include the 'x' bit), and the first line must begin with #! followed by the pathname for the Python interpreter.

The first is done by executing 'chmod +x scriptfile' or perhaps 'chmod 755 scriptfile'. The second can be done in a number of ways. The most straightforward way is to write

```
#!/usr/local/bin/python
```

as the very first line of your file — or whatever the pathname is where the Python interpreter is installed on your platform.

If you would like the script to be independent of where the Python interpreter lives, you can use the "env" program. On almost all platforms, the following will work, assuming the Python interpreter is in a directory on the user's $PATH:

```
#! /usr/bin/env python
```

Occasionally, a user's environment is so full that the /usr/bin/env program fails; or there's no env program at all. In that case, you can try the following hack (due to Alex Rezinsky):

```
#! /bin/sh
""":"
```

Gotcha

Don't do this for CGI scripts. The $PATH variable for CGI scripts is often very minimal, so you need to use the actual absolute pathname of the interpreter.

```
exec python $0 ${1+"$@"}
"""
```

The disadvantage is that this defines the script's __doc__ string. However, you can fix that by adding

```
__doc__ = """...Whatever..."""
```

2.64 How do you remove duplicates from a list?

Generally, if you don't mind reordering the List:

```
if List:
    List.sort()
    last = List[-1]
    for i in range(len(List)-2, -1, -1):
        if last==List[i]: del List[i]
        else: last=List[i]
```

If all elements of the list may be used as dictionary keys (for example, they are all hashable), this is often faster

```
d = {}
for x in List: d[x]=x
List = d.values()
```

Also, for extremely large lists you might consider more optimal alternatives to the first one. The second one is pretty good whenever it can be used.

2.65 Are there any known year 2000 problems in Python?

I am not aware of year 2000 deficiencies in Python 1.5. Python does very few date calculations and for what it does, it relies on the C library functions. Python generally represents times either as seconds since 1970, or as a tuple (year, month, day, ...), where the year is expressed with four digits, which makes Y2K bugs unlikely. So as long as your C library is okay, Python should be okay. Of course, I cannot vouch for *your* Python code!

Given the nature of freely available software, I have to add that this statement is not legally binding. The Python copyright notice contains the following disclaimer:

STICHTING MATHEMATISCH CENTRUM AND CNRI DISCLAIM ALL WARRANTIES WITH REGARD TO THIS SOFTWARE, INCLUDING ALL IMPLIED WARRANTIES OF MERCHANTABILITY AND FITNESS, IN NO EVENT SHALL STICHTING MATHEMATISCH CENTRUM OR CNRI BE LIABLE FOR ANY SPECIAL, INDIRECT OR

CONSEQUENTIAL DAMAGES OR ANY DAMAGES WHATSOEVER RESULTING FROM LOSS OF USE, DATA OR PROFITS, WHETHER IN AN ACTION OF CONTRACT, NEGLIGENCE OR OTHER TORTIOUS ACTION, ARISING OUT OF OR IN CONNECTION WITH THE USE OR PERFORMANCE OF THIS SOFTWARE.

The good news is that *if* you encounter a problem, you have full source available to track it down and fix it!

2.66 I want a version of map that applies a method to a sequence of objects! Help!

Get fancy!

```
def method_map(objects, method, arguments):
    """method_map([a,b], "flog", (1,2)) gives [a.flog(1,2), b.flog(1,2)]"""
    nobjects = len(objects)
    methods = map(getattr, objects, [method]*nobjects)
    return map(apply, methods, [arguments]*nobjects)
```

It's generally a good idea to get to know the mysteries of map and apply and getattr and the other dynamic features of Python.

2.67 How do I generate random numbers in Python?

The standard library module "whrandom" implements a random number generator. Usage is simple:

```
import whrandom
whrandom.random()
```

This returns a random floating point number in the range [0, 1). Other specialized generators are also in this module:

```
randint(a, b) chooses an integer in the range [a, b]
choice(S) chooses from a given sequence
uniform(a, b) chooses a floating point number in the range [a, b]
```

To force the random number generator's initial setting, use

```
seed(x, y, z) set the seed from three integers in [1, 256)
```

There's also a class, whrandom, which you can instantiate to create independent multiple random number generators. The module "random" contains functions that approximate various standard distributions. All this is documented in the library reference manual. Note that the module "rand" is obsolete.

2.68 How do I access the serial (RS232) port?

There's a Windows serial communication module (for communication over RS 232 serial ports) at:

http://www.python.org/ftp/python/contrib/System/siomodule.README

http://www.python.org/ftp/python/contrib/System/siomodule.zip

For DOS, try Hans Nowak's Python-DX, which supports this, at:

http://www.cuci.nl/~hnowak/

For UNIX, search Deja News (using **http://www.python.org/search/**) for "serial port" with author Mitch Chapman (his post is a little too long to include here).

2.69 Images on Tk-Buttons don't work in Py15

They *do* work, but you must keep your own *reference* to the image object now. More verbosely, you must make sure that, say, a global variable or a class attribute refers to the object.

Quoting Fredrik Lundh from the mailinglist: Well, the Tk button widget keeps a reference to the internal photoimage object, but Tkinter does not. So when the last Python reference goes away, Tkinter tells Tk to release the photoimage. But since the image is in use by a widget, Tk doesn't destroy it. Not completely. It just blanks the image, making it completely transparent... And yes, there was a bug in the keyword argument handling in 1.4 that kept an extra reference around in some cases. And when Guido fixed that bug in 1.5, he broke quite a few Tkinter programs...

2.70 Where is the math.py (socket.py, regex.py, etc.) source file?

If you can't find a source file for a module it may be a builtin or dynamically loaded module implemented in C, C++, or other compiled language. In this case you may not have the source file or it may be something like mathmodule.c, somewhere in a C source directory (not on the Python Path).

Fredrik Lundh (**fredrik@pythonware.com**) explains (on the Python-list): There are (at least) three kinds of modules in Python: 1) modules written in Python (.py); 2) modules written in C and dynamically loaded (.dll, .pyd, .so, .sl, etc); 3) modules written in C and linked with the interpreter; to get a list of these, type:

```
import sys
print sys.builtin_module_names
```

2.71 How do I send mail from a Python script?

On UNIX, it's very simple, using sendmail. The location of the sendmail program varies between systems; sometimes it is /usr/lib/sendmail, sometimes /usr/sbin/ sendmail. The sendmail manual page will help you out. Here's some sample code:

```
SENDMAIL = "/usr/sbin/sendmail" # sendmail location
import os
p = os.popen("%s -t" % SENDMAIL, "w")
p.write("To: cary@ratatosk.org\n")
p.write("Subject: test\n")
p.write("\n") # blank line separating headers from body
p.write("Some text\n")
p.write("some more text\n")
sts = p.close()
if sts != 0:
    print "Sendmail exit status", sts
```

On non-UNIX systems (and on UNIX systems too, of course!), you can use SMTP to send mail to a nearby mail server. A library for SMTP (smtplib.py) is included in Python 1.5.1; in 1.5.2 it will be documented and extended. Here's a very simple interactive mail sender that uses it:

```
import sys, smtplib
fromaddr = raw_input("From: ")
toaddrs  = string.splitfields(raw_input("To: "), ',')
print "Enter message, end with ^D:"
msg = ''
while 1:
    line = sys.stdin.readline()
    if not line:
        break
    msg = msg + line
# The actual mail send
server = smtplib.SMTP('localhost')
server.sendmail(fromaddr, toaddrs, msg)
server.quit()
```

This method will work on any host that supports an SMTP listener; otherwise, you will have to ask the user for a host.

2.72 How do I avoid blocking in connect() of a socket?

The select module is widely known to help with asynchronous I/O on sockets once they are connected. However, it is less than common knowledge how to avoid blocking on the initial connect() call. Jeremy Hylton has the following advice (slightly edited):

To prevent the TCP connect from blocking, you can set the socket to non-blocking mode. Then when you do the connect(), you will either connect immediately (unlikely) or get an exception that contains the errno. errno.EINPROGRESS indicates that the connection is in progress, but hasn't finished yet. Different OSes will return different errnos, so you're going to have to check. I can tell you that different versions of Solaris return different errno values.

In Python 1.5 and later, you can use connect_ex() to avoid creating an exception. It will just return the errno value. To poll, you can call connect_ex() again later — 0 or errno.EISCONN indicate that you're connected — or you can pass this socket to select (checking to see if it is writeable).

2.73 How do I specify hexadecimal and octal integers?

To specify an octal digit, precede the octal value with a zero. For example, to set the variable "a" to the octal value "10" (8 in decimal), type:

```
>>> a = 010
```

To verify that this works, you can type "a" and hit enter while in the interpreter, which will cause Python to spit out the current value of "a" in decimal:

```
>>> a
8
```

Hexadecimal is just as easy. Simply precede the hexadecimal number with a zero, and then a lower- or uppercase "x". Hexadecimal digits can be specified in lower- or uppercase. For example, in the Python interpreter:

```
>>> a = 0xa5
>>> a
165
>>> b = 0XB2
>>> b
178
```

2.74 How to get a single keypress at a time

Here is an answer for UNIX. There are several solutions; some involve using curses, which is a pretty big thing to learn. Here's a solution without curses, due to Andrew Kuchling (adapted from code to do a PGP-style randomness pool):

```python
import termios, TERMIOS, sys, os
fd = sys.stdin.fileno()
old = termios.tcgetattr(fd)
new = termios.tcgetattr(fd)
new[3] = new[3] & ~TERMIOS.ICANON & ~TERMIOS.ECHO
new[6][TERMIOS.VMIN] = 1
new[6][TERMIOS.VTIME] = 0
termios.tcsetattr(fd, TERMIOS.TCSANOW, new)
s = ''    # We'll save the characters typed and add them to the pool.
try:
    while 1:
        c = os.read(fd, 1)
        print "Got character", `c`
        s = s+c
finally:
    termios.tcsetattr(fd, TERMIOS.TCSAFLUSH, old)
```

You need the termios module for any of this to work, and I've only tried it on Linux, though it should work elsewhere. It turns off stdin's echoing and disables canonical mode, and then reads a character at a time from stdin, noting the time after each keystroke.

2.75 How can I overload constructors (or methods) in Python?

(This actually applies to all methods, but somehow the question usually comes up first in the context of constructors.) Where in C++ you'd write

```cpp
class C {
    C() { cout << "No arguments\n"; }
    C(int i) { cout << "Argument is " << i << "\n"; }
}
```

in Python you have to write a single constructor that catches all cases using default arguments. For example:

```python
class C:
    def __init__(self, i=None):
```

```
        if i is None:
            print "No arguments"
        else:
            print "Argument is", I
```

This is not entirely equivalent, but close enough in practice. You could also try a variable-length argument list, for example:

```
    def __init__(self, *args):
        ....
```

The same approach works for all method definitions.

2.76 How do I pass keyword arguments from one method to another?

Use apply. For example:

```
class Account:
    def __init__(self, **kw):
        self.accountType = kw.get('accountType')
        self.balance = kw.get('balance')
class CheckingAccount(Account):
    def __init__(self, **kw):
        kw['accountType'] = 'checking'
        apply(Account.__init__, (self,), kw)
myAccount = CheckingAccount(balance=100.00)
```

2.77 What module should I use to help with generating HTML?

Check out HTMLgen written by Robin Friedrich. It's a class library of objects corresponding to all the HTML 3.2 markup tags. It's used when you are writing in Python and wish to synthesize HTML pages for generating a Web or for CGI forms, etc.

It can be found in the FTP contrib area on python.org or on the Starship. Use the search engines there to locate the latest version. It might also be useful to consider DocumentTemplate, which offers clear separation between Python code and HTML code. DocumentTemplate is part of the Bobo objects publishing system (**http:/www.digicool.com/releases**) but can be used independently of course!

2.78 How do I create documentation from doc strings?

Use gendoc, by Daniel Larson. See **http://starship.skyport.net/crew/danilo/**

It can create HTML from the doc strings in your Python source code.

2.79 How do I read (or write) binary data?

For complex data formats, it's best to use the struct module. It's documented in the library reference. It allows you to take a string read from a file containing binary data (usually numbers) and convert it to Python objects; and vice versa.

For example, the following code reads two 2-byte integers and one 4-byte integer in big-endian format from a file:

```
import struct
f = open(filename, "rb")  # Open in binary mode for portability
s = f.read(8)
x, y, z = struct.unpack(">hhl", s)
```

The '>' in the format string forces bin-endian data; the letter 'h' reads one "short integer" (2 bytes), and 'l' reads one "long integer" (4 bytes) from the string.

For data that is more regular (such as a homogeneous list of ints or floats), you can also use the array module, also documented in the library reference.

2.80 I can't get key bindings to work in Tkinter

An oft-heard complaint is that event handlers bound to events with the bind() method don't get handled even when the appropriate key is pressed.

The most common cause is that the widget to which the binding applies doesn't have "keyboard focus." Check out the Tk documentation for the focus command. Usually a widget is given the keyboard focus by clicking in it (but not for labels; see the taketocus option).

2.81 "import crypt" falls

(UNIX) Starting with Python 1.5, the crypt module is disabled by default. In order to enable it, you must go into the Python source tree and edit the file Modules/ Setup to enable it (remove a '#' sign in front of the line starting with '#crypt'). Then rebuild. You may also have to add the string '-lcrypt' to that same line.

2.82 Are there coding standards or a style guide for Python programs?

Yes, Guido has written the "Python Style Guide." See **http://www.python.org/ doc/essays/styleguide.html**

2.83 How do I freeze Tkinter applications?

Freeze is a tool to create stand-alone applications (see 2.28). When freezing Tkinter applications, the applications will not be truly stand-alone, as the application will still need the tcl and tk libraries.

One solution is to ship the application with the tcl and tk libraries, and point to them at run-time using the TCL_LIBRARY and TK_LIBRARY environment variables.

To get truly stand-alone applications, the Tcl scripts that form the library have to be integrated into the application as well. One tool supporting that is SAM (stand-alone modules), which is part of the Tix distribution (**http://tix.mne.com**). Build Tix with SAM enabled, perform the appropriate call to Tclsam_init etc. inside Python's Modules/tkappinit.c, and link with libtclsam and libtksam (you might include the Tix libraries as well).

2.84 How do I create static class data and static class methods?

(Tim Peters, **tim_one@email.msn.com**) Static data (in the sense of C++ or Java) is easy; static methods (again in the sense of C++ or Java) are not supported directly.

STATIC DATA

For example,

```
class C:
    count = 0   # number of times C.__init__ called
    def __init__(self):
        C.count = C.count + 1
    def getcount(self):
        return C.count  # or return self.count
```

c.count also refers to C.count for any c such that isinstance(c, C) holds, unless overridden by c itself or by some class on the base-class search path from c.__class__ back to C.

STATIC METHODS

Static methods (as opposed to static data) are unnatural in Python, because

```
    C.getcount
```

returns an unbound method object, which can't be invoked without supplying an instance of C as the first argument.

The intended way to get the effect of a static method is via a module-level function:

```
    def getcount():
        return C.count
```

If your code is structured so as to define one class (or tightly related class hierarchy) per module, this supplies the desired encapsulation.

Gotcha

Within a method of C,

```
self.count = 42
```

creates a new and unrelated instance vrbl named "count" in self's own dict. So re-binding of a class-static data name needs the

```
C.count = 314
```

form whether inside a method or not.

Several tortured schemes for faking static methods can be found by searching DejaNews. Most people feel such cures are worse than the disease. Perhaps the least obnoxious is due to Pekka Pessi (**mailto:ppessi@hut.fi**):

```
# helper class to disguise function objects
class _static:
    def __init__(self, f):
        self.__call__ = f
class C:
    count = 0
    def __init__(self):
        C.count = C.count + 1
    def getcount():
        return C.count
    getcount = _static(getcount)
    def sum(x, y):
        return x + y
    sum = _static(sum)
C(); C()
c - C()
print C.getcount()  # prints 3
print c.getcount()  # prints 3
print C.sum(27, 15) # prints 42
```

2.85 __import__ ('x.y.z') returns <module 'x'>; how do I get z?

Try

```
__import__('x.y.z').y.z
```

For more realistic situations, you may have to do something like

```
m = __import__(s)
for i in string.split(s, ".")[1:]:
    m = getattr(m, I)
```

2.86 Basic thread wisdom

If you write a simple test program like this:

```
import thread
def run(name, n):
    for i in range(n): print name, i
```

```
for i in range(10):
    thread.start_new(run, (i, 100))
```

none of the threads seem to run! The reason is that as soon as the main thread exits, all threads are killed.

A simple fix is to add a sleep to the end of the program, sufficiently long for all threads to finish:

```
import thread, time
def run(name, n):
    for i in range(n): print name, i
for i in range(10):
    thread.start_new(run, (i, 100))
time.sleep(10) # <----------------------------!
```

But now (on many platforms) the threads don't run in parallel, but appear to run sequentially, one at a time! The reason is that the OS thread scheduler doesn't start a new thread until the previous thread is blocked.

A simple fix is to add a tiny sleep to the start of the run function:

```
import thread, time
def run(name, n):
    time.sleep(0.001) # <-------------------!
    for i in range(n): print name, i
for i in range(10):
    thread.start_new(run, (i, 100))
time.sleep(10)
```

Some more hints:

Instead of using a time.sleep() call at the end, it's better to use some kind of semaphore mechanism. One idea is to use a Queue module to create a queue object, let each thread append a token to the queue when it finishes, and let the main thread read as many tokens from the queue as there are threads.

Use the threading module instead of the thread module. It's part of Python since version 1.5.1. It takes care of all these details, and has many other nice features too!

2.87 Why doesn't closing sys.stdout (stdin, stderr) really close it?

Python file objects are a high-level layer of abstraction on top of C streams, which in turn are a medium-level layer of abstraction on top of (among other things) low-level C file descriptors.

For most file objects f you create in Python via the builtin "open" function, f.close() marks the Python file object as being closed from Python's point of view, and also arranges to close the underlying C stream. This happens automatically too, in f's destructor, when f becomes garbage.

But stdin, stdout, and stderr are treated specially by Python, because of the special status also given to them by C: doing

```
sys.stdout.close() # ditto for stdin and stderr
```

marks the Python-level file object as being closed, but does *not* close the associated C stream (provided sys.stdout is still bound to its default value, which is the stream C also calls "stdout").

To close the underlying C stream for one of these three, you should first be sure that's what you really want to do (for example, you may confuse the heck out of extension modules trying to do I/O). If it is, use os.close:

```
os.close(0)    # close C's stdin stream
os.close(1)    # close C's stdout stream
os.close(2)    # close C's stderr stream
```

2.88 What kinds of global value mutation are thread-safe?

(Adapted from c.l.py responses by Gordon McMillan & GvR) A global interpreter lock is used internally to ensure that only one thread runs in the Python VM at a time. In general, Python offers to switch among threads only between bytecode instructions (how frequently it offers to switch can be set via sys.setcheckinterval). Each bytecode instruction — and all the C implementation code reached from it — is therefore atomic.

In theory, this means an exact accounting requires an exact understanding of the PVM bytecode implementation. In practice, it means that operations on shared vrbls of builtin data types (ints, lists, dicts, etc) that "look atomic" really are.

For example, these are atomic (L, L1, L2 are lists, D, D1, D2 are dicts, x, y are objects, i, j are ints):

```
L.append(x)
L1.extend(L2)
x = L[i]
x = L.pop()
L1[i:j] = L2
L.sort()
x = y
```

```
x.field = y
D[x] = y
D1.update(D2)
D.keys()
```

These aren't:

```
i = i+1
L.append(L[-1])
L[i] = L[j]
D[x] = D[x] + 1
```

> Operations that replace other objects may invoke those other objects' __del__ method when their reference count reaches zero, and that can affect things. This is especially true for the mass updates to dictionaries and lists. When in doubt, use a mutex!

2.89 How do I modify a string in place?

Strings are immutable, so you cannot modify a string directly. If you need an object with this ability, try converting the string to a list or take a look at the array module.

```
>>> s = "Hello, world"
>>> a = list(s)
>>> print a
['H', 'e', 'l', 'l', 'o', ',', ' ', 'w', 'o', 'r', 'l', 'd']
>>> a[7:] = list("there!")
>>> import string
>>> print string.join(a, '')
'Hello, there!'
>>> import array
>>> a = array.array('c', s)
>>> print a
array('c', 'Hello, world')
>>> a[0] = 'y' ; print a
array('c', 'yello world')
>>> a.tostring()
'yello, world'
```

2.90 How can I pass on optional or keyword parameters from one function to another?

Use 'apply', like:

```
def f1(a, *b, **c):
    ...
def f2(x, *y, **z):
    ...
    z['width']='14.3c'
    ...
    apply(f1, (a,)+b, c)
```

Appendix B: What's On the CD?

Running the CD

The Prima License

The Prima User Interface

The CD that accompanies this book contains Python (Linux and Windows version), tools (such as HTMLgen and Grail), a list of Python Frequently Asked Questions (FAQ), and sample modules and scripts.

Running the CD

To make the CD more user-friendly and take up less of your disk space, no installation is required. This means that the only files transferred to your hard disk are the ones you choose to copy or install.

CAUTION

This CD has been designed to run under Linux. You may open and navigate the CD in any Operating System that has a graphical HTML viewer, however, only one Windows executable is present.

Linux

1. Open the CD tray and insert the CD.
2. As root, type the following at the command line: ***mount /dev/cdrom /tmp*** (replace */tmp* with wherever you want to mount the CD).
3. Start an X session (*startx* in most cases).
4. Open Netscape Navigator.
5. Choose Open from the File menu, and then click the Browse button.
6. Browse to start_here.html.

Windows 95/98/NT4

1. Insert the CD in the CD-ROM drive, and close the tray.
2. Go to the Control Panel and double click the CD-ROM Drive.
3. Open start_here.html (works with Netscape and Internet Explorer)

The Prima License

The first window you will see is the Prima License Agreement. Take a moment to read the agreement, and click the "I Agree" button to accept the license and proceed to the user interface. If you do not agree with the license, click the "I Disagree" button and the CD will not load.

The Prima User Interface

The opening screen of the Prima user interface contains a two-panel window. The left panel contains the structure of the programs on the disc. The right panel displays a description page for the selected entry in the left panel.

Resizing and Closing the User Interface

To resize the window, position the mouse over any edge or corner, hold down the left mouse button, and drag the edge or corner to a new position.

To close and exit the user interface, select File, Exit (your specific X setup may have a unique graphical means of closing Netscape).

Using the Left Panel

If you want to view a Tool, click /Tools. A drop-down menu appears containing the various Tools on the CD. Same goes for Scripts, Modules, and Help. Then simply click the tool you wish to download or view. It opens in the right window.

Using the Right Panel

The right panel displays a page that describes the entry you chose in the left panel. Use the information provided to provide details about your selection—such as what functionality an installable program provides. To download the particular file, follow the directions that come up in the left panel.

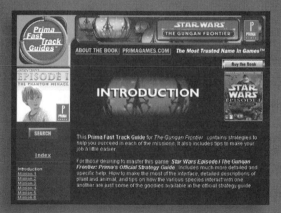